A CHAPTER OF MEDIÆVAL HISTORY

A CHAPTER OF MEDIÆVAL HISTORY

THE FATHERS OF THE LITERATURE OF FIELD SPORT AND HORSES

BY THE RT. HON. D. H. MADDEN

M.A., HON. LL.D., HON. LITT.D.,

SOMETIME
VICE-CHANCELLOR OF THE UNIVERSITY OF DUBLIN

O, like a Book of Sport thou'ld read me o'er ;
But there is more in me than thou understand'st.
Troilus and Cressida

KENNIKAT PRESS
Port Washington, N. Y./London

A CHAPTER OF MEDIAEVAL HISTORY

First published 1924
Reissued in 1969 by Kennikat Press
Library of Congress Catalog Card No: 74-91048
SBN 8046-0658-7

Manufactured by Taylor-Publishing Company   Dallas, Texas

PREFACE

IN an introductory chapter it is told how this book came to be written and why it assumes the title of a chapter of mediæval history, not as a record of events, but as a supplementary chapter by which the reader may be assisted in coming to an understanding of the great age of chivalry and the chase.

The pages of this volume afford evidence of the debt which it owes to former workers in the same field of research, more especially to Mr. Harting and to the late Mr. Baillie-Grohman; always ready to give friendly assistance to a fellow-worker.

To my friend Louis Purser, Senior Fellow of Trinity College, Dublin, and formerly Professor of Latin in the University, I am deeply indebted, not only for valuable suggestions, but for the encouragement which I gained from his approval during the progress of the work.

The reader of the chapter entitled 'Gaston Phœbus and Froissart' will find at p. 107 a note of the manner in which reference is made to the work on which it is founded, Lord Berners's translation of the chronicles.

Another writing of the fourteenth century, from which much may be learned of the spirit of that time, especially of religion in connection with the chase, is the Roy Modus and Royne Racio. M. Blaze's edition, admirable otherwise, is not paged, but the leaves are numbered, and the reader of these pages who desires to consult the original, if he substitutes f. lxxii *v.* for the noting at p. 59, will by the numbering of the leaves be able to find a passage referred to in the text which has been regarded as noteworthy.

D. H. MADDEN.

THE ORCHARD,
EAST SHEEN.

CONTENTS

A CHAPTER OF MEDIÆVAL HISTORY

CHAPTER I

INTRODUCTORY

A GOOD many years ago I was led to search through old-world books on Sport and on Horses for an explanation of the numberless allusions to these pursuits that I found scattered throughout the works of Shakespeare, for the perfect understanding of which something seemed to be needed beyond what had been supplied by critics and commentators. I had the good fortune to have gained, during several seasons, some practical knowledge of the sport of hunting the wild red deer which has been from time immemorial carried on in accordance with ancient usage in the Forest of Exmoor. The result of my somewhat discursive reading, in the light of the practical experience thus acquired, was embodied in a book which was first printed in the year 1897, entitled *The Diary of Master William Silence, A Study of Shakespeare and of Elizabethan Sport.*

Success in getting together for the purpose of my work a number of treatises printed in the fifteenth, sixteenth, and seventeenth centuries on country life, field sports, and horsemanship, acquired at a time when copies were more easily procurable than now, led to a desire to make the collection, if not complete, at all events representative. Occupied in spare moments of time in making a *catalogue raisonné* of a collection which attained respectable proportions, I came to understand what a real thing this long-forgotten literature had been in its day, and to understand the place that it once had held in the estimation of some of the greatest intellects of the Middle Ages and next succeeding centuries.

It was a revelation to find that Albertus Magnus, the Universal Doctor, was the father, not only of scholastic philosophy, but of the mediæval literature of Sport and of Horses.

In arranging mediæval works on horses in chronological order, according to the dates of composition, the treatise of Albertus Magnus was found to occupy the first place. In another division of the catalogue, in which books on field sports were noted, the primacy of his treatise *De Falconibus* was contested by one book only, the *De Arte Venandi cum Avibus* of the emperor Frederick II., attributed to the year 1245.

It was interesting to find, contending for the pride of place among mediæval writers on sport and horses, the great emperor, of whom a contemporary historian writes as ' Stupor Mundi Fredericus '; one ' whose name has ever since lived in history as that of the most wonderful man in a wonderful age ';* and a philosopher who,

* Freeman, *Historical Essays.*

alone among thinkers, holds a place among the elect few in the history of the world who are not only esteemed 'great,' but have acquired by common consent a right to appropriate the word as if it were a part of the name by which they are known. Later on, I found among contributors to my collection men of letters such as the humanist De Budé, better known by his latinised name Budæus, according to sir Richard Jebb the most learned Greek scholar of his age, surpassing in this branch of learning even the great Erasmus; and 'the grave' Thuanus, whom Gibbon accounts his master, whose history of his times was so highly esteemed by Dr. Johnson that he was about to undertake the task of translating it, so far relaxed his gravity as to write a poem on falconry in Latin verse, which was often reprinted and translated, and which, in the sixteenth century, took rank as a classic.

The estimation in which the book of sport was held by the great men of the Middle Ages is shown by the ambition of monarchs and princes to be known as authors, and the success which they attained is evidence of the earnestness with which they applied themselves to the task.

Gaston Phœbus, comte de Foix, was the author of *La Chasse*, ' the most important hunting book of any country that has come down to us from the Middle Ages.'* Gaston had the good fortune to be immortalised in the pages of Froissart. The romantic nature of this, the most characteristic prince of his time, won the

* Baillie-Grohman, *Master of Game*, Bibliography.

life-long admiration of Disraeli. Gaston became
known to him on his journey to Scotland in 1825,
when he found Froissart a most entertaining
travelling companion. The impression was a lasting one, for in *Lothair*, written in 1870, a principal
character is an illustrious painter, descended
from a noble Gascon house, and whose name
is Gaston Phœbus; and in *An Unfinished Novel*,
printed in vol. v. of the *Life*,* Lord Gaston, son
of a great noble, has a part allotted to him which
is plainly intended to be a leading one.

Disraeli's appreciation of Froissart is thus
expressed in a letter addressed to Mr. John
Murray: ' I find Froissart a most entertaining
companion, just the fellow for a traveller's
evening; and just the work too, for it needs
neither books of reference nor accumulation
of MS.'*

This reference to Froissart as supplying ' work '
which could be comfortably done on a journey,
in the absence of books of reference and without
accumulation of MS., suggests that the writer
thought of Gaston Phœbus, by whose character
he had been impressed, and his story as told by
Froissart, as the subject of a mediæval romance.
I owe to the courtesy of Disraeli's biographer,
Mr. Buckle, the knowledge that his papers afford
no evidence of this ' work ' having been undertaken, and a few years later a less interesting
subject was found in *Alroy*.

Gaston, as made known to us by Froissart and
in his own book on the chase, fills a larger proportion of these pages than is allotted to any

* *Life*, by Monypenny and Buckle, vol. i., p. 64.

other subject; and this for several reasons. He holds the first place among mediæval writers on the chase; and a study of the old-world literature of field sport is mainly interesting in so far as it enables us to understand the character and ideas of the men by whom it was written. Of no man of his time have we a fuller and more intimate knowledge than of Gaston, from what he tells us in his writings and by his acts, and from a portrait drawn by a consummate artist inspired by the belief that his work would be handed down to coming generations.

Foremost among the rulers who contributed to the literature of sport was the great emperor Frederick II., of whose treatise on falconry Mr. Harting writes: ' To master this is to acquire a liberal education in the art of hawking.' There was also John I. of Portugal, whose elaborate *Livro da Montaria* remained in manuscript until 1918, when it was published, carefully edited, by order of *Da Academia das sciencias de Lisboa.*

It would have been well for Charles IX. of France if he had been unknown in history, save as the friend and correspondent of Ronsard, and the author of the *Livre de Roy Charles, de la Chasse du cerf,* a work which an editor, who was also a high authority on ancient sport, regards as a classic.

So highly esteemed was the literature of sport, that monarchs and princes who were not themselves authors took a pride in having their names associated with works written by learned clerks at their command. The earliest Spanish treatise on hunting, penned about the year 1340, is stated on the title-page of the first printed edition (1582) to have been written by command of the king, *Don Alfonzo de Castilla, de Leon, ultimo destre nombre.* Alphonso XI. of Castile died in 1350, at the age of thirty-eight, but not before he had won distinctions as a soldier and as an administrator.

An interesting work on country life, which forms a connecting-link between the treatises of the classical age and the mediæval book of sport, was written in 1307 at the request of Charles II., king of Sicily, by Petrus Crescentiensis, a learned lawyer and eminent citizen of Bologna, and translated into French by the direction of Charles V. of France; and, later on, we find the great scholar Budæus writing at the request of Francis I. of France a treatise in Latin on the hunting of the hart, by way of proof that an appropriate word could be found in that language for every one of the numberless terms of art in venery which were then in use.

Our royal house of Plantagenet was distinguished by interest in the chase, and the oldest treatise of the art of venery in the English language was written between the years 1406 and 1413 by Edward, second duke of York, who fell in the battle of Agincourt in 1415. This book was not printed until the year 1904, but it was well known in manuscript in the time of Shakespeare, and respect for the author as an authority on the chase may have led him, in defiance of history, to transform the traitor Aumerle, the discomfortable cousin of Richard, 'smouldered to death' at

Agincourt, into the hero of whose glorious death in battle we read in Henry IV.

Between the ages in which princes, philosophers, and scholars devoted themselves to the literature of the chase and the days in which we live, there 'lies a gulf of mystery which the powers of the historian will never adequately bridge.' Of the men of those ages, Froude finely says: 'They cannot come to us, and our imagination can but feebly penetrate to them. Only among the aisles of the Cathedral, only as we gaze upon their silent figures sleeping on their tombs, some faint conceptions float before us of what these men were when alive; and perhaps in the sound of bells, that peculiar creation of mediæval age, which falls upon the ear like the echo of a vanished world.'

In the language of the chase, borne to us by the sporting literature of the Middle Ages, we may catch an echo of sounds, articulate once, and familiar to the ear as 'holy bells that knolled to church.' Gaston Phœbus was buried at the foot of the high altar of the Friary at Orthez, with great pomp, amidst the lamentations of his people. Of this church and of his tomb *etiam periere ruinæ*. But were we permitted to gaze on a silent figure, sleeping on his tomb, the image of one whose beauty was deemed comparable to that of Phœbus Apollo, we could gain no idea of the man and of his daily life, like to that derived from companionship in his writings with one whose strong personality makes itself apparent throughout his pages.

The chase, with the literature in many languages,

in prose and in verse, to which it gave birth, was regarded by our ancestors of the Middle Ages in a spirit of seriousness, which twentieth-century readers find it difficult to understand, for they find no suggestion of the existence of this spirit in the literary or political histories of the time. Some assistance in realising the place which it held in the life of the day may be gained from an acquaintance with the forest laws of mediæval Europe and the royal establishments connected with the chase. These departments of state were kept up on a scale of magnificence corresponding to the estimation in which the chase was held, and similar establishments were maintained by noblemen and gentlemen, proportioned to their position and means.

The magnificence of the illustrations with which the manuscripts of the great mediæval books of sport were adorned testifies to the respect in which the subject was held. The art of the illuminator and miniaturist is seen at its best when applied to the decoration of the *Master of Game*, of the *Roy Modus*, or the *La Chasse* of Gaston Phœbus. The beautiful reproductions of these illuminations contained in Mr. Baillie-Grohman's *Sport in Art* enables the reader of that interesting volume to trace the history of art in its application to the illustration of books of sport, in manuscript and in print. The reader cannot fail to observe the contrast between the wealth of decoration which was lavished on mediæval manuscripts and the poverty of the woodcuts which in a subsequent age were considered good enough for so important a work as the *Vénerie* of Jacques du Fouilloux, printed in 1561.

It is not too much to say that an account of the manners and occupations of the Middle Ages is not complete without a chapter devoted to a subject which was regarded of such importance, on which such an expenditure of wealth was lavished, and which gave birth to a literature to which poets, philosophers, and princes loved to contribute. For such a chapter I have searched in vain through the works of the historians who have written of the centuries during which the chase and its literature stood so high in general repute.

If Hallam, when he took in hand to give to the world a *View of the State of Europe during the Middle Ages*, had approached his task in the spirit of Macaulay, he would have realised that a historian who would give to his readers ' a true picture of the life of their ancestors ' ought ' not to pass by with neglect even the revolutions which have taken place in dress, furniture, repasts, and public entertainments,' and that he might even spare ' a few pages from military evolutions and political intrigues for the purpose of letting us know how the parlours and bedchambers of our ancestors looked.'

But when Hallam wrote, the dignity of history sat enthroned. References consistent with the maintenance of this dignity are made by him to the forest laws; to charters of the forest; and to the excessive passion for sports of the field, with its disastrous results; but the literature of the chase was deemed unworthy of notice, either in a

historical view of the Middle Ages or in a treatise
on the literature of Europe in the fifteenth, sixteenth, and seventeenth centuries, when the
books included in the collection of the present
writer were, for the most part, written. This
literature, in regard to mere bulk, is a considerable
one, and for some of the writers immortality was
predicted by admiring contemporaries. But not
one of them has found admission, even to pages
devoted to miscellaneous writings, in which so
insignificant a literary treasure as the second
edition of Gerard's *Herbal* may be found enshrined.
De Thou and Turberville are, indeed, mentioned:
one as a historian, and the other as a poet. But
no mention is made of a poem by Thuanus—the
version of his name adopted by De Thou—which
was often reprinted in Latin and in Italian, and
edited with the same care that is devoted to an
ancient classic. So high was the reputation of this
poem that Mr. Harting, writing of the work of the
emperor Frederick II. and worthily magnifying the
office of writer on falconry, goes so far as to say
that English translations of 'the Emperor's work
and of De Thou's celebrated poem would form
acceptable additions to the well-known series of
Latin classics for English readers.' Turberville's
Booke of Faukonrie, as the most important
English treatise on the subject, had a higher
claim to recognition than his volume of poems,
none of which, indeed, are as good as the
spirited verses in praise of hawking contained in
his *Booke*.

It is true that but few of the old-world books of
sport can lay claim to literary merit. But in

this respect they compare favourably with the books on sorcery and demoniacal possession recorded by Hallam, of which it is said that 'the greater part are contemptible to any other light than as evidences of the state of human opinion.' A far saner and healthier state of human opinion and one more worthy of note is that which found expression in the mediæval literature of sport, in the vernacular languages, and also, under the influence of the Renaissance, in Latin versification, founded on the best models of the classical period. Of this long-forgotten literature, in which eminent ecclesiastics and men of letters loved to exercise their ingenuity and taste, something will be found in these pages.

No work on the chase comparable to the French classics was written in England during the Middle Ages. The language of venery, for centuries after the conquest, was Norman French, and the laws and practices of woodcraft appear to have been transmitted verbally in that language until the reign of Edward II., when a short treatise in French was written, attributed to his huntsman, Twici, which has survived. The earliest treatise on the chase in the English language is a translation of the *La Chasse* of Gaston Phœbus, adapted to the use of English masters of game.

The *Book of St. Albans*, although devoid of literary quality and never of much account as a treatise on woodcraft, is interesting from the position held by the editions of 1486 and 1497 in the history of printing in England. To it, also, appertains the honour of containing the earliest work written by an Englishwoman which

2

found its way into print—the doggerel verses on hunting attributed to Dame Juliana Barnes, or Berners, whose personality has been the subject of industrious but fruitless inquiry.

It must be admitted that in a collection of works upon field sports written in England up to the end of the seventeenth century scarcely one is included deserving of attention, from either the distinction of the writer or the literary quality of his work.

There is, indeed, one glorious exception. The *Compleat Angler* of Izaak Walton opens with 'A conference betwixt an Angler, a Hunter and a Falconer, each commending his recreation.'

Piscator speaks well of angling; but his successor of to-day, in commending his recreation, might add that angling alone of field sports has inspired a work that was not only a useful practical treatise in its day, but a classic, known and beloved, and begetting love for its author, wherever the English language is spoken.

The English literature of the chase, although otherwise of little moment, has a historical value which is lacking in more important works of the kind written in other countries. In it we can trace the making of the English nation by a union of the Norman conquerors with the older inhabitants of the island, to whom the language of venery was an unknown tongue, to be acquired by study of the book of sport. This knowledge was imparted by the *Book of St. Albans* and a host of followers, of whose service in this behalf something is said in a following chapter.

It need hardly be said that the sketches contained in this volume are not offered as a serious contribution to the history of the literature of old-world sport and of horses. If they have any value or interest, it is by way of enabling a twentieth-century lover of country pursuits to realise the place that they held in the life of our ancestors; and they may aid us in coming on speaking terms with great men of our race, between whom and ourselves there is scarcely a connecting-link, beyond the bond of a common humanity. The scholar who knows his Horace, if he were to encounter Mæcenas on the *Via Sacra*, would find no difficulty in conversing with him on the topics of the day, some trifling difficulties of accent and pronunciation having been overcome; and there are some among us who would bear themselves creditably in a walk through the groves of Academus. But on what topic of common interest could he address the great unknown who conceived the glory of Chartres ? The greatness of this man is of a different order from the greatness of Homer. But they have this in common: in the ages following Homer an epic poet wrote as he was inspired by Homer, and the utmost to which the modern cathedral builder can aspire is to reproduce in some degree the great conceptions of the Middle Ages.

There were two institutions, nearly akin, dear to the hearts of the great men of the age when Europe was awakening from the torpor of the dark ages—the years in which Albertus Magnus and Frederick II. wrote of falconry and of horses—Chivalry and the Chase.

If France was 'the fountain of Chivalry' she was as truly the mother of *La Grande Chasse*, and into both she breathed the same spirit, an influence which, up to the present day, affects English-speaking people throughout the world. To Somerville the chase is

The sport of Kings
Image of war without its guilt.*

The tournament was a livelier image of war than the hunting field, but in both lessons were learned of the courage, endurance, honour, and discipline which go to make a good soldier.

The fourteenth century was the great age of chivalry and of the chase. In the opening years of the Hundred Years' War, the earliest of the great French classics, the *Roy Modus*, was written by some learned clerk at the request—there is reason to believe—of a great nobleman of Normandy who came to England as a prisoner after the battle of Poitiers, and who holds a foremost place in the *Chronicles* of Froissart. And in the same century a gentle and joyous deed of arms for thirty days between the flower of French and English chivalry took place at St. Ingilbert, in time of truce, for which 'Sir John Holland, brother to the King of England, and more than sixty knights and squires with him,' arrived at Calais, having ' sent over their horses and harness both for peace and war.'†

There was much in common between the spirit of chivalry and that of *La Grande Chasse*. It was through the systematised observances of the chase and the honourable obligations which they

* *The Chase.*   † Froissart, iv., pp. 109–132.

imposed on sportsmen that courtesy became an element in the capture and destruction of animals *feræ naturæ*.

'It was in France that venery was first regulated, and pursued with well-defined ceremonials and acquired a vocabulary of its own, and in France the Art of Venery was first considered a science.'* Of Gaston de Foix, Mr. Baillie-Grohman writes: 'His book is characterised all through with that spirit of fair play and love of sport which, indeed, could scarcely be absent from that of a great knight in the most flourishing period of chivalry.'

Of taking beasts by gins, Gaston speaks unwillingly, 'for I should not teach to take beasts unless it be by nobleness and gentleness, and to have good disport, so that there be more beasts, and that they be not killed falsely.' Of the various manners of taking beasts by 'falseness,' he writes: 'I will speak no more of this chase, for it is one pertaining to villains, to the common people, and to the peasants.'

In the opinion of Hallam the best school of moral discipline which the Middle Ages afforded was the institute of chivalry. 'There is something perhaps to allow for the partiality of modern writers upon this interesting subject; yet our most sceptical criticism must assign a decisive influence to this great source of human improvement. The more deeply it is considered, the more we shall become sensible of its importance.'† The castles of superior lords were schools of chivalry in which the sons of gentlemen, as

* *Master of Game*, p. 199.   † Hallam, chap. ix., pt. 11.

pages from the age of seven, and at fourteen as esquires, ' at once learned the whole discipline of their future profession, and imbibed its emulous and enthusiastic spirit.' Instruction in the mysteries of venery was part of this liberal education, and its moral importance was fully recognised. Froissart tells us that when king John of France was a prisoner in England Gace de la Buigne, an ecclesiastic of an old Norman family, the author of a work on venery, was entrusted with the education of the King's son Philip, so that the Prince, ' being learned in sport, might avoid the sin of idleness and learn good manners and virtue.'

Of the strong tincture of religion which entered into the composition of chivalry from the twelfth century and of ' another ingredient equally distinguishing, a great regard for the female sex,' Hallam discourses in a strain of unwonted eloquence, and adds: ' Three virtues may particularly be noticed as essential to the character of a knight, loyalty, courtesy, and munificence.'

Courtesy was the distinctive characteristic of the great days of chivalry and of the chase. The courtesy shown by the Black Prince to king John of France when his prisoner at Poitiers is remarkable only from the distinction of the actors. All the knights English and French entertained their prisoners, questioning them ' upon their honour what ransom they could pay without inconvenience and easily gave them credit; and it was common for men to say that they would not straiten any knight or esquire, so that he should not live well and keep up his honour.'

But it must be remembered, if we are to enter into the spirit of the Middle Ages, that, in the words of Freeman, 'the chivalrous spirit is above all things a class spirit. The good knight is above all bound to courtesy towards men, and more towards women, of a certain rank: he may treat all below that rank with any degree of scorn and cruelty.'

Gibbon writes of a revolution which had taken place in European states between the age of Charlemagne and that of the crusades in which 'the service of the infantry was degraded to the plebeians;' the cavalry formed the strength of the armies; and the honourable name of 'miles,' or soldier, was confined to the gentlemen who served on horseback, and were invested with the character of knighthood.*

The sharp distinction of class that was thus created was accompanied by another distinction, the line of division being nearly the same. The question of ransom entered so largely into the life of a mediæval soldier that it was often spent in a fight for gain, not glory. That mercy should be shown to a conquered foe who was under the degree of knight, and unable to come to ransom, was no part of the code of chivalry. The truth of this statement is often borne in upon the student of Froissart: when he finds a conquered army divided into two classes, those who can pay, and those who cannot; the latter, unless of knightly rank, are mercilessly butchered, and the former courteously ransomed.

* *Decline and Fall*, chap. lviii.

Although a kindred spirit inspired chivalry and *La Grande Chasse*, a treatise on the former would be out of place in these pages, but a note may be permissible on chivalry, as we find it in Froissart.*

The strong tincture of religion which Hallam found in the composition of chivalry entered into every phase of mediæval activity and thought. It is not possible to come to a full understanding of the Middle Ages in their art, their poetry, their philosophy, or even their book of sport, unless the subject be studied in sympathy with the spirit of the time.

During the millennium which followed the fall of the Roman empire the religion which acknowledged the pope of Rome as its head was the religion of christendom. Heresies sprang up and were suppressed; antipopes flourished for a time and were forgotten, but Rome ruled throughout the centuries with ever-increasing authority.

The power of this church was at its greatest height and its influence upon thought and action most clearly discernible when the great French classics of the chase were written.

To the modern reader of *La Chasse* the solemn invocation with which it opens would appear out of place, and more suited to a religious work than to a book on hunting. But as he reads on he comes to understand the religious purpose with which the book was written. Gaston's purpose is to proclaim to the world that the true sportsman makes the best of both worlds; he is free from

* Note A, Chivalry in Froissart.

temptation to mortal sins, for they have their origin in the slothful idleness which is not possible to a diligent sportsman.

Gaston was an understanding lover of the dog, and when he came to write of the hound he did so seriously, beginning with these words: *Et puis par la grâce de Dieu parleray de la nature des chiens qui chassent et prennent bestes.*

In the *Roy Modus et Royne Racio*—the most interesting of the mediæval books of sport—the king discourses of the science of woodcraft while the queen draws religious and moral conclusions from his teaching, and in no part of her teaching is the religious spirit in which it is conceived more apparent than in her moralising on the final cause of the creation of the hound and of the hart.

St. Eustace was the patron saint of hunters, and the legend of his miraculous conversion by sight of the crucifix between the antlers of a hunted hart was first told of him. He was a Roman soldier of noble birth, and the story of his conversion is told in the *Golden Legend*.

St. Hubert, who lived in the eighth century, was a mighty hunter. He was buried in the heart of the great forest of Ardennes, and he also became patron saint of hunters.* The story of his conversion, similar to that told of St. Eustace in the *Roy Modus*, is carved in marble over the doorway of the beautiful chapel dedicated to St. Hubert, in the garden of the château of Amboise.

* *Lives of the Saints*, Baring Gould, i., p. 74.

By degrees St. Hubert took the place of the older patron saint. The chapels in the forests were naturally dedicated to St. Hubert, who lay in the forest of Ardennes. Mr. R. E. Prothero, in *Pleasant Land of France*, writes of a chapel in the forest of Fontainebleau, built, according to tradition, by Henri IV., where the ceremonial of blessing the hounds on St. Hubert's day (November 3) was carried on, to the time of the third Napoleon.

In a book instinct with the feeling of mediæval sport the Duchesse d'Uzès tells of the celebration of St. Hubert's day, and from what she says it may be concluded that the estate of the writer is not the only one on which this mediæval custom survives.

She writes (p. 59) of a day in the hunting season which is somewhat different from other days—Saint Hubert's day:

Tous les équipages ne la fêtent pas aussi pompeusement, mais j'en connais où la cérémonie est vraiment imposante : grand' messe solonnelle, à l'église du village, les trompes en sont la seule musique, tous les veneurs en tenue sont au premier rang, les piqueurs offrent et portent le pain bénit ; à l'issue de la messe, on monte à cheval prestement, on entoure la meute, le prêtre lui donne la bénédiction, et en route pour l'attaque !

The work of the duchess is illustrated with pictures of the incidents of the chase which recall the miniatures of fourteenth-century manuscripts, gaining in accuracy what they lose in richness of colouring. In one we see the pack (*meute*) held in couples in the courtyard of a fine feudal château, while surpliced priests and acolytes, having issued, with a goodly congregation, from an adjoining church, await the commencement of the ceremony. (*La Chasse à Course*, Paris, 1912.)

The religious purpose of the *Roy Modus* goes beyond the moralising of the queen; the whole treatise is founded on the belief that the sports of the field are a divinely appointed order in which Providence has provided for each man the kind of sport that is best fitted to his nature. King Modus, before instructing his pupils in woodcraft, impresses on them the duty, *Dieu servir premièrement;* and when a pupil asks which is the first of sports he is told that men vary in taste and in capacity for sport and in means; therefore different kinds of sport have been ordained by Providence, suited to each man's inclination and to his position in life.

Le Romans des Déduits is a treatise in which instruction in virtue and good living is imparted in the form of a treatise on falconry; written by command of King John the Good when a prisoner in England, for the instruction of his young son, Philip, who was also a prisoner.

After the Middle Ages instruction in religion and virtue formed no part of the sportsman's library. Religion no longer inspires the writer of the book of sport. The older classics of the chase were followed and superseded by the *La Vénerie* of Jacques du Fouilloux, published in 1561, of which twenty-four editions are noted by Souhart. (*Bibliographie des Ouvrages sur la Chasse.*) But the spirit of the Middle Ages had fled; and instead of the glorious illustrations, of which manuscripts of the fourteenth century were deemed worthy, we have poor woodcuts.

The spirit neither of religion nor art inspired this famous book, the third of the French classics, from which much of the English literature of the chase was borrowed, and a comparison of this product of the sixteenth century with its forerunners of the fourteenth may assist in realising the change that had come over the writers on the chase.

Jacques du Fouilloux was a jovial provincial seigneur, of whom it is recorded that he met the king on his entry into Poitiers with fifty of his sons, of whom only one was born in wedlock. The irrelevances of this writer were unlike those which we find in the work of Gaston Phœbus. Instead of discourses on religion and morality, we have a long poem by the author entitled *L'Adolescence de Ieqves du Fouilloux*, in which he tells the tale of a love affair with a beautiful shepherdess.

The frontispiece to *La Vénerie* represents the author on his knees presenting his work to the king, a youth of about twenty years. A few courtiers are present, and the queen, with ladies in attendance, is seen on a balcony. What seems her head the semblance of a Marie Stuart hat has on, and the rude woodcut is intended as a portrait of Mary.

The book was not published until after the death of Francis II., when it was dedicated to Charles IX., then about nine years of age; but no change was made in the frontispiece, so little regard was then had to the illustration of a printed book.

The *Noble Arte of Venerie*, published in 1575, was

largely copied from this book. Most of the wood-cuts in the *Noble Arte* are reproductions of those in *La Vénerie*, but some are original, and amongst them one represents queen Elizabeth, mounted, in a hawking party. When the second edition was printed in 1611, loyalty to king James suggested that he should take the place of Elizabeth, but thrift forbade the production of a new woodcut, and the plate was altered so as to admit of his inclusion, but so carelessly as to admit also a considerable part of the queen's attire.

With religion, art disappears from the book of sport. The rapid production of books by the printing press rendered it impossible to apply to each copy the art of the illuminator and miniaturist, then in highest perfection; although the reservation of a blank space for illumination in early copies suggests that the decoration of printed books was not despaired of.

The sense of religion with which the field sports of the Middle Ages were affected had a humanising influence, by uniting all classes in a common service and a common source of pleasure. Unlike chivalry, field sport did not belong to a single class. The allotment in the *Book of St. Albans* of a distinct hawk to each class in society from the prince to the yeoman, and even to the unclassed ' poor man,' had a meaning which was in accordance with the religious teaching of the *Royn Racio*, and the clerk by whom the following words were written points out how the sporting instinct of the poor may be gratified in the taking of birds as a means of living: *Les poures qui de ce se vivant y prennent ausi grant plaisance* (*Roy Modus*).

Henry V., on the eve of Agincourt, thus spoke to each soldier who should shed his blood with him:

> be he ne'er so vile,
> This day shall gentle his condition.
> (*King Henry V.*, Act IV., Scene 3.)

and in the same spirit Gaston Phœbus declares every true sportsman to have the true quality of gentleman.

As time went on the institution of chivalry became more and more unsuited to the conditions of the warfare of the day. In the time of its decadence it was disfigured by extravagance and affectation. The would-be gentleman, who bought a Book of Sport to learn something of the hawking language, discoursed of heraldry and the blazoning of arms, as he was taught by the manuals of gentlemanlike learning which were in vogue up to the end of the seventeenth century.* The language of heraldry was affected by the Shallows and Slenders of the day, without strict regard to accuracy. This did not escape the notice of Shakespeare.

SLEN.: They may give the dozen white luces in their coat.
SHAL.: It is an old coat. . . .
SLEN.: I may quarter, Coz.
SHAL: You may by marrying.
　　　It is marrying indeed, if he quarter it.†

The age of chivalry and of *La Grande Chasse*, with its forms and ceremonies, passed away, but 'the spirit of chivalry left behind it a more valuable successor. The character of knight gradually sub-

---

* Treatises on the ' Blasing of armys ' formed part of the *Book of St. Albans ;* of Peacham's *Compleat Gentleman ;* and Blome's *Gentleman's Recreation.*

† *Merry Wives*, i., 1, 16.

sided in that of gentleman; and the one distinguishes European Society in the sixteenth and seventeenth centuries, as much as the other did in the preceding ages. . . . Time has effaced much of this gentlemanly, as it did of the chivalrous character.'* Although much has been taken away, much remains, and from a common source, the French nation, and English-speaking people throughout the world have derived a spirit of chivalry in warfare and in sport which is wanting in nations of purely Teuton origin. To the civilising influences of chivalry and of the chase, infused into the upper classes by the Norman invaders, another civilising influence was added by which the population of England was more generally affected. The spirit of courtesy is innate in the tribal system of the Celt as surely as in the Norman institution of chivalry. Dr. Johnson, a typical Englishman, observing among the Highlanders of Scotland the courtesy that is also found among the peasantry of Ireland, attributed it to the influence of the clan system. 'Civility seems part of the national character of Highlanders. Every Chieftain is a monarch; and politeness, the natural product of royal government, is diffused from the laird through the entire clan.'† When Dr. Johnson visited the Highlands of Scotland, evidences of the former existence of the tribal system were apparent which have long since disappeared from England and from Ireland. But characteristics and qualities acquired in the infancy of a people, like the ideas and habits of childhood, seem to be infused into the blood; they survive the lapse of centuries, and

* Hallam, *Middle Ages*, chap. ix., pt. II.
† *A Journey through the Western Highlands.*

radicaı changes in forms of government, and conditions of life. The peoples of English origin throughout the world are sometimes spoken of as the Anglo-Saxon race. But they are not of purely Teuton origin. To the gentlemen of Elizabeth's time who, in the words of Harrison (*Description of England*, 1577), were 'not knowen to have come in with William Duke of Normandie,' there had come, in the course of four centuries, a large admixture of Norman blood. Recent research has shown that the Celtic inhabitants of Britain were not exterminated by the Saxon invaders in the manner supposed by the earlier writers. Of the England which was brought into existence by the Anglo-Saxon invasion they formed a substantial element, especially in the Western counties, where, in the laws of Ine, King of Wessex, we find special legislation for the protection of the native British.

The British soldier of to-day reckons among his ancestors the hardy barbarian of the north, by whom the great Roman empire was overthrown. But he is also the outcome of civilising influences, among which, with the infusion of Norman and Celtic blood, the traditions of the chase should not be forgotten. The spirit of chivalrous fair play—even to the hunted quarry—which had its origin in the Middle Ages, passed into the popular games and pastimes of later years. The name of the great national games of England has by common consent been taken as typical of honest sport, and negation of the spirit of this game, in a homely phrase, is the severest comment that can be passed on foul play or treachery in warfare, politics, or sport.

The Book of Sport holds the honourable position of a branch of literature which received distinction and appreciative notice from Shakespeare. When Hector unarmed visits the tents of the Greeks, Achilles says to him:

Now, Hector, I have fed my eyes on thee. I have with exact view perused thee, Hector, and quoted joint by joint.

Then follows:

HECT.: Is this Achilles?
ACHIL.: I am Achilles.
HECT.: Stand fair, I pray thee; let me look on thee.
ACHIL.: Behold thy fill.
HECT.: Nay, I have done already.
ACHIL.: Thou art too brief; I will the second time,
As I would buy thee, view thee limb by limb.
HECT.: O, like a book of sport thou'ld read me o'er;
But there is more in me than thou understand'st.*

To Shakespeare the Book of Sport meant more than a grammar and dictionary of the hawking and hunting languages, uses to which it was put by the would-be gentleman of the Tudor age.

The collection of old-world books on sport and horsemanship upon which these pages are founded had its origin in an attempt to extract from them something by which light might be thrown on Shakespeare's modes of thought and forms of expression. Many of the works contained in this collection were written in the sixteenth century, when the literature of the chase attained to general popularity. But the spirit of the Middle Ages continued to inspire the Book of Sport, and the influence of this spirit is discernible up to the end of the seventeenth century.

* *Troilus and Cressida,* iv., 5, 231.

3

CHAPTER II

ALBERTUS MAGNUS AND THE HORSE

'OUR public libraries are cemeteries of departed reputations, and the dust accumulated upon their untouched volumes speaks as forcibly as the grass that waves over the ruins of Babylon.'

These words were written by Hallam in the year 1818 of the scholastic philosophy, so famous for several ages. Since they were written, the grass that then waved over the buried cities of Babylon, Troy, and Cnossus, has been disturbed, and long-buried treasures of rare interest have been dug out of the ruins. Writing in 1848, Hallam owns that he did not, when he wrote these words, anticipate the attention which the books of the schoolmen were to attract in modern Europe. 'For several years past,' he adds, 'the metaphysicians of Germany and France have brushed the dust from the Scholastic volumes.'

Hallam's words are still true of another long-buried mediæval literature. It had as its Father the great man to whom the scholastic philosophy owes its origin, and it had in its day a reputation, different indeed from that of the works of the schoolmen, but perhaps more widely diffused.

That Albertus Magnus was the Father of scholastic philosophy is well known. That he was also the father of the mediæval literature of field sport and horses is a fact which, when understood, brings out in its true proportions the life and character of this most human of schoolmen, and throws light on some of the stories and legends that have clustered around his name. His great work, in which he systematised the philosophy of Aristotle, and adapted it to the requirements of ecclesiastical dogma, was the foundation of the philosophy of his famous pupil St. Thomas Aquinas, whose system, according to Professor Seth, ' is simply that of Albert, rounded to a greater completeness, and elaborated in parts by the subtle intellect of the younger man.'* His reputation in his own time was unrivalled. He was acclaimed Albert the Great, the Universal Doctor; a tribute to his all-embracing knowledge. Albert died in 1280. Dante, writing about twenty years later, places him in the Heaven of the Sun at the right hand of Thomas of Aquin, among the fathers and doctors of the church.

The studies and writings of this extraordinary man were not confined within the limits of theology and philosophy. With the exception of Roger Bacon, he was the most learned man of his age in natural and experimental science. His writings on these subjects fill five of the twenty-one folio volumes in which his collected works were printed in 1657. He was accredited with achievements so varied as the invention of artillery, and the construction of the plans for Cologne cathedral. The marvellous results of his experiments and his mechanical skill won for him the character of magician, not only with the vulgar, but with his disciple Ubrech d'Engel, who writes *In rebus magicis*

* *Ency. Brit.* (eleventh edition), *Albertus Magnus.*

expertus fuit. He was the subject of many traditions and legends, some of which are noted by his biographer, Dr. Joachim Sighart. Others of a more curious character, to one of which I shall presently refer, are related by Bayle in his *Dictionary*.

One of the legends recorded by Dr. Sighart is as follows: ' His pupil Thomas, led by curiosity to explore the secrets of the master's workshop in his absence, found himself face to face with the enchanting figure of a young girl, which addressed to him the salutation *Salve, Salve, Salve*. Believing that the prince of hell was sporting with him, Thomas broke the image into pieces, exclaiming, "Begone, Satan!" When he was flying from the room he met the master, who thus addressed him: "Thomas! Thomas! What have you done? You have destroyed the labour of thirty years." '

Dr. Sighart believes that there was a foundation of fact for this, as for other legends and traditions. He finds it difficult to doubt that ' Albertus manufactured automatons that were able to pronounce certain words, and to move a few paces; for he so frequently speaks of these things, and goes into so many details that we are obliged to take his words in their literal sense.'

I cannot find that any of the biographers or eulogists of this man of many-sided genius have accorded to him the primacy in the literature of horses and mediæval sport, and yet his claim to it is indisputable.

Some time between the years 1262 and 1280, when Albertus was teaching at Cologne, he gave to the world an elaborate work, in the manner of his master, Aristotle, entitled *De Animalibus.*

This treatise is of purely scientific character, until the writer in treating of quadrupeds in alphabetical order (Lib. XXII.) comes to the word *equus*, when the work from a work on natural science becomes a practical treatise on horses and farriery under the title *De infirmitatibus equorum*, occupying many closely printed folio pages in the copy in the possession of the present writer.* This is succeeded by short notes on other quadrupeds. Lib. XXIII. is concerned with birds, and at the word *falco* there is interposed a practical treatise on falconry in all its branches divided into twenty-four chapters, which became the textbook on this branch of sport during the Middle Ages. Having circulated in manuscript during more than two centuries it was printed in Rome in 1478 by the title of *Albertus Magnus De Falconibus, Asturibus et Accipitribus. In Opere De Animalibus.*

The treatise *De infirmitatibus equorum* does not appear to have been separately printed, but it also must have had a wide circulation in manuscript. For I find it referred to as a classic by a well-known authority on horsemanship, writing in the year 1573. Claudio Corte, a celebrated professor of horsemanship, brought from Italy by Robert Dudley, earl of Leicester, was for a time in the service of Elizabeth. Returning to Italy, he published in 1573 his work on horsemanship entitled *Il Cavallarizzo*. Among writers whose works were of great service to him he mentions Albertus Magnus, and as it is not likely that a ponderous folio on natural philosophy

* Venice, 1519.

formed part of his library, it is reasonable to conclude that he, and the mediæval horse masters
who consulted the work of Albert, had access to it
in manuscript in a separate form.

When we find a great philosopher or dramatist
interrupting the course of his teaching, or literary
work, by references to sport and to horsemanship
founded on the personal experience of the writer,
we turn with interest to the history of his life,
in search of an explanation of such unexpected
irrelevance. In the instance of Shakespeare an
explanation is suggested by the years of early
manhood spent in Stratford-on-Avon, with traditions of trouble connected with deer, and of
resort to the care of horses as a means of earning
a livelihood. Scanty as is the information which
has come down to us in regard to the early life
of Albertus, it is sufficient to suggest an answer
to our inquiries, and in his case also history is
supplemented by tradition and legend.

He was born in the year 1193 at Lauinger in
Suabia: a membei of the noble house of Bollstadt.
' The days of his childhood are surrounded with
an almost impenetrable darkness.' So writes
Dr. Sighart, adding that it could not be doubted
' that the body of the youth acquired at that period
in the exercises of a chivalrous life an energy,
suppleness, and strength which imparted to his
mind in later life, and even till he was far advanced
in years, the vigorous impulse of a wonderful
activity.' (*Life*, Eng. Trans., London, 1876.)

The University of Padua was founded in 1222
by the Emperor Frederick II., Duke of Suabia,
and Albertus, son of one of his Suabian nobles,

became a student. He was then twenty-nine years of age. It seems strange that a youth of such promise was not sent to a university at an earlier age. There was then no university in Germany, but the University of Bologna, of which Albertus afterwards became a member, had been founded in the eleventh century.

The fact that Albertus passed in his father's castle of Bollstadt some twelve years which were ordinarily spent in a university by youths of his condition, has had some interesting consequences. It enabled the future doctor to acquire the practical knowledge of horses and hawks to which he makes claim in his writings, and it has, as we shall see, given rise in modern times to some curious theories and speculations. There would have been no reason to doubt that the years between the ages of seventeen at which students usually entered the universities, and twenty-nine, when we find him at Padua, were spent in his father's castle in the enjoyment, like other noble youths, of the field sports and manly exercises to which his energetical disposition and great physical strength would naturally incline him, even if we had not his own statement that his knowledge of the art of falconry was derived from practical experience as well as from a study of the best authorities, and that what he wrote on horses, and the many infirmities to which they are subject, came from himself. The exact date at which Albertus put into writing the result of his experiences of horses and hawks cannot be ascertained. It is probable that these treatises were written before he entered the University of Padua. In the early years of manhood his intellectual powers and literary instinct would have lain fallow in the castle of Bollstadt if they had not been made to yield this harvest. His various occupations during the later years of his life are well known. From Padua he joined the Dominican preaching order. He taught and preached in the cities of Cologne, Hildesheim, Strasburg, Friburg, and Ratisbon. With intervals, he taught in a school at Cologne from 1243 till his death in 1280. He had reluctantly accepted the bishopric of Ratisbon, but after a few years he resigned the bishopric and in 1262 returned to his office of teacher in the convent at Cologne. The composition of his *De Animalibus* is attributed to some time between that date and his death in 1280.

At no time during the years of strenuous life as student, preacher, and teacher of philosophy, would it have been possible for Albert to have acquired, as falconer and horseman, a practical knowledge of the keeping of hawks and the curing of horses. But the memories of early life, and of the sports and pursuits in which he first found a field for the exercise of the powers of research and exposition of which he was conscious, were ever with him. He had carefully preserved what he had written of his favourite pursuits, and when in the course of a scientific treatise on natural history he came to the words *equus* and *falco*, he became once more Albertus of Bollstadt, and took delight in letting the world know what these words meant to him.

To the learned world of the day this was foolishness which the great doctor might well have forgotten. But to Albert it was part of his nature.

In the light of his reminiscences of the sports and exercises of his early years, and of legends, the truth of which matters not, when they are understood as evidences of the nature and character of the man of whom they related, we obtain a glimpse of one to whom the word myriad-minded might be applied without a sense of disproportion. For Albert, though he wrote in prose of theology and of philosophy, was at heart both a sportsman and a poet.   Dr. Sighart says of one of his works, his *Mariale :* ' It is less a dogmatic and learned treatise than a poem, in which the imagination, like an industrious bee, gathers from every object of creation, and from the flowers of science the honey of its arguments in her praise.'

As Jeremy Taylor is the Shakespeare of Divines, so the great Albert is the Shakespeare of Schoolmen.   Like Shakespeare he was true throughout his life to his first love.   Shakespeare wrote no prose treatise on sport or on horses in the years of early manhood passed at Stratford.   But in a poem which he calls ' the first heir of my invention ' we find a pen-and-ink sketch of the perfect English horse which may be compared with the ideal horse of Albertus (*post*, p. 41) ; a representation so exact in all details that Professor Dowden asks, ' Is it poetry or a passage from an advertisement of a horse sale ?'

In the same poem we find the story of a hare hunt, unsurpassed in truthfulness and vigour, and in his latest plays—in *The Tempest* and in *Cymbeline*—he dwells as lovingly on horses and hounds as in the days of *Venus and Adonis* and *Love's Labour's Lost*.

Though Albert's *De Falconibus Asturibus et Accipitribus* is a practical handbook of falconry, the strong personality of the writer makes itself manifest, and in his indebtedness for instruction to the falconer of the great emperor Frederick II., we have a link connecting the earliest and greatest of the mediæval writers on field sport. The treatise begins with an elaborate description of the various kinds of long-winged hawks (falcons), noble and ignoble, including one named *Sacrum*— which Symmachus calls *Britannicum* — which loves man and sporting dogs (*canes venaticos*) and takes a pride in hunting its best when they are with it. Then follows the practical part of the work. Cap. 17 treats of the management and training of falcons. Cap. 18 of the treatment of the various diseases of falcons according to Gulielmus, the falconer of king Rogerus. This Gulielmus was to Albert the great authority as regards both long-winged and short-winged hawks. His *dicta* are treated with the highest respect. He tells us that he adopts, in the first place, the results of the experience of Gulielmus, adding a little of his own.*

Here we see that Albert's treatise is not a mere compilation from the writings of others. Something is added as the result of his own experience, and he does not hesitate to point out errors into which his masters have fallen.

He cannot, he says, pass over in silence an assertion of Aquila, of Theodotio, and of Symmachus, associated with them. ' They call all

---

* *Precipue experta Gulielmi regis Rogerii falconarii secuti sumus, pauca de nostris adjicientes.*

kinds of short-winged hawks "falcons." They define them as being of four species, placing the goshawks, as of the first excellence, in the first species, placing the lesser goshawk which we call " tercel " (*tercellinum*) in the second species, the sparrow hawk (*nisum*) in the third species, and the musket (*muscetum*) in the fourth species. The fact that the tercel is found in the airie of the goshawk (*accipitris*) proves that it is quite impossible to agree with them; also the musket is found in the airie of the sparrow hawk, and accordingly the goshawk and the tercel differ only as to sex, not as to species; the goshawk is the female and the tercel is the male. The sparrow hawk and the musket differ in the same way; the sparrow hawk is the female and the musket is the male.'

The terminology of falconry has perplexed not only poets and dramatists, but even learned lexicographers, for we find the great Dr. Johnson thus misquoting,

> A falcon towering in *his* pride of place
> Was by a mousing owl hawked at and killed.

And in that vast storehouse of accurate information now happily within measurable distance of completion, we read ' falcon-gentle, a name applied to the female and young of the goshawk,' an error corrected in a note prefixed to the fourth volume.*

* Emendation. ' The falcon-gentle is the female of the peregrine, not of the goshawk . . . and the male is the tercel-gentle ' (D. H. Madden, *Diary of Master William Silence*, 1897, p. 376).

I cannot refrain from noting that it fell to the lot of Albertus Magnus more than six centuries ago to correct an error of the same kind, occurring in a kind of literature where we should least expect to find it, not a dictionary compiled by men of letters, but practical treatises on the art of falconry.

The ' falcon ' is the female of the long-winged species. The males of the hawks principally used in falconry—the peregrine and goshawk— were called ' tiercels ' or ' tercels ' because (it is said) they are smaller than the females by one third; the male of the nobler species—the pere- grine—being distinguished by the addition of the word ' gentle.' The male of the goshawk is the tercel.

The writers from whom Albert dissents, misled probably by the difference in size, treated the tercel as of a different species. The mistakes of the authorities from whom Albert dissents were twofold; they called the females of both kinds ' falcons,' and they treated the tercel as of a different species from the goshawk, and the musket from the sparrow hawk.

It is interesting to find the youth who was to become the great schoolman Albertus confuting the errors of these masters of the art, not by a process of scholastic reasoning, but by an experi- mental interrogation of nature. Climbing to the airie of a sparrow hawk in the forest of Bollstadt, he observed a musket flying out of it, and thence- forth he found it impossible to agree with the theorists, who, from a consideration of the difference in size between it and the sparrow hawk, satisfied themselves that they must be of different species.

Thus by a plain tale the theories of Aquila, Symmachus, and Theodotio were put down.

The child is father of the man, and in the youthful Albert we find the characteristics which are discernible in the learned doctor of Cologne. An earnest student, he mastered the literature of falconry which had even then attained respectable dimensions: a sportsman, he brought the *dicta* of the masters of the art to the test of his own experience; and a natural philosopher, he corrected errors in their natural history of birds of prey by the result of his personal observation of their habits.

Neither king Rogerus, nor king Ptolemy with his ancient correspondents, may have had any existence in fact, but there is no question as to another of Albert's masters, the emperor Frederick II. Next to the authority of the great Gulielmus he ranks the experience (*experta*) of the emperor and of his falconer. This falconer is not named, and the treatise of the emperor is not referred to. It is more than probable that Albertus was a disciple in the art of falconry of this unnamed falconer. If so he studied in a famous school. A practical interest in falconry was hereditary in the princes of the house of Hohenstaufen, dukes of Suabia. Frederick Barbarossa, duke of Suabia, was elected emperor in 1152. He is said to have introduced falconry into Italy from the East, and there can be no doubt that he introduced it also into his native Suabia, for we find in his grandson, Frederick II., duke of Suabia, a famous professor of the art, and Manfred, son of the second Frederick, completed his father's treatise, which was left unfinished at his death.

The unnamed falconer of Frederick II. did not, like the great Gulielmus, commit to writing his *experta*, or those of his masters. It is not at all likely that Albert had access to the unfinished manuscript of the work of the emperor, from which his work is not copied. It is more probable that the *experta* were communicated by the falconer to Albert while he was still in the Suabian castle of Bollstadt. He may be taken to have commenced falconry some fifteen years before he entered the University of Padua—that is to say, about the year 1274. Frederick died in 1250. If his falconer had been then forty years of age, he may well have been the great authority at whose feet the young Suabian nobleman sat, and from whom he learned the *experta* of his master.

Albert's treatise on horses is, as its title denotes, a practical manual of farriery. It has this special interest that it is wholly the result of the personal experience of the writer. It is interpolated in the twenty-second book of the *De Animalibus* when the author comes to the quadruped *equus*. It is not, like the work on falconry, subdivided into numbered chapters, but in the table of contents prefixed to the copy in the possession of the present writer the chapters relating to the horse are distinguished by the title *De infirmitatibus equorum et de curatione earumdem*, and at the end of the treatise these words are added: *hac de cura equorum sunt a nobis*. Apart from this distinct statement, there is much in the writer's treatment of the subject to show that it is the result of practical experience. Albert does not hold himself responsible for the paragraph which follows those words, but with this exception the treatise is wholly his own.

The views of Albertus on the points of a horse are expressed in terms for which I have endeavoured to find suitable equivalents in the English language. The words which I have chosen are not in every instance those that would be adopted by the writer of a Latin-English dictionary. For example, *siccus* when used of the head of a horse is intended to convey the idea which we express by the word ' fine '; and the characteristics of the horse which possesses *meritum*, as described by Albertus, suggest what we understand by the term ' quality.'

In regard to horses, four matters are taken into consideration, that is to say, shape, good looks, quality, and colour (*forma : pulchritudo : meritum . color*).

Shape; when the body is powerful and hardy, and the height corresponds with the strength; the flanks lengthy, the buttocks round; the whole body knotted, as it were, with thick and numerous muscles; the legs strong and firm, extending clean (*equaliter*) from the knee to the foot, without knottiness, swelling, or any tenderness, without any growths: the foot, moreover, level with a smooth surface—that is, not rough—round, with hollow hoof, touching the ground all round.

Good looks are when the head is small in comparison with the body, and very fine (*siccus*), so that the hide, as it were, shines over the bones (*immineat*, cf. *imminente luna*, Hor., od. 1.4.5). Eyes, large, so to speak, projecting from the head.

Ears short and pointed, reaching forward, as it were. Nostrils wide, plunged deeply in the water when he is drinking; crest high; mane thick, tail large and long; and in the body a thorough roundness with general firmness.

As regards quality (*meritum*), it is accounted good that he should be very spirited, digging up and tearing the ground under his feet, neighing, his limbs quivering, for this is a sign of courage; one that is easily aroused from extreme repose and easily stayed and quieted from the greatest excitement.

The natural colour of the horse that is caught in the forests is dun; a dark line stretching from his head to the tail. But, among those which are domesticated, the blacks, the chestnut, and sometimes the white are found to be good; likewise the grey that have black and white hair dappled, as if small circles were intermingled.

This is the ideal horse of Albertus, and with it may be compared a picture of the perfect English horse, drawn with pen and ink as

> when a painter would surpass the life
> In limning out a well-proportioned steed.

The mane of the horse of Albert is thick, otherwise the description of the horse of Adonis might serve as a rendering into English poetry of the Latin prose of Albert:

So did this horse excel a common one,
In shape, in courage, colour, pace and bone.
Round-hoofed, short-jointed, fetlocks shag and long,
  Broad breast, full eye, small head, and nostril wide,
High crest, short ears, straight legs, and passing strong,
  Thin mane, thick tail, broad buttock, tender hide;
Look what a horse should have, he did not lack.

Ven. & Ad., 289-290.

'This is an animal liable to many diseases.'
Thus writes Albert, and Shakespeare was of the
same opinion, for according to Grumio, Petruchio
would marry for money 'an old trot, though she
have as many diseases as two and fifty horses'
(*Taming of the Shrew*, i. ii. 81).

It is not easy to identify all the diseases to
which horseflesh is subject, which with their
appropriate remedies are enumerated in detail
by Albert. But about *Lambistus* and *farcina*
there is no doubt. These terms of art are thus
englished by Shakespeare: 'troubled with the
lampas, infected with the fashions.' According
to Gervais Markham 'farcin' or the 'farcy'
is 'of our ignorant smiths called the fashions.'

Although Albert's treatise had a high reputation
in the Middle Ages, and was, as we have seen,
regarded as a classic up to the sixteenth century,
it was never printed in a separate form. This
may be accounted for by the great popularity of a
work entitled *Marescalciæ Equorum* of Laurentius
Ruffus or Rusius, written in 1462, and printed
in 1490. This treatise was frequently reprinted,
and its popularity and extensive circulation may
account for the fact that the older treatise of
Albertus, with other treatises on horses noted by
Mr. Huth in his *Bibliographical Record of Hippo-
logy*, were allowed to remain in manuscript.

Turning from history to tradition, we find that
some circumstances connected with the early
life of Albertus and also with his closing years
seemed so strange as to supply the foundation
of a legend. This legend, handed down through
the Middle Ages, reached Bayle in the form of a

story that ' he was miraculously converted from an ass into a philosopher, and afterwards from a philosopher into an ass' (*Dictionary*).

There was some difficulty to be overcome before Albert was led to devote himself to the study of philosophy and theology. The least probable explanation is that adopted by some of his biographers, when they ' speak of grave difficulties which fettered the progress of his studies; a certain dullness of apprehension; clouds which obscured his mind, and kept him in the lowest place among his fellow disciples.' This explanation is rightly rejected by Dr. Sighart. ' How, indeed, can it be supposed that Albert, studying at Bologna, should show himself wanting in facility and talent after having devoted himself for ten years at Padua to philosophical studies with a success that merited for him the glorious surname of Master ?' According to the legend the difficulties which beset Albert were miraculously removed by a heavenly visitant, while he was at the same time assured that all his knowledge was destined to disappear before his death. ' After this apparition,' says Bayle, ' he showed a prodigious deal of wit, and improved in all sciences with a quickness which astonished all his masters, but three years before his death he forgot in an instant all he knew and being at a stand in a lecture of divinity at Cologne, and endeavouring in vain to recall his ideas, he was sensible that it was the fulfilment of the prediction.'

Albert died at Cologne in 1280 at the age of eighty-seven. That he lost his memory some time before his death may be accepted as a historical fact, and as the foundation of the legend, so far as it relates to the conversion of the philosopher before his death into an ass. But from what previous state of life and .feeling was Albert converted into a philosopher ? Not assuredly from a condition of stupidity. Is it not more probable that a longing to return to the field sports of Suabia, the love of which abode with him throughout his life, may have been a real difficulty in the way of Albertus when he resolved to join the Dominican order ? Pursuits which in the eyes of the learned doctors of Padua were foolishness were not forgotten when in Cologne he taught philosophy to St. Thomas, and systematised and Christianised the philosophy of Aristotle, and the choice which converted Albertus of Bollstadt, falconer and horse master, into the great preacher and universal doctor, may well have been attributed by the pious begetters of legend to a direct interposition of Providence.

The early experiences of this great schoolman and his lifelong devotion to the pursuits of his youth may be compared with the history of a famous scholar of a later date, who was a leading humanist in the revival of learning. Guillaume Budé, better known by his latinised name Budæus, ' was beyond question the best Greek scholar of his day in Europe, being superior in this respect to Erasmus, though no rival to him in literary genius.'* He was born in 1467, the son of *Jean Budé, Signeur d'Yerre de Villiers-sur-Marne, Marly et autres lieux.* He spent three years at the University of Orleans. 'After he returned to his

* Sir Richard Jebb, *Cambridge Modern History*, i., p. 576.

father's home, he lost much more time; he spent his days in hunting and the pleasures of youth, but quitted them after some years, and had such an inclination for learning that the ardour where-with he applied himself to study is not to be ex-pressed ' (Bayle, *Dictionary*). In this respect his history resembles that of another youth of noble birth, whose early years were devoted to sport and horsemanship, and who betaking himself to study, *sero sed serio*, and becoming the greatest scholar of his age, did not disdain to be known as the author of a work on sport. Albertus Magnus lived in the age of legend, Budæus in that of bio-graphy. Accordingly Bayle records of Albert the ancient legend that he was miraculously converted from an ass into a philosopher, while of Budæus, he tells us, following a contemporary biographer, that he was happily changed from an idler to a student.

Some recent biographers in defiance of testimony have invented a date for the birth of Albertus, in order to make the events of his life fit in with their preconceived ideas of what ought to have been. This is quite in accordance with the practice of certain classes of literary critics and of expert witnesses. But in this instance their theories are hopelessly at variance with historic fact. They regard it as unlikely that a student entering a university at the age of twenty-nine should have become the greatest scholar of his age. The probability therefore is that Albert came to Padua when he was about seventeen, and as the university was not founded until 1222, it follows that he could not have been born in 1193.

The reasoning is good of its kind, but it is unfortunately opposed to testimony not only as to his birth, but as to the circumstances of his death. It is a historical fact that Albert attained a great age and that he survived his faculties. If he was born at the date invented by these theorists, 1206, he would have been seventy-four at the time of his death, a good old age, but not one that would have been recorded as extraordinary. Nor is it likely that death at that age would have been preceded by three years of loss of memory from senile decay. The authentic date is retained by Dr. Sighart. In the note on Albertus Magnus in the *Encyclopædia Britannica* the date is thus stated: ' ? 1206–1280 . . . the date of his birth generally given as 1193 is more probably 1206.'

The date of the birth, even of a great man, is a matter of fact. In the absence of evidence of fact, or in the face of contradictory testimony, regard may be fairly had to probability. But in the case of Albert, historic testimony and probability point in the same direction. The years of early manhood, spent in the castle of Bollstadt before he entered the University of Padua, at the age of twenty-nine, are the only years of his life in which it would have been possible for Albert to have acquired the practical knowledge of horses and of falconry to which, in later years, he laid claim, in works each of which took rank as a recognised authority.

The literature of the *Haute École* lies beyond the scope of this volume. It had its origin in the middle of the sixteenth century when the famous *Ordini di Cavalcare* was published by Frederico

Grisone, whom all the writers on horsemanship acknowledge as their master. Italy was the source of the new literature of horsemanship, whence riding-masters were imported into England and France, who became authors of well-known treatises.

The spirit of the Middle Ages yet lingered in the elaborate and somewhat fantastic exercises of this school of horsemanship, and in the famous illustrations which adorn the pages of the *Maneige Royal* of Pluvinel (1623), and of the great work to which the marquis—afterwards duke—of Newcastle devoted the years of exile between his defeat at the battle of Marston Moor and the restoration of his pupil, Charles II., to the throne of England (*Methode de dresser des Chevaux Anvers*, 1657).

CHAPTER III

LE LIVRE DU ROY MODUS AND LA GRANDE CHASSE

THIS is the most interesting of the old-world Books of Sport. Not only is it the earliest and most famous of the great French classics, but it is of literary and historical value; for the author has, with consummate skill, interwoven with instruction in the mysteries of woodcraft a trenchant satire directed against abuses in Church and State. We also catch a glimpse of life in Normandy in the early years of the fourteenth century, for a poetical interlude introduces us not only to courtly knights, with dames who discourse in verse of the merits of the sports to which they were devoted, but also to rustic hunters and falconers, after a good day's sport, quarrelling in homely prose over the comparative merits of the same sports, and then, warmed by the generous wine of their host, coming to blows in the kitchen of a village inn.

The authorship of the *Roy Modus* has been the subject of industrious research by writers in England as well as in France. 'About the authorship of this important work there has waged quite as much controversy as about the date of its composition, and numerous bibliophiles have studied and written upon the question.'* Curiosity

---

* Baillie-Grohman, *Master of Game*, Bibliography.

49

has been stimulated by the inclusion in two manuscripts, one of which is as ancient as 1379, of a kind of anagram in which letters are contained in a *rosace*. We are told that the letters in the outer part of the *rosace*, when properly arranged, indicate the name and surname of the ' maker ' of the book, *de celui qui c'est livre fist ;* the letters in the inner circle those *du clerk qui son songe escript.**

In an inquiry into the authorship of a work the first witness to be called is the book itself. The testimony of the book ought to be accepted in the absence of evidence to the contrary, for experience shows that in the vast majority of cases it is deserving of credit. Literary forgeries are not unknown, but they are few in number. There are such things as literary conventions and devices, but they are not designed to deceive, and they, in fact, deceive none but the extremely simple-minded. Indeed, they are often of great value in the discernment of truth, where the authorship has to be discovered of a book, which, like the *Roy Modus*, contains no direct statement on the point.

The *Roy Modus* contains statements of fact and also conventions. When the author states that he had seen king Charles IV. hunting in the Forêt de Breteuil, it has been reasonably inferred that he was recording a reminiscence of a former king. Charles IV. died in 1328, and, as a manuscript is extant written in 1379 which contains

* This anagram is reproduced in M. Blaze's edition of the *Roy Modus*. It will also be found in Mr. Harting's *Bibliotheca Accipitraria*, and in facsimile in an elaborate note in the bibliography appended to Mr. Baillie-Grohman's edition of the *Master of Game.*

the whole of the work, it follows that it was completed before that date. From internal evidence, which has been accepted as conclusive, it is evident that the book was written in Normandy. The problem of the authorship was to discover in Normandy, living between the years 1328 and 1379, a possible author to whom the work could be attributed consistently with the literary quality of the work and the indications of the *rosace*.

For more than five hundred years the riddle of the *rosace* remained unsolved. If a promising *nom* and *surnom* had been evolved by a skilful manipulation of the letters in the outer circle, chronology intervened and the illusion was dispelled by an impossible date. At last, in the year 1880, M. Victor Bouton, Héraut d'Armes, by a happy discovery raised the inquiry from an attempt to solve an ingenious puzzle to the level of an interesting literary investigation.

In a curious poem, *Le Trésor de la Vénerie*, written in 1394 by Messire Hardouin de Fontaines-Guerin, he found coupled with the name of Gaston Phœbus, comte de Foix, that of another noble sportsman and *acteur*, the comte de Tancarville.

Gaston Phœbus, comte de Foix, was the author of a famous work *La Chasse*, the second in date of the French classics. The word *acteur* was in use when Hardouin wrote in the sense of 'author.' Gace de la Buigne, in his *Romans des Déduits*, writing of the book on falconry of the 'great St. Denys,' calls the author *acteur*.

> Un acteur qui fut de grand pris
> Qui fut evesque de senlis.

112228

The word is evidently applied by Hardouin in the same sense to Gaston Phœbus and to de Tancarville. They are both celebrated as authors, *acteurs*.

Hardouin wrote in 1394, and it is probable that at that time the connection of de Tancarville with the *Roy Modus* was an open secret, for his interest in the literature of sport is attested by writers of the day.

De Tancarville was a great Norman nobleman who played an important part in the Hundred Years' War. He is often mentioned by Froissart. At the battle of Poitiers he and his son were taken prisoners with king John, whom he accompanied to England, where we shall find him recognised as an authority in regard to the literature of the chase.

When we first meet with the count in Froissart he is one of the members of the special council of the king of France sent by him ' to the council of England, which was then holden at London for the performance of the King of England's homage ' for the duchy of Aquitaine. Charles IV. had died in the year 1328. With him the senior male line of the house of Capet became extinct, and the crown, according to the rule of succession which came to be known as the Salic law, laid down by the French lawyers and adopted by the peers of France, passed to Philip VI. of Valois, to the exclusion of the claim of Edward III. of England, through his mother Isabella, daughter of Philip, the father of Charles IV. Apart from the Salic law, which excluded succession to the crown through a female, there were manifest infirmities in the title of Edward. It was not asserted for some years after the death of Charles, and Edward did homage to the king of France for Guienne.

It was in the autumn of 1339 that the comte de Tancarville, with other great lords of France, arrived in England and tarried all the winter, for it was not until the following May that the matter was concluded. On the arrival of the mission from France there was ' great consultation and much dispute about this homage, and murmuring by many who said that the king their lord was nearer by true succession of inheritance to the crown of France.' After the departure of the mission these murmurings took a definite form. Edward, by the advice of his council, put forward his claim, and the Hundred Years' War began.

In the early years of the war de Tancarville took an active and prominent part. He is several times mentioned by Froissart as acting with the constable of France; we find him foremost in the great host which the duke of Normandy brought with Gascons against the duke of Lancaster. He was sent with the constable of France as envoy from the duke to the king. In the battle of Poitiers ' King John with his own hands did very many great deeds, . . . near to the king there were taken the earl of Tancarville,' and at the famous supper given to the French king by the Black Prince on the day of the battle, ' the prince caused the king and his son, the lord John of Bourbon, the lord John d'Arbois, the earl of Tancarville (with four others) to sit at one table, and other lords, knights and squires at other tables ' (Froissart, Globe ed., 128, 131).

We next meet with de Tancarville at the court of king Edward III. Gace de la Buigne, an ecclesiastic of an old Norman family, accompanied king John to England after the battle of Poitiers, and the sporting education of king John's son Philip was entrusted to him. The king was removed in 1359 from the Savoy to Hereford, and the sporting priest then began his *Romans des Déduits*, written at the command of the king, ' so that the young prince Philip being learned in sport, might avoid the sin of idleness, and learn good manners and virtue.' The priest introduces as much moral advice as possible into his verse. There is a long discussion, characteristic of the age, on the comparative merits of hunting and hawking. The king holds a council, in which he is advised by knights, in favour of each sport. Among these advisers is the comte de Tancarville, described as knowing as much of one pastime as of the other, and as passionately devoted to both. King Edward of England is spoken of as one ' who knows no master in the science of hunting, and cedes the place of honour to no one in valour on the battle field.' Finally, choice is made of one to teach the laws of falconry and hunting to those at the French court. It is the comte de Tancarville who is to remain in England, and he is requested by the others to thank the king on their behalf for his judgment.

When we find de Tancarville taking part in the decision of a literary contest as to the comparative merits of hunting and hawking, we are not sur-

prised to find him a few years later mentioned by
Hardouin among the writers on field sports.

Independently of the testimony of Hardouin,
Mr. Harting was led for several reasons to attribute
the authorship of the *Roy Modus* to de Tancarville.
' His identity is sufficiently indicated by the letters
in the rosace.' The letters can be read as indi-
cating not the name, but the office of the making
of the books, from which his name may be learned.
The office is that of *régent régisseur*, which is
stated to have been held by de Tancarville; and
to arrive at the name through the office may have
been part of the puzzle. The count, who died in
1384, was alive at the date attributed to the
book, and, it may be added, he was a *grand
seigneur* of Normandy, where the book was written.
Mr. Harting also relies on the introduction of the
name of de Tancarville into the *Roy Modus*, a
matter of which more will be said hereafter, and
on the fact that he is specially mentioned as an
authority on falconry by a contemporary, Pero
Lopez de Ayala, in a work written in 1386. This
last consideration is entitled to great weight, for
if there had ever been a book on falconry written
by a man so famous as the comte de Tancarville
it is inconceivable that it should have been
allowed to pass out of remembrance, when works of
men like Gace de la Buigne, Hardouin, and Lopez
de Ayala survived, and except the *Roy Modus*
there is no known production of the fourteenth
century that could possibly be attributed to him.

On the other hand, Mr. Baillie-Grohman in
an important note* offers convincing reasons for

* *Master of Game*, Bibliography.

his conclusion that it is difficult to attribute the
composition of the work to ' a grand seigneur,
actively engaged, as he was, as a high functionary
at court, and employed with important missions
by his sovereigns and living at a time when his
country was distracted with the English invasions
and the internal feuds in Brittany, as well as
between the houses of Burgundy and Orleans.'
Even clearer evidence that the *Roy Modus* was
not altogether the composition of the comte
de Tancarville is afforded by the book itself.   For
the clerk by whom it was written, when he had
completed his work so far as it was concerned
with the sports of the field, addresses the reader
in his proper person, and tells the story of how
the continuation of the work came to be written,
in a manner which excludes the idea of authorship
by the comte de Tancarville.

In endeavouring to solve the riddle of the
rosace we may call in aid a custom of the Middle
Ages in accordance with which the name of some
great personage was associated with a treatise
on field sports, written by his direction and under
his patronage.   Jean de Malon, comte de Tancarville, was not a royal personage, like Charles III.
of Sicily, Francis I. of France, or Olonzo of Castile,
by whose command famous books were written.
But he was a great man at the court of France.
The ruined castle of Tancarville is an imposing
object on a lofty rock rising above the Seine,
between Havre and Rouen.   Such a man may
well have commanded the services of a learned
clerk to give to the world his sporting lore in
literary form.   De Tancarville was not a mere

sporting country gentleman, like Du Fouilloux, the author of the latest of the French classics. He had a wide experience of affairs in England and in France, and it is not surprising to find that he inspired into his work on field sport reflections on state and church of a kind that are absent from the ordinary book of sport.

In contemporary literature de Tancarville appears not only as a famous sportsman, but as the arbiter in an intellectual contest between the champions of different kinds of field sports. It is in this character that he appears in the *Roy Modus*, into which a poetical interlude is introduced, which would have no connection with the work unless it was devised for the purpose of presenting to the apprehension of the reader, in their proper persons, the originator of the work, to whom it owed its existence, and the learned clerk by whom it was composed. The riddle of the *rosace* must be read with the interpretation of the poem; and to read the poem aright, its place in the book must be understood.

The book brings us back to the golden age of a fabled king, the father of the art of venery. This was a convention common to many of the mediæval writers on sport and horsemanship.*

---

* It is a common literary device, in mediæval works of sport, to introduce an imaginary king as its patron. An ancient French manuscript on falconry, dated 19th Août, 1284, was a translation of a Latin work attributed to one Dancus, who was supposed to have been king of Armenia; it was printed in Paris in 1883 by the title of *Le livre du Roi Dancus*. As to the author, the editor concludes: *Nous devons donc penser que le roi Dancus et ses partenaires sont cousins germains du bon roi Artus de Bretagne, et des héros de la Table Ronde, c'est*

Dame Juliana Berne s in the *Boke of St. Albans*
instructs her pupils in the lore of Tristram.

> Wheresoevere ye fare by fryth or by fell;
> My dere chyld take hede how Trystam do you tell
> How many maner bestys of venery there were;
> Lystyn to youre dame and she shall you lere.

King Modus reigned in the happy time when

> Au temps du riche roy Modus
> Fut bien le monde en paix tenus.

Method, the king, represents systematised experience. He is wedded to queen Reason, *car
bonne manière fort sans raison, raison sans bonne
manière.* In some introductory verses the different
parts taken by Method and Reason in the affairs
of life are set forth:

> Modus a toutes emperique
> Par quoy scet les arts mécaniques.

But in the chase, as in the grave affairs of life,
mere experience, unaided by reflection, is of no
avail, and so,

> Sur toutes choses terriennes
> Sarrazines on crestiennes
> Ont Modus, Racio, pouvoir
> Riens sans eulx l'on ne peult savoir.

In the first of the quaint woodcuts in which
M. Blaze reproduces in reduced form the miniatures of an ancient manuscript, king Modus sits

---

a dire, des personages de pure invention. Albertus Magnus,
in his work on falconry, mentions among the ancient authorities on the sport the falconer of a king Rogerus, whose identity has never been discovered, and he speaks of a certain
Ptolemy of Egypt, a patron of falconry, who seems to be
equally mythical.

enthroned. Before him are his listening ' apprentices,' one of whom is ready to write down the words of wisdom which proceed from his lips,' and the treatise begins thus: *Aux temps que le Roy Modus donnoit doctrine de tous diduis il disait à les aprentiss.*

As in many other ancient treatises on sport—including that of our dame Juliana Bernes—instruction is given in the form of question and answer. The king explains to his disciples how, all men not being of the same will or courage, our Lord God ordained many kinds of sport so that every man is able to find a kind of sport in which he may find pleasure suitable to his nature and condition of life. *Car les ungs appartiennent aux riches.*

King Modus has two classes of disciples in his school of venery, the nobles who can afford to keep hounds and hawks, and the poor, whose sports are of a humbler nature, but who are also deserving of attention. *Le roy Modus donna manière comment on pouroit prendre toutes manières de bestes et d'oiseaulx des quelles l'une manière aprent aux nobles que sont puissans d'avoir chiens et filets et autres choses nécessaires, et les autres au poures qui ne sont mie puissans d'avoir chiens ne filets* (f. 13, r.).

The king begins with the chase of the stag *à force des chiens.* This is the finest of sports, and it occupies by far the largest proportion of the book. There are elaborate directions as to the harbouring of a warrantable stag. One of the woodcuts represents the assembly *comment les veneurs sont assemblée.* The outdoor dinner or

5

assembly, as it was called, was a prominent feature in the day's work, in England and Italy as well as in France, when a solemn hunting was organised by a prince or great lord. The *Noble Art of Venerie* contains a woodcut illustration of ' the place when and how an assembly should be made ' in the presence of queen Elizabeth, of whom a recognisable likeness is presented, and a fine engraving of a more elaborate entertainment is to be found in *Venaria Reale* (Turin, 1674). Then follows the chase of the stag, and the reward of the hounds, *la cuirée* (quarry); *comment on dont faire la cuirée aux chiens.*

The author treats, but not with the same elaboration, of the chase of the hind, the fallow buck, the roebuck, the hare, the wild boar, the wild sow, the wolf, the fox, and the otter. These are the ten beasts of venery.

Addressing his apprentices as those who were able to enjoy and maintain the kinds of sports which he had explained to them, he refers them to queen Racio for some special teaching, *doctrine en espécial*, which she is ready to impart, and in the meantime he announces to his apprentices of noble birth that he proposes to show his less mportant and poorer apprentices, *a mes petite poures aprentis*, some kinds of sport which cost little, and which they are able to maintain.

L'aprentis demande à la Rayne quelles sont les moralités et figures qui puent estre trouvées et figurées ès dix bestes dont le roy Modus nous a démonstré toute la vénerie. The teaching of queen Racio is a special feature of the *Roy Modus*. I find no ' moralities ' like it in other mediæval books of sport. There is, indeed, a passage, already quoted, from the *Romans des Déduits* of Gace de la Buigne, which suggests that instruction in *La Vénerie* was part of a liberal education in good manners and virtue. But the good queen Racio does not confine herself to lessons in morals. She deals with affairs of church and state. It is said by M. Blaze that in one of the ancient manuscripts of the *Roy Modus* the queen appears in state seated by the king, and it is interesting to find a writer in the middle of the Hundred Years' War assigning to a woman, in high command, the moderating power of reason.

> Ne pape, ne roy, ne prelaz
> Ne peuvent riens faire en nul cas
> Ce n'est de la puissant vertus
> De Racio et de Modus (f. 1, v.).

The teaching of the king on the chase as a providential institution, adapted to each class of the community, has been already quoted (*ante*, p. 59), and the queen's more detailed moralising may be reserved for a subsequent page.

Before the king proceeds to instruct his class of poor apprentices, he has something to say to his humble neighbours who are interested in the destruction and capture of wild animals, not for sport, nor as a means of earning a livelihood, but by way of protection against their ravages and for other practical reasons. *Le roy Modus commença a parler au poures non puissans d'avoir chiens et filez pour mener les déduits telz comme il avait dict et devise* (f. 69, r.). Eight chapters of the book are devoted to instructing those who have not hounds how to take animals with slight assistance from nets, and to suggesting many devices by which wild animals may be captured. A poor man approaches the king and says to him, ' Sire, I live near a forest, and I suffer much from a wild boar that comes to my garden; kindly advise me how I may take him.' The king enters into elaborate details as to the construction of a pitfall, and the manner in which the beast is to be enticed to it. Another poor man asks how he is to get rid of the wolves who are so numerous that they destroy his cattle, and is instructed in a rather barbarous manner of killing them by mixing needles in food left in their way. A third poor man is told of a mode of baiting a trap by which the destructive roe deer in the forest near his house may be taken. A poor man, who had no means of taking a hare save by a single net that he possessed, is instructed as to how to use this net to best advantage. Another poor man is told how he may take quantities of rabbits by smoking them out of the rabbit holes, and another is instructed in the best way of capturing the squirrels which do so much mischief in his garden.

A poor man whose hens were eaten by a fox asks the king how he could be taken, and is instructed as to how he can be driven out of his earth and captured. Lastly, a poor man asked the king how he could take badgers. ' Poor man,' said king Modus, ' what harm do badgers to you?' ' Sire,' said the poor man, ' they do me no harm, but I never had shoes that lasted me so long as those that are made of the hide of badgers.' ' And I will tell you,' said Modus, ' how you can take all the badgers in your part of the world.'

The king's plan is to place a kind of purse-net in the entrance of the badgers' earth in which they are captured when driven in by dogs, or if the poor man has no dog, if he visits the earth in the morning, he will find a badger, or perchance, two or three in the purse-net

The next part of the book is introduced with the words : *Cy devise comment le roy Modus monstre à ses escoliers la science de faulconnerie.* The teaching of *Roy Modus* on the science of falconry is not followed by moralities of the queen, and it does not seem to have been so highly esteemed by later authorities as the part of the work which is concerned with the mysteries of woodcraft (ff. 76-100).

Then follows an interlude which is interesting and instructive, not only from the picture which it presents of rural life in the Normandy of the day, but from the light thrown by it on the question of the authorship of the work. The scene is laid in an hostelry, the resort of rustic sportsmen. Filled with enthusiasm for their favourite sports, and also with the good wine of their host, the hunters and falconers, from argument, come to angry words, and then to blows. The falconer hits the huntsman on the head with his lure, the huntsman replies with a stroke of his hunting horn, when one of the company says: ' You are fighting about nothing, for the matter which you dispute was discussed by two ladies, who caused their arguments to be expressed in rhyme, and sent to the comte de Tancarville for his decision, and of it I have with me the writing.'

Then comes a suggestion which is unanimously

adopted. They are all to dine at the hostel on the following day. The huntsmen are to contribute venison to the repast, the falconers wild duck (*oyseaux de rivière*) and two or three herons. On these terms the combatants are to make peace, and drink to each other. The expense of the dinner will be only the cost of the wine and bread. After dinner the decision will be read, and the successful party will pay for the bread and wine.

At the end of the next day the sportsmen met for dinner, and became so merry and so full of good wine, blowing the horn and hilloing,* like falconers and huntsmen, that the townsmen came running together. Peace having thus been made between the combatants, the peacemaker produces his roll, and reads.

The arguments of the ladies and the decision of de Tancarville fill fifteen pages of M. Blaze's reprint, concluding with the words, *Explicit le jugement que fist le Comte de Tancarville.*

The verses, though commonplace enough, are interesting from the simplicity and good faith in which they are written, and also for the light that they throw on the manners of the day, and on the interest which was taken by all classes of society in Normandy in the sports of the field. In them we pass from the rude revelling of hunters and falconers in the village inn, to the company of *chevaliers* and their *dames*, who discuss the merits of their favourite sports in gentler fashion. The verses begin with an argument between two young and beautiful ladies: a master of hounds and a keeper of hawks.

* ' Hillo, ho, ho, boy ! come, bird, come' (*Hamlet*, I., v., 115).

> Ung argument
> De deux dames joesnes et beaux
> L'une avoit chiens, l'autre ayseaulx (f. 103, r.).

The knightly husbands of these dames took a deep interest in the discussions that had been so ably carried on by their wives. For reasons that after the lapse of six centuries remain equally intelligible, it is thought prudent that the decision between the two ladies should be left to an outsider, and the husband of one of the ladies suggests as arbiter one whose knowledge of hounds and hawks was unrivalled and whose good faith is beyond question.

> Car il est sages et loyaulx
> Et si scet de chiens et d'oiseaulx
> Plus que nul homme, a mon devis,
> Et n'a en lui barat ne guille,
> C'est le Comte de Tancarville.

The dames joyfully accept the count as judge. But how are their arguments to be reduced to writing and presented to the judge in literary form? This was evidently beyond the power of the knights, who had listened with delight to the arguments of their wives. Then *ung des chevaliers qui fut sage* suggests as envoy to the comte a clerk whom he knows, than whom no one is better qualified to act as messenger, and to put the arguments of the dames into writing.

> Je crois qu'il n'a en ceste ville
> Nul homme qui mieulx sceust faire
> Ung message, ne qui mieulx sceust retraire
> Tout ce que vous vorriez dire;
> Et bien scet ditter et escripre
> Mieulx que nul homme à mon advis (f. 114, r.).

The clerk is called, and readily accepts the office. He then finds de Tancarville at Blandi* with a newly taken falcon on his wrist.   He presents an apology from the ladies for not sending their names, but the comte regards himself as in duty bound to do their behest.

> Dont dist le comte, par ma foy
> Je ne say qui les dames sont;
> Mais, j'ay a cuer bien parfout
> Voulenté de furnit et faire
> Tout ce qu' aux dames possoit plaire (f. 116, r.).

The ancient manuscript seems to be defective, for in the middle of the judgment of the count a *lacuna* is noted by M. Blaze, but enough remains to justify de Tancarville's presentation of himself as *preux chevalier,* and also the confidence that has been placed in him as an arbiter.   Acting on the principle laid down by Bacon in his essay on judicature, he awards civil commendation to the argument of one lady while he gives judgment in favour of the other.

> Celle qui parle des oiseaulx
> Dit vérité; ils sont plus beaux
> Et sont de plus nette nature
> Que ne sont les chiens, sans mesure.

---

* *Les ruines du Château de Blandy existent encore dans le village qui porte ce nom, a trois lieuses nord-est de Melun. Le château appartenant autrefois aux vicomtes de Melun, Comtes de Tancarville. C'est là qu'en* 1417 *Guillaume iv. comte de Tancarville, maria sa fille Marguerite Jacques de Harcourt, baron de Montgomery, et lui donna pour dot sa seigneurie de Blandy. Le comte de Tancarville, dont il est question dans le Livre du Roy Modus, était probablement l'aieul ou le bisaieleul de Guillaume* IV. (M. Blaze).

But the question which he has to decide is not which is the fairer, the falcon or the hound, but which of the two sports is the finer.   He holds that the sport which appeals to seeing is more enjoyable than that which is the result of hearing. But the advocate of the hound can say that more enjoyment is derived from hearing and seeing combined than from seeing alone.   On this ground the count rests his decision, given under his seal with commendable brevity, in words of art which may be attributed to the clerk.

> Pour lui donne mon jugement,
> Et par arrest lui est rendu
> Si prye à tous qu'il soit tenu.

Explicit le jugement que fist le comte de Tancarville.*

Justice has not been done to the authors of the *Roy Modus*—the maker of the book, and the clerk by whom it was written—for the ingenuity with which they have in the interlude presented to the reader the personalities indicated by the letters of the *rosace*.

* M. Blaze tells us in his *Preface* that Guillaume Crestin, a poet of the sixteenth century who had a great reputation, and was placed by a critic named Tory above Horace, Virgil, and Dante, rendered the dialogue of the two ladies on hounds and hawks into poetry of his day.   This version, *très inférieure à l'originel qui, du moins se recommande par la naïveté du style*, was published by Crestin as an original work, and not as an imitation of the *Roy Modus*, from which M. Blaze concludes that the *Roy Modus* was little known to the learned of the sixteenth century, for not one of them denounced the plagiarism.   The book was naturally unknown to readers of that century.   It was not studied as literature; as a Book of Sport it had been superseded by the popular work of Du Fouilloux, published in 1561, and it had not yet attracted the attention of archæologists.

In the Comte de Tancarville of the interlude who *scet de chiens et d'oiseaulx plus que nul homme*, we see the famous lover and patron of sport, the grand seigneur at whose instance the book was written; *celui qui c'est livre fist*.

The name of the composer of the book—the *clerc qui son songe escript*—is not found in the interlude, but the contemporaries of de Tancarville would have had little difficulty, with the aid of the *rosace*, in identifying the man of letters in a neighbouring town who was worthy of the character given to him in the interlude and also of commemoration in the *rosace*, an honour which would never have been accorded to a mere scrivener who had no share in the composition of the work.

The interlude is followed by some chapters to which I have found none corresponding in other mediæval works of sport (ff. 118-120). In an earlier part of the book we have seen a great nobleman, typified by king Modus, instructing his humble neighbours how they may best safeguard their fields and gardens from the ravages of the beasts of venery which are protected in the interests of sport, and how they may take a few rabbits or a hare for the pot or a badger for the sake of his hide (*ante*, p. 62). This is quite in accordance with the conception of the courtesy of the *grand seigneur*, in the great age of chivalry and sport. But in these chapters king Modus condescends to instruct a class of apprentices, of his neighbours, how they may earn an honest livelihood, and at the same time enjoy some of the pleasures of sport. This he does at the request of *les poures apprentis*. The chapter is entitled : *Cy après devise comment on prent toutes manières d'oyseaulx,* and tells of what in the English books is called ' fowling,' as distinguished from falconry. Its final cause was not enjoyment for the sportsman, but the earning of money by the fowler, or providing meat for the host, and Gervais Markham's treatise on fowling bears the suggestive title of *Hunger's Prevention.*

Yet, as the clerk says, the sporting instinct of the poor may find gratification in the taking of birds as a livelihood by the methods which he points out, *Les poures qui de ce se vivent y prennent ausi grant plaisance, et pour ce q'ils y prennent leur vie en eux.* It is interesting to find among these methods ' springes to catch woodcocks ' (*videcos*), of which M. Blaze reproduces an illustration from his ancient manuscript, depicting a peasant setting a ' springe,' certainly in sight of the bird, for it stands close by ready to insert its long bill in the noose. Among the birds by the taking of which poor men may live are included hawks for the great man's mews, as well as partridge, woodcock, and pheasants for his table.

In those chapters the writer seems to speak to the poor apprentice in his proper person, and in a manner which suggests that, although written at the instance of his patron, and in accordance with the design of the book, this part of the book was in a special manner the work of the clerk, who may have been, in his younger days, of the class from whom these apprentices were taken. The teaching, however, is sound, founded on that given by the king in the earlier part of the book: *J'ai pris ma matière du Roy Modus.*

The book concludes with the moralising of queen Racio on birds, *Comment la royne Racio moralise sur les oyseaux*. The queen's reflections on the ten beasts of the chase follow the king's instructions on the science of venery. But as the moralising forms a separate part of the work, and is not intermixed with the king's instructions, it may be conveniently presented in a collected form.

L'aprentis demands a la Royne quelles sont les moralites et figures qui puent estre trouvées et figurées es dix bestes donc le roy Modus nous a démmstré toute la Vénerie (f. 61, v.). The queen explains that of those ten beasts, five are called sweet (*doulces*) and five stinking (*puans*). The sweet are the stag, the hind, the fallow buck, the roebuck, and the hare.

As to the stag, the ten points of his head were given to him by God to protect him from three foes—mankind, hounds, and wolves. These ten points represent the ten commandments of the law which Jesus Christ gives mankind as a defence against three foes—the flesh, the devil, and the world—between which commandments God manifested himself crucified to St. Eustace (f. 62, r.). M. Blaze reproduces in a woodcut a miniature which represents a crucifix uplifted on the head of a stag. The ten commandments corresponding to the ten points of the antlers of the stag are to be found in the margin of the page. They are not those of the decalogue, but maxims taken from the teaching of Christ. One is—

> Et si ne fais rien à aultrui
> Que tu ne presisses pour ty.

The stag is a symbol, not only of the clergy, *gens d'église*, who have the sacrament within their ten fingers and hold God high above their heads, but of good men, *tant clers comme lays*, who live ordered and chaste lives, and observe the commandments of God, keeping them in their heads.

Lessons may be derived from the other sweet beasts of venery. The fallow buck and roebuck carrying antlers signify crowns, and can be assigned as symbols of emperors, kings, and of the nobility whose duty it is to uphold the faith, wherefore they are called *chevaliers de l'église*.

The hind suggests a simple nature, with little sense. The hare has her dwelling in the fields. These two beasts are likened *aux trois estats*, and represent those who labour, by whom all others live, *Ce sont les gens de labeur, qui labeurent ce de quox les autres vivent.*

The queen then moralises *des cinq bestes puans, et les figures qui sont a prisent au monde*, and firstly of the wild boar, the representative of the stinking, as the stag is of the sweet beasts of venery (f. 64, r.). He bears ten points which represent the ten commandments of the law of antichrist. A curious woodcut represents a wild boar at the foot of the trunk of a tree with ten short branches, on the top of which antichrist is seated, easily recognisable by his cloven foot and diabolical countenance. The ten branches represent his ten commandments, which are given in the margin of the page.

Of these one is:

Fais à ton corps tous ses délis
Il n'est point d'autre paradis.

The ten characteristics of the wild boar, and their analogy to the principles of antichrist, as announced in his ten commandments, afford a text on which queen Racio founds an excellent discourse. She then proceeds to moralise on somewhat similar characteristics of the wild sow, *pour en faire example.*

The queen then considers the character and properties of the wolf. ' The character of the wolf is that by nature it destroys the sheep. By wolves I mean those who enjoy the property of Holy Church, who have the cures of souls (f. 66, r.), who should be shepherds, and are wolves. By sheep, I mean the good folk who live under them in their parishes with little sense or reason, because they see in their priests so many vices, to their destruction in soul and body by the bad example which they see in them. Again, for further proof that they are bad shepherds, and that they may be well called wolves, there are many of them who seize the sheep that they ought to protect, and take and kill them; that is to say, they seize and hold their parishioners, and truly kill them, when they hold them in mortal sin. Again, wolves have another characteristic, for when they have spent their days in going hither and thither in ill-doing, and they have come to eventide, they howl and congregate, and their howling is an ugly affair, causing great horror and alarm; then they take themselves off, and go, some one way and others another. So do the bad shepherds, who wander all day in dissolute haunts, leaving their sheep to go to the tavern, and when it is evening they go to holy church, dirty and tipsy, and set up such a howl in saying vespers, that they become a laughing stock.*

'Undoubtedly, bishops will answer for it for sending wolves to keep their flocks instead of shepherds; one cannot see or imagine a more horrible or wicked thing in this world than to see among the others one who is worthy. For he can consecrate and handle the body of Jesus Christ. There is peril when the wolf holds the lamb in his hands.'

The queen's moralising on the fox is not prompted by the *sæva indignatio* aroused by the negligent pastor who leaves his flock, unconfessed and unshriven, in the mortal sin into which they have been led by his bad example; by the dissolute monks who bring disgrace on their order; and by the worst offenders of all, the bishops who send wolves instead of shepherds to tend the flocks of the church.

The subtlety of the fox affords the queen a text for her next discourse (f. 67, r.). It is in a lighter vein—in the manner of Addison rather than of Swift. He is a master of every kind of deceit and craftiness. His practices are popular, and generally imitated. *Reynard a par tout le monde traigné sa queue.* The three estates, clerics, nobles, and *gens de labeur*, have for the most part studied in this school. The queen is specially hard on lawyers and public officials. Advocates

* Ainsi font les mauvais pasteurs que errent tout jour ès lieux dissolus, et laissent leurs brebis, et vont en la taverne; et quant il est vespre, ils vont en sainte église saoulz et yvres, et s'assemblent et font une grant urlerie en disant vespres tellement que chacun se moque d'eulx (f. 66, r.).

of the ecclesiastical and lay courts *sont parfais en la science de reynard, et en lisent tous les jours en ordinaire, et combien que officiers royaulx, et Cathédraux ayent esté gouvernés par la doctrins reynard.*

Of the remaining *beste puans*, the otter lives on fish and is amphibious. Akin to him are double-faced flatterers of both sexes. People of this sort may be said to fish beneath streams, and to take fish when by flattery and play they abstract the property of their masters. The discourses on the *beste puans* ends in a fabled compact between the fox and the otter, by which they become masters of wood and water. Of the apologue M. Blaze writes:

Lisez au feullet LXVIII le dialogue du renard et de la loutre, vous y trouverez un naturel, une simplicité de style dignes de Lafontaine: c'est un apologue fort agréable, et par le sens caché qu'il renferme, et par la manière dont il est presenté. Si notre grand fabuliste l'avait connu certainement il en aurait enriché son immortel recueil.

At the conclusion of the king's lessons on falconry, the queen moralises *sur les oyseaulx* (f. 137, r.). In birds of prey she finds analogues of the three enemies of mankind—the world, the flesh, and the devil. The king had shown how men take birds by means of bird-lime. This the queen compares to the fatal attraction of the flesh, and here she spares the *grans seigneurs* as little as she did the priests, the advocates, and the officials of her time. In discoursing on birds the queen is not so elaborate or so interesting as when she moralises on the beasts of the chase. This is the conclusion of the whole matter, told in words which are now as easily understood as when they were written nearly eight centuries ago:

Si tu te vuel diffendre de ces trois ennemis, c'est assavoir du deable, du monde et de la char, soit garni de trois choses, c'est de foy, d'espérance et d'amour, et sois armé de trois armentes, c'est de confession, de repentance, et de satisfaction. Ainsy ces ennemis ne te parront nuyre ni grever (f. 139, v.).

The part of the *Roy Modus* which contains the instructions of the king to his apprentices and the moralising of the queen is complete in itself, and, with the exception of the poetical interlude which is inserted between the lessons on falconry and those on fowling, it is a treatise in prose on field sport in all its branches. M. Blaze reproduces in his edition this part only of the work, which includes all that is of interest in regard to the literature of field sports. The manuscripts from which the *Livre du Roy Modus* was printed contained some additional matter, the work of the same hand, my knowledge of which is derived from the bibliography of sport appended to the *Master of Game*. The clerk tells us that, in the year 1338, having copied the book of sports on the 4th of April, he was very desirous of finding some pleasant matter with which he might fill the parchment with which he had been furnished. So Mr. Baillie-Grohman understands the words *matere plaisant de la quelle je pensoie aempler mon livre*.

As he walked in perplexity through a forest he rested at the foot of a tree, where he had a dream in which he saw king Modus and queen

6

Racio. Encouraged by this vision he proceeds to write the continuation of the book. The second part is an allegorical vision, entitled *Le Songe de Pestilence*. Having written down his vision the clerk found that he still had some leaves of parchment to spare, and 'the book finishes with an account of the courts of Charles V.'s reign, the persons who figured in the chief events not being mentioned by name, but under allegorical pseudonyms' (*Master of Game*, p. 222).

Having done with *le livre des déduits*, the scribe, addressing the reader in his proper person, while still within the region of convention, tells us that he wrote the first part of the work, as he had found it, according to the ordinances of king Modus, in a very ancient book, *Comment je l'avoie veu et trouvé en ung livre bien achien sy comme il roy Modus les avoit ordinnez*. Commentators have sought in vain for a trace of this ancient writing. It may well be that king Modus and this ancient book were parts of the same convention, and equally devoid of existence in the world of fact, and in them we may discern the count and the notes on his beloved field sports, which he entrusted to a scribe who had skill to put into literary form the experiences and ideas of his patron.

The continuation of the *Roy Modus* is of interest in regard to the question of authorship, for this part of the work could not with any degree of probability be attributed to the comte de Tancarville. Even in the first part of the book there are passages in which the clerk who wrote it stands revealed. The comte de Tancarville, a great peer of France, an honoured guest at the courts of France and England, would never have written as the clerk did of having seen king Charles IV. hunting in the forest of Breteuil. Justice Shallow talked familiarly of John of Gaunt on the strength of having seen him once in the tilt yard.* The clerk, to do him justice, did not presume on this acquaintance with Charles IV. Had de Tancarville been present in the forest, his recollection of the royal hunting would have been very different from that recorded by the clerk, for he certainly would have been of the king's party.

The *Livre du Roy Modus* is written in a clear style. There are few words that are now obsolete, and where it is free from the technicalities of the chase a student of modern French can read it without difficulty. The French of Rabelais, who wrote two centuries later, presents much greater obstacles to the ordinary reader.

It is interesting to compare the French of the *Roy Modus* with the English of a contemporary work: *The Vision of Piers Plowman*, written in 1362, at a time when the English language was in course of formation. In literary significance the works are very different. One is a fine allegorical poem, and the other a popular book of sport. But there are some points of resemblance between these writings and their authors. Each was the composition of an unknown clerk, whose identity the most careful research has failed to discover, while conjecture has, in both cases, taken the place of knowledge. The seer

* 2 *Hen. IV.*, iii., ii., 346.

of the *Vision of Piers Plowman* on the May morning on the Malvern hills, and the clerk who on the 4th of April, 1338, dreamed dreams at the foot of a tree in a Norman forest, had much in common. Each wrote as a pious Christian and loyal son of the church, without any quarrel with the established order of things in church or state, and each was moved to righteous indignation by the abuses and iniquities which he saw in both. The Lady Meed, with Falsehood and Flattery of the vision, were apt students in the school of Reynaud, and with them we find, among the crowd, advocates of the court of Arches. The author of the *Vision*, with the Norman clerk, holds responsible the bishops, who suffer abuses to prevail. The dignity of labour is recognised in the person of Piers, the honest ploughman, as queen Racio finds in certain of the *bestes doulces*, the type of *les gens de labeur, qui labeurent et de quoy les autres vivent.*

In the *Vision* Reason moralises and discourses. He is an adviser sent for by the king, who set him on the bench between him and his son, where they talked wisely for a long time. The gallant author of the *Roy Modus* assigns the part of Reason to a woman. The *Vision* had many readers until the English in which it was written was no longer understood. The *Roy Modus* was widely circulated in manuscript before the age of printing. Before the year 1379 the lessons of *Roy Modus* and the discourses of *Royne Racio* had travelled as far as the remote court of Orthez, for in that year Gaston Phœbus began to write *La Chasse*, in which he borrows largely from the writing of the devout Norman clerk.

The author of the *Roy Modus* was a reformer, but not of the type of Wyclif or Huss. He is concerned with matters of discipline, morality, and episcopal control, but not with questions of theological dogma. How far the spirit in which he wrote of these matters prevailed in France during the fourteenth century is an interesting inquiry calling for an acquaintance with the intellectual condition of France during that period which the present writer does not possess.

The *Royne Racio* and her moralising would appear to be part of the general design of the book, attributable to the author, and not to the scribe. They are found in the part of the work which concludes with the words *Explicit le livre des déduits,* etc., and not in the supplement, which is undoubtedly the work of the clerk.

In the comte de Tancarville and in the author of the *Roy Modus* the features of one and the same man may be discovered. By the comte de Tancarville I mean the man of whom Froissart, Hardouin, de Ayala, and the composer of the *Interlude* wrote. By the author of the *Roy Modus* I mean him by whom the book was designed *fist,* and whose ideas on field sports and on abuses in church and state were interpreted and expressed in literary form by the clerk, whom I have called the scribe. The comte was no mere sportsman. He was an acknowledged authority on the literature of sport. He had an acquaintance, at first hand, of matters of state, and he might easily be credited with an interest in the abuses which had crept into church and state. He is presented to us in the *Interlude* as a model of honour and knightly courtesy—a very perfect knight. *Il est sages et loyalx . . . et n'en lui barat ne guille.* A humble scribe comes to him with a request from two unknown ladies to act as arbiter in a controversy as to the merits of the sports to which they are devoted. He is not only in duty bound to serve these ladies, but he has a heartfelt pleasure in so doing. *J'ay a cuer bien parfont voulenté.* In him we see the courtesy of a true gentleman and sportsman in the heroic age of chivalry and of *La Grande Chasse.* We find the same qualities of courtesy and consideration for others in the author of the book as in the count. It is a profound saying of Tennyson that every man imputes himself, and the qualities of the comte de Tancarville are imputed to the *Roy Modus.* The king teaches the poor whose fields and gardens are ravaged by beasts of venery how to capture these beasts, and also how to take a few rabbits and hares for their own use. He also instructs a class of poor apprentices in certain pursuits by which they can earn a livelihood, and at the same time have some of the enjoyment of sport. The *rosace* affords evidence of the same courtesy and consideration, for in it a place is found not only for the author by whom the book was made, but also for the clerk, who acted as scribe.

It is pleasant to think that in *Roy Modus* we may see the type of a great French nobleman in his relations to his humble neighbours and followers, amid all the miseries of the Hundred Years' War. Such a man Jean de Melun, *Vicomte et Comte de Tancarville,* grand Chamberlain of France, may well have been. Around the life of de Tancarville—a grand seigneur of France; the most famous sportsman of his time; the mirror of courtesy and knightly gallantry, to whom it was a heartfelt pleasure to do the bidding of an unknown dame; fighting by the side of his king in the battle of Poitiers; an honoured guest at the table of the Black Prince and in the court of Edward of England—the Great Magician might have woven a romance of the Middle Ages exceeding in interest even *Quentin Durward*—not the greatest work of Scott, but surely the first of historical novels—and in it we might have caught a glimpse of the gracious lady whose wisdom and goodness suggested to the author, the queen Racio, without whose guidance and advice the experience of king Modus would have been fruitless.

As a treatise on the chase the *Roy Modus* was excelled by the work of Gaston Phœbus, written in 1347. The copious irrelevancies of the earlier work, to which it owes its interest as literature, impaired its usefulness as a practical work, and later writers on the subject place the work of Gaston on a higher level. Both these classical writers were superseded by the practical treatise of Jacques du Fouilloux, published in 1561. But the *Roy Modus* holds its place as the original authority on the observance of *La Grande Chasse*, and the terms of art which came into use:

Si dans tous les pays du monde la grande chasse porte le nom de chasse française, c'est au Roy Modus qu'il faut en attribuer l'honneur. La plupart des termes de vénerie dont on se sert de nos jours se trouvent dans son livre. Le Roy Modus les a consacrés, et la mode qui change si souvent en France ne leur a point fait sentir son influence (M. Blaze).

CHAPTER IV

PETRUS CRESCENTIENSIS AND SPORT IN ITALY

NONE other of the treatises on country life and field sports attained the popularity of a work written by Peter of Crescentia in the year 1307, entitled *De omnibus Agriculturæ partibus, et plantarum animaliumque partibus et utilitate.* The author was a citizen of Bologna. In an all too short preface he tells the story of his life, and the circumstances under which his book came to be written. By it we are not only attracted to the personality of the writer, but afforded an insight into life in one of the great city democracies of Lombardy at an interesting period of its history.

To him a peaceful and tranquil life was the greatest of earthly blessings for mind and body. Bad men do not value it, and if it should fall to their lot they destroy it by pride or some other vice, which may bring them a short-lived prosperity. But the peaceful and meek, though they may suffer awhile, survive their trouble, and, having found favour with God and men, in the long-run inherit the land. ' And so,' he says, ' I, by birth Peter, of Crescentia, a citizen of Bologna, who spent the whole of my youth in the study of logic, medicine, and natural science,

in the end sweated (*insudavi*) at the noble science
of Law.' Desirous of a quiet life after the lamentable division (*flendum schisma*) in that rarely
good city, known in every part of the world by
its true and appropriate name *Bononia id est
bona per omnia*, and recognising that when unity
and peacefulness had been exchanged for dis-
suasion, hatred, and jealousy, he ought not to be
mixed up in the affairs of that perverse schism,
for thirty years he went round diverse provinces,
with their rulers, freely dispensing justice to the
subjects and honest advice to the rulers, while
doing his utmost to preserve the states in the
enjoyment of their rights, and in a peaceful
condition. He also studied many books, ancient
and modern, by learned authors, and inspected
the various operations of the cultivators of the
soil. At length, when, by the grace of God the
state had been to some extent reformed, becoming
weary of such extended journeying and the confinement which it involved, he returned home.
Recognising, with Tully, that of all sources of
revenue, none were better than agriculture, none
more fruitful, none greater, none more worthy
of a man of liberal culture, and also that in
it may be found a peaceful life, alike free from
indolence and inoffensive to one's neighbours,
he was led to apply his mind, heartily, to the
cultivation of the land, perceiving the advantage and pleasure that were derived from being
thoroughly informed on the subject and the dis-
advantages of careless cultivation, following the
old ways, without well-regulated industry. Also,
the learning on the subject had been handed

down by the old writers in an obscure and imperfect form, and was almost unknown to those of his time. So with the help of Almighty God he undertook his work.

In a dedication to Charles II., king of Sicily, written *Bononiæ ex rusculo nostro suburbano*, Crescentius (for so the name is usually written) tells us how his book was undertaken at the request of the king. The author was in a difficulty from his public duties as a citizen of Bologna in trying times, *impeditus quidem multis et arduis rei publicæ Bononienvis negotiis*, but he felt that he could not refuse to undertake the task, although it was far beyond his power. And so, though over seventy years of age, he betook him to his country home, in order that he might, with the help of Almighty God, meet the wishes of the king. He adds that his work had met with approbation from the highest authorities in his own university of Bologna, in natural science, and especially from medical men, who have a special interest in what grows in the soil, for from it they derive the material that they employ.

The author's preface suggests some questions to be answered.

What was the lamentable schism that for so many years deprived Bologna of the services of so valuable a citizen, and how was unity at length restored to the distracted city ?

How came it that a learned lawyer of Bologna was able to devote the years of his life between forty and seventy to the work of a circuit-going judge, in ' provinces ' outside the commune of which he was a citizen ?   Whence did he derive authority to administer justice to the subjects of these external provinces ?

How came the citizen of an independent state to write to the king of Sicily as his sovereign, whose bidding he was bound to obey ?

In a singular feature of the jurisprudence of the Lombard cities—the introduction of judges from a different commune—we find an explanation of the account given by Crescentius of his judicial work, and also an answer to a more interesting inquiry: How came it that the Doge and principal citizens of Venice submitted the decision of an important suit to a learned lawyer, not of their city, and summoned from another commune ? In Crescentius of Bologna we find the prototype of Bellario, also of Bologna, and we can see how it comes about that Bellario was summoned to Venice, not from that city, but from Padua.

Bologna was one of the foremost of the cities of northern Italy, which having freed themselves from the rule of bishops, and afterwards of counts, had become united in the famous Lombardy league. The cities which singly were unable to resist the power of the Emperor Frederick Barbarossa succeeded, when united, in obtaining the peace of Constance (1183) by which the independence of the Lombard republics was recognised.

In each of the cities of this league—more than thirty in number—there was established a system of popular government, which, in its origin and in its fall, furnishes one of the most interesting and instructive chapters of history.

Crescentius became a citizen of Bologna at an

important period of its history. The long struggle
of the Lombard cities against the Swabian emperors was over, ' those heroic days of medieval
Italy when the names of Guelf and Ghibelin were
no unmeaning badges of hereditary feud, but
were the true and speaking watchwords of the
highest principles that can stir the breast of
man.'* In those days the Guelph stood for the
opponent of the emperor, the champion of the
independence of the cities of the Lombard league.
In the contest between Frederick II. and the
popes, the emperor was supported by the Ghibel-
lins, while the popes were associated with the
Guelfs, so that the term 'Guelf and Ghibellin'
came to be applied to a supporter of the pope or
of the emperor.

In Bologna, in the lifetime of Crescentius, these
words, once of grave import, had lost their significance. 'The names of Guelph and Ghibelin
indeed are still heard, but they now carry with
them no more of meaning than the Shanavests and
Caravats of a nearer field of discord' (Freeman).
By their association with the rivalry of great
houses in the Lombard cities they had become
mere faction cries. The intensity of the hostility
between the Montagues and Capulets in the
Lombard city of Verona gains a new significance
when we recognise in these families the leaders
of the Guelfs and the Ghibelins. The Montecchi
(Montagues), once powerful in Verona, were in the
end destroyed by the tyrant Esselino. The
Capuletti (Capulets), the leading Guelfs of
Cremona, were by a tradition which found itself

* Freeman, *Historical Essays.*

connected with the story of Romeo and Juliet erroneously brought to Verona.*

In Bologna the family of Geremei were the leaders of the Guelfs and the Lambertazzi of the Ghibelins. The city of Bologna and its university were Guelf. Thus arose the *flendum schisma* which brought such misery on the city. In 1274 twelve thousand persons, members of that party, were expelled from Bologna. The unity and peace which the city had enjoyed in its struggle for independence were exchanged for envy, hatred, malice, and all uncharitableness, with acts of violence, over which Crescentius in his desire to make peace draws a veil. At length the state of affairs was so far improved by the expulsion of the Lambertazzi, the supporters of the Ghibelins, that Crescentius, weary of the life of journeying and confinement which he had been living for thirty years, returned to his home; where, as it would appear from his address to the king, he was actively employed in restoring tranquillity to the city. He is described on the title-page to the copy of his work in the possession of the present writer (Basiliæ, 1549) as *princeps Reipub. Bononiensis*, probably one of the notables who were associated with the *Podesta* in the administrative business of the city. But his heart was in his little suburban farm, where he realised not only the happiness of a life spent in the cultivation of the soil, but the importance of knowledge to the successful cultivation of the soil. So he applied his mind to the subject, and his book is the result.

* W. F. Butler, *The Lombard Communes*.

The resemblance of the self-governing communes of the Lombard league to the autonomous cities of Greece has been often noted. But there was a cardinal distinction. In Greece the full and perfect sovereignty of each separate city was the fundamental idea. The Italian cities were overshadowed by the idea of the universal dominion of the empire, which from time to time manifested itself in a practical form, and in the time of Crescentius the autonomy of Bologna was not inconsistent with a kind of overlordship in the king of Sicily.

Charles I., son of Louis VIII. of France, was not only ruler of Provence and Anjou, but, as the result of a fierce struggle with Manfred, natural son of the Emperor Frederick II., was established as the king of the Two Sicilies, and lord of many cities of Lombardy, including Bologna. His son Charles II. was not successful in retaining these dominions. After some unsuccessful warfare, by the peace of Castabellota in 1302, he gave up all claims to Sicily. 'Charles spent his last years quietly in Naples, which city he improved and embellished.'* It would appear that he retained, with Naples, the overlordship of the Lombard cities, and it was during the peaceful close of his life that he entered into communication with Crescentius.

There was another remarkable difference between the independent existence of the communes of Lombardy and that of the Grecian republics, and in it may be found the solution of one of the questions suggested by the account of

* *Ency. Brit.:* Tit. Sicily.

his life given by Crescentius. For an Athenian citizen to speak of having spent his life in administering justice in the other cities of Greece would be a manifest absurdity. To an Italian novelist of the fourteenth century, it was a matter of course. Indeed, the magistrate by whom justice was administered in criminal matters in each commune was necessarily taken from another city.

Frederick Barbarossa, in the days of his tyranny, had invaded the independence of the city by appointing, in place of the elected consuls, an imperial officer called *Podesta*. This office was abolished when the cities rebelled against Frederick. After the peace of Constance, ' from experience, as we must presume, of the partiality which their domestic factions carried into the administration of justice, it became a general practice to elect, by the name of *Podesta*, a citizen of some neighbouring state as their general criminal judge and preserver of the peace ' (Hallam, *Middle Ages*). His freedom from local influences was insured by requiring that he should be of a noble family unconnected with the city in which he was to act, of which his wife could not be a native. He could have no relation residing within the commune, nor could he eat or drink in the house of any citizen.

In the decision of civil suits the same principle was adopted. In the free municipalities of Lombardy the magistrates were ' chosen from among the citizens, and the succession to office was usually so rapid that almost every freeman might expect in his turn to partake in the public government,

and consequently in the administration of justice '
(Hallam). In the discharge of this duty the
citizens were aided by a learned civilian from one
of the universities, most commonly from Bologna,
whose decision on questions of law appears to
have been accepted as final. There was no regular
judicial system or body of judges, but we find in
a Lombard commune the essentials of the administration of justice according to the law of
England, by which the decision of questions of
fact is the privilege of the citizens, who do not
interfere in matters of law, the determination of
which is reserved for a class of experts who have
acquired a qualification in the law school: in
England of one of the Inns of Court, in Lombardy
of one of the universities.

Hallam points out that when justice was
administered by the citizens of a commune ' the
laws were rude and the proceedings tumultuous,
and the decisions perverted by violence. The
spirit of liberty begot a stronger source of right;
and right, it was soon perceived, could only be
secured by a common standard ' (chap. iii.,
pt. i.). Such a standard was supplied by the
Roman law, as embodied in the system of Justinian,
and knowledge of this system, which found its
way to adoption in most of the nations of Europe,
was principally derived from the University of
Bologna.

This university, founded in the eleventh century, acquired a European reputation. Early
in the next century a professor named Irnerius
opened a school of civil law in the university, and
the study of law having thus revived, made a

surprising progress; ' within fifty years Lombardy was full of lawyers, on whom Frederic Barbarossa and Alexander III., so hostile in every other respect, conspired to shower honours and privileges.   The schools of Bologna were pre-eminent throughout this country for legal learning' (Hallam, *Middle Ages*).

It was the duty of a civilian, duly qualified by the university, to supply the standard by which the magistrates were to be guided in the adjustment of civil claims.

The novel from which Shakespeare borrowed the trial scene in the *Merchant of Venice** tells us something of the functions and authority of a learned doctor from Bologna.   Ansalto, a merchant of Venice, godfather of the hero, Giannetto, in order to provide his godson with funds for an adventure by which he was to win a wealthy bride, who lived at Belmonte, had given to a Jew a bond for ten thousand ducats to be paid on a certain day, the penalty being the same as Shylock's bond.   Giannetto wins the lady, and they pass the time so pleasantly that the day nominated in the bond passes unnoticed.   When Giannetto realises the position he starts for Venice with a hundred thousand ducats, given to him by his loving bride.   The lady of Belmonte, whom I shall call Portia, follows in a lawyer's habit attended by two servants.   Biannetto had offered money, up to a hundred thousand ducats, but

---

* A story in the *Pecorone* of San Giovanni Fierentino, a novelist who wrote in 1378.   A translation epitomised by Dr. Johnson is printed in the fifth volume of the *Variorum* edition of Shakespeare (1821).

the Jew insisted on his pound of flesh. Portia, arriving in Venice at an inn, announces herself as a young lawyer who had finished his studies at Bologna. ' The lawyer caused a proclamation to be made that whoever had any law matters to determine, they should have recourse to him: so it was told to Giannetto, that a famous lawyer was come from Bologna, who could decide all cases in law.' Giannetto proposed to the Jew to apply to this lawyer. ' With all my heart,' says the Jew, ' but let who will come, I will stick to my bond.' They came to this judge and saluted him. ' Giannetto did not remember him, for he had disguised his face with the juice of certain herbs.' After a conversation in which the Jew insists on his strict rights, they ' go to the tribunal appointed for such judgments,' where the Jew obtains the measure of justice that was meted out to Shylock.

What this ' tribunal ' was the novel does not tell us, but it was no doubt the court in which the governor and magistrates of the city were assembled awaiting the coming of the duly qualified civilian, whose arrival in the city had been proclaimed. Such a tribunal was formed by the Doge and Magnificos of the commune of Venice. Before it appeared Shylock and Bassanio. The Jew insists upon his legal rights.

> If you deny me, fie upon your law!
> There is no force in the decrees of Venice;
> I stand for judgment: answer; shall I have it ?
> (*Merchant of Venice*, IV., i., 101.)

The issue thus raised is clearly one of law. It is a question of the interpretation and effect of a legal document, and the court, as then 'constituted, was not competent to deal with such a matter. It must be determined by a qualified civilian, and so the duke rules, and judgment could not be given

> unless Bellario, a learned doctor,
> Whom I have sent for to determine this,
> Come here to-day.

This ruling is strictly in accordance with the procedure in the courts of the communes of Lombardy.

Shakespeare has been accused of exceeding the bounds of probability in this scene. Dr. Johnson writes: ' The doctor and the court are here somewhat unskilfully brought together. That the duke would on such an occasion consult a doctor of great reputation is not unlikely, but how should this be foreknown by Portia ?'

Shakespeare, from his reading of the novel, grasped by the intuition of genius the reality of the situation, which escaped the grasp of the learned commentator. Bellario was sent for, not to advise the duke, but to determine the suit, and the decision of the supposed doctor speaking with this authority is accepted as final.

The presence of a learned doctor summoned for the decision of the suit would be foreknown by Portia, precisely as a lady of high intelligence residing in an English county would foreknow that she would find a judge of the High Court presiding at the assizes. But how did she know that the doctor would be her cousin Bellario ? The learned doctor to whom the duke had applied was well known to the magistrates of the city. He is spoken of as an old friend. ' Come you from old Bellario ?' the duke asks of the young doctor by whom he is represented. Bellario was Portia's cousin, and she would naturally know that the duke when in a difficulty would certainly send for his ' old Bellario.'

Crescentius writes of the communities in which he had administered justice, and assisted the governing bodies with his advice, with affectionate regard. We can well believe that this feeling of regard would be reciprocated, and that after his thirty years of service, ' old Crescentius,' and none other, would be summoned when an important suit had to be determined.

But why did Shakespeare not follow the novelist in introducing the learned civilian as of Bologna ? And why was his representative, Balthasar, a learned doctor, from Rome ? The answer is the same as that given by Dr. Johnson to a lady who asked him why he defined ' pastern ' as the ' knee ' of a horse. But there is this difference. Ignorance as to the parts of a horse's leg might lead to mistaken treatment. But for the purposes of the dramatist it was immaterial at what university Bellario had obtained his qualification as doctor of law.

Shakespeare, when he borrowed a plot from Italian novel, English chronicle, or the *Iliad* of Homer, was concerned only with essentials, and never troubled himself about mere accessories. For the development of the plot it was essential that Bellario should be within easy reach of Venice, and so he was sent for to the neighbouring Padua, and not to the distant Bologna. Balthasar was a doctor of Rome. Shakespeare would naturally suppose—if he thought of it at all—that as

English advocates qualified by studying in London, so an Italian lawyer acquired his qualifications in the capital city of Rome. He did not know that Italy had long enjoyed the priceless boon of a multitude of universities, a privilege the value of which is better understood now than it was a century ago. Italy had in the Middle Ages twenty-one universities, and from this source sprang the revival of learning the blessings of which were shared by the other nations of Europe. Scotland, with a population of not more than 500,000, had four, and from them was derived an intellectual force which, extending through all classes of society, brings Scotsmen to the front wherever they may be found.

The work of Crescentius is founded on treatises on country life, which, circulating in manuscript, were popular for many centuries before they were collected and printed by the name of *Libri de Re Rustica*. The authors are M. Porcius Cato, known as Censor, 234-14 B.C.; Terentius Varro, 116-28 B.C., the most learned Roman of the Ciceronian age; Junius Columella, a contemporary of Seneca, who died A.D. 65; and Palladius, whose date is uncertain, but it is most probable that he lived in the middle of the fourth century of the Christian era (Smith, *Class. Dict.*). These treatises were very popular in the Middle Ages, and the most famous of them was the *De Re Rustica Libri Tres* of Varro.

Varro was the father of the literature of country life, a position which justifies his inclusion in the present chapter, for, although he gives no evidence of interest in field sports, the subject is included in the mediæval treatises of which his work was the model, and his character and work are full of interest. He was of the party of Pompey, but his vast learning earned for him, after the battle of Pharsalia, the forgiveness of Cæsar, who employed him in the collection and arrangement of the great library which he was forming. Although Varro's name appeared in the list of the proscribed by the second triumvirate, he had the good fortune to escape and to be permitted to spend the rest of his life in tranquillity and in literary work. He died at the age of eighty-seven, having written, according to his own statement, four hundred and ninety books. Of these two only have come down to us, of which *De Re Rustica* alone is complete. It was ' written when the author was eighty years old, and is the most important of all the treatises upon ancient agriculture, being far superior to the more voluminous production of Columella, with which alone it can be compared ' (Smith). The vitality of this treatise was marvellous. Alone among the many works of its author it survived, unimpaired, the wholesale destruction and mutilation of manuscripts of the classical age, during the dark ages, which caused the loss of so many literary treasures. The printing-press renewed its youth, and introduced it to a wider range of readers, for we find that, with its companion treatises, the work of Varro was translated into French and Italian, and that up to the end of the eighteenth century editions of the collection, carefully annotated by eminent scholars, continued to appear.*

* The first edition was printed by Nicholaus Jenson, Venice, 1472. Brunet notes five editions in the fifteenth century,

Varro is to Crescentius *egregius philosophus*, and he is often referred to as an authority. Indeed, his work might be described as ' Varro up to date.' The modern element is most apparent in the chapters on the capture of wild beasts and the taking of fish.

This great scholar and charming writer is among the many men eminent in letters and also in affairs who are noteworthy as contributors to the literature of country life. His name occurs often in Cicero's correspondence with Atticus, and from the way in which he is spoken of we can form an idea of the personality of the man: self-asserting, jealous and unlovable; but a man to be accounted with.

Atticus urged Cicero to find a place for Varro in one of his dialogues, and after some demur he was introduced as a principal character in *Academica Posteriora*. Then there was a question about the person to whom the work should be dedicated. Cicero wishes for Varro, especially because he desired it.

But he is, as Atticus knows—and here what Patroclus says of Achilles is quoted—a terrible man, ready to blame the guiltless.* Cicero thinks that he sees how Varro would look when making

---

but his list is not exhaustive, for the earliest edition in the possession of the present writer, *Regii, impensis Dionysii Bertochi* 1496 *fol.*, is not included. It was produced with a copious commentary under the title of *Libri de Re Rustica* by the press of P. Junta, in Florence in 1515, and reprinted with some additions by the representatives of Junta in 1521. The volume continued to be reprinted up to 1797, and there were also translations in French and Italian.

* *Iliad*, xi., 654.

some such complaint ' as that I had given a more important part in the dialogue to myself than to him.' However, he does not despair of being approved by Varro, and he is reconciled to the idea of the dedication to him being retained ' as you and I have gone to the expense of procuring folio sheets,' *quoniam impensam fecimus in macrocolla.** Such a man was no welcome visitor when he dropped in unexpectedly, especially if the company had been discussing him. *De Varrone loquebamur ; lupus in fabula* — ' Talk of the devil,' writes Cicero to Atticus (*Ep.* 636, p. 144). When reading these letters one cannot help thinking what a priceless literary treasure my lamented friend Robert Tyrrell could have given us, in an *Imaginary Conversation* between Cicero and Atticus on the subject of Varro, his moods, and his literary aspirations.

Classical writers in *De Re Rustica* owe their inclusion in the present collection to the chapters in which they treat of the horse. Varro has a short chapter, *De Equis et equabus*. There is another, *De Canibus*, in which he divides them into two genera, *unum venaticum et pertinet ad feras bestias*, the other including watchdogs and sheep-dogs. But there is no suggestion of horsemanship or of sport, beyond the mere destruction or capture of wild animals.

The earliest works on field sports and country

* Cicero to Atticus, *Epist.* 642, in the *Correspondence of M. Tullius Cicero*, by Robert Yelverton Tyrrell, Litt.D., etc., sometime Regius Professor of Greek in the University of Dublin, and Louis Claude Purser, Litt.D., etc., sometime Professor of Latin in the same University, vol. v., second edition, p. 156.

life were written in Latin, for it was at that time
the language of educated men. The vulgar
tongues of the European nations, then in course
of formation, were not, as yet, employed in
literary composition. But there is a marked
difference in the Latinity of the different authors.
Albertus Magnus wrote of horses and hawks in
the style, severe and clear, of his philosophical
writings. Frederick II. wrote in the same language, but his style was so rough and unpolished
that the editor of the first printed edition of his
works on falconry (Paris, 1596) thought it necessary to offer as an excuse for the defects of his
style the age in which he lived. *Impolitiam et
asperitatem scriptionis seculum excusat, quam
rerum diligens tam verborum negligens.*

In the centuries before the revival of learning,
and the study of the great writers of the classical
age which it brought about, the Latin ordinarily
written was devoid of literary quality. Crescentius
wrote in the easy style of one to whom Latin was
the language in which he thought and wrote.
He wrote also as a scholar whose style had been
formed by a study of the best authors. But
there is an absence of the conscious imitation
which is apparent in the writings of Latinists of
a later date. Of this an example is afforded
by the *De rebus in Hibernia gestis* of Richard
Stanyhurst, an excellent scholar educated at the
famous school in Kilkenny, where in subsequent
years Swift, Berkeley, and Congreve were school-
fellows. Stanyhurst's style is learned, but artificial, in which fine phrases borrowed from
Cicero are imbedded like plums in a pudding.

The work of Crescentius is treated as a book of sport by the compilers of catalogues, and it contains chapters which entitle it to be so regarded. In Liber X. he writes : *De diversis artibus capiendi animalia fera*. This book contains thirty-nine chapters, some of which deal with the capture of wolves, stags, and hares, and tell of snares, traps, and pitfalls. Wild beasts are taken either because they are dangerous or because they are good for food. Cap. XXIX. tells us of wild beasts *qualiter canibus capiuntur*. Hares are found and taken by trained hounds, also wild goats, and sometimes stag with the assistance of skilfully placed nets, *principue auxilio retiarum magnarum positarum in locis unde fugantur*. But there is no suggestion of the noble art of venerie which in France was, in the time of Crescentius, held in honour as a divinely ordained source of human happiness.

Fish are caught in nets and similar engines. They are also taken by means of a baited hook. Here some words suggest that the good Petrus had the spirit of a sportsman, and that he might have enjoyed an occasional day's fishing in the Po when summoned from Bologna to Venice to determine some important suit. But the idea is at once dispelled when we find him describing with realistic detail, suggestive of personal experience, how fish are caught with quicklime; how the lime is put in a bag; how a small pool of standing water is selected; how two men vigorously move the bag containing the lime throughout the water; and how all the fish come blindly to the surface of the water, and are easily taken by the hand. He tells also of a terrible kind of strokehaul, by which large fish may be taken, to be used from a boat, or even when standing on the bank, if the fisherman catches a glimpse of a fish in muddy water.

Crescentius considered it necessary for the completeness of his work on country life that he should in some sort handle sport. But his heart was in his life-work, journeying throughout the communes, dispensing justice and counselling their rulers, and in the days of retirement in his little suburban farm.

The only true field sport of which he treats in detail is the art of falconry; naturally, for it was the only mediæval sport which was successfully pursued in Italy. His chapters are suggestive of a tribute to the popularity of the sport, and are of little other significance. To him, the father of falconry was the mythical Dancus or Daucus, *rex Daucus, qui divino intellectu novit naturam accipitrum et falconum*, and he makes no mention of the historical introducers of the sport into Italy—the Suabian emperors of the house of Hohenstaufen.

It is as the prototype of the modern popular treatise on country life with illustrations, rather than from its literary merit, that the *Agricultura* of Crescentius owes its unique position in the history of literature. The manuscripts appear to have been illustrated with miniatures which were reproduced in the woodcuts of the early printed editions—useful and practical, but devoid of the beauty with which the great French classics of the chase were adorned. The success that was attained by the work of Crescentius is shown by the early date at which it found its way into print. The first edition was published in Augsburg in 1471 by the title of *Ruralium Commodorum Libri XII*. Six editions in the original Latin, printed in the fifteenth century, are noted by Mr. Harting. It had already been translated into French in the year 1373 at the request of Charles V., known in history as the 'Wise.' No stronger proof of his wisdom could be given than his introduction into France, amid the devastations of the Hundred Years' War, of a practical treatise on the cultivation of the soil, for every reader of Froissart must be struck by the oft-recurring statement that some of the most fertile parts of France were laid waste and remained uncultivated for several years. The first printed edition of the French translation was in Paris in 1486. Mr. Harting notes seven up to the middle of the sixteenth century, when it was superseded by the *Maison Rustique*. There was also a German edition of which ' several were printed at Strassburg about the end of the fifteenth century and earlier ' (Harting, *Bibliotheca Accipitraria*).

The treatise was translated into the vulgar tongue of Italy at a date which is uncertain, but which is probably shortly after the book was written. The earliest printed edition appeared in Florence in 1478 under the title *Il libri della Agricoltura*. Thirteen editions of this translation from 1478 to 1805 are noted by Mr. Harting, adding that there were probably others, in which he is certainly right, for there is in the collection of the present writer an edition not noted by him, printed in Venice in 1519, with the title *Piero Crescentio de Agricultura vulgare*.

The French translation of the work of Crescentius was the model on which *L'Agriculture et Maison Rustique de Maistres Charles Estienne et Jean Liebault* was founded. In the first edition, published in 1564, Estienne appears as the author, the name of Liebault being added in 1566 and in subsequent editions.

This book attained a popularity eclipsing that of its predecessors by Varro and by Crescentius. Appearing in the age of printing, it was immediately and frequently reproduced. Souhart notes upwards of one hundred editions, not including translations in Italian, German, and English. With it was generally printed a treatise on the taking of the wolf, *La chasse du Loup necessaire à la Maison Rustique*.

This work never became popular in England. It was translated by the title of *Maison Rustique, or the Countrey Farm*, by Richard Surflet, Practitioner in Physicke (London, 1600), and in 1616 Gervais Markham brought out an edition of the book with the same title, in which ' the husbandry of France, Italy, and Spaine was reconciled and made to agree with ours here in England.' The work was regarded as of little value. It was never reprinted, and is interesting only as evidence of the extraordinary industry of the compiler.

Italian is the only Romance language that has produced no great treatise on the chase, and in this it followed the tradition of the classical age of Italy. The few books on hunting that were written in that language in later years are noteworthy only on account of the illustrations with which they are profusely adorned. The *Delle Caccie* of Raimondi, first published in 1621, has some vigorous woodcuts, and later editions contain a number of copperplate engravings, but as a book of sport it is unworthy of notice.

The *Venaria Reale* of count Amadeo di Castellamonte (1672-74) is valued by collectors on account of its rarity and its illustrations, of which Mr. Baillie-Grohman writes: ' It is to be hoped, for the sake of Italy's reputation, that some of these do not represent actuality, but are imaginary scenes ' (*Sport in Art*, p. 220). In the engraving entitled *Morte del cervo* we see the hart—a sorry ' rascal '—stoned to death when set up at bay by the hounds. *La curea* is enacted in the presence of a motley crowd, joined by ladies in full court dress, arriving in coaches drawn by six horses, in time to see the rewarding of the hounds.

Falconry, a field sport not of native growth, took deep root when planted in Italian soil. This will be told in the chapter entitled ' The Emperor Frederick II. and Falconry.'

CHAPTER V

GASTON PHŒBUS AND FROISSART

GASTON PHŒBUS, COMTE DE FOIX, was the embodiment of the spirit of his age; and Froissart the chronicler, who shows ' of the very age and body of the time his form and pressure.'

' I rejoice you have met with Froissart,' Gray wrote to a friend; ' he is the Herodotus of a barbarous age; had he but the luck of writing in so good a language, he might have been immortal.'

Whether the word ' barbarous ' is rightly applied to the age of Dante; of Petrarch; of Wyclif, one of the makers of English prose; and of Chaucer, the father of English poetry, it is needless to inquire. For our present purpose it is enough that it is the age of Froissart, a writer who, in the opinion of the grave and judicial Hallam, takes rank with the greatest historians of Greece and Rome; one who ' by his picturesque description and fertility of historical invention may be reckoned the Livy of France,'* and ' who equals Herodotus in simplicity, liveliness, and power over the heart';† and who was beloved alike of Gibbon (*post*, p. 113) and of Scott, who writes of Edward Waverley: ' The splendid pages of Froissart,

---

* *Literature of Europe.*   † *Middle Ages.*

with his heart-stirring and eye-dazzling descriptions of war and of tournaments, were among his
chief favourites.'*

In the exercise of these great literary powers
Froissart was at his best when in a happy hour
of the year 1388 he rode forth in company with
sir Espang de Lyon to the court of Gaston at
Orthez in quest of tales of knightly valour.

He was then about fifty years of age. Born
in Valenciennes of a family connected with the
neighbouring town of Beaumont, the seigneurie
of a younger branch of the house of Hainault, his
connection with Hainault and the lords of Beaumont had a determining influence on his life and
fortunes.

Jean Sire de Beaumont had been patron of a
canon of Liège called Jean le Bel, whose chronicles,
written at the instigation of his lord, became in
course of events the foundation of the work
undertaken by Froissart at the command, as he
tells us, of the grandson and successor of this
lord of Beaumont.

The canon was 'in his life days well beloved
and of the secret council with the lord, sir John of
Hainault, who is often remembered, as reason
requireth, here after in this book.'

It was indeed as reason required that sir John
of Hainault was remembered by le Bel and by
Froissart, for he was the ' only begetter ' of their
chronicles. For many years he was remembered
by them as the chivalrous champion of queen

* 'The passages concerning whose (Edward Waverley) course
of reading were imitated from recollections of my own '
(*Waverley:* General Preface to Novels).

Isabella and the friend of England, and Froissart writes with evident regret of the traitorous calumny by which he was led to desert, and to fight in the battle of Poitiers against the Black Prince, the son of the chronicler's beloved patron, queen Philippa.

When queen Isabella had failed to obtain the aid of her brother, Charles IV. of France, against the evil advisers of her husband, Edward II., she came with her son Edward to Valenciennes, the court of the count of Hainault, and there found an enthusiastic champion in his younger brother, the lord of Beaumont. Sir John, being, as the chronicler tells us, ' young and lusty, desiring all honours,' wept to hear of the queen's dolours, and said, ' Certainly, fair lady, behold me here your own knight, who shall not fail you to die in the quarrel ' (p. 7).*

He promised to conduct the queen and her son to England, and to do his best to bring her to her estates, and he kept his word. He comes on the stage in Marlowe's *Edward II.*, but he lives in Froissart. The count of Flanders and his council thought that the enterprise was right high and perilous, but howsoever they blamed or counselled him the gentle knight would never change his purpose, but said ' he had but one death to die, the which was in the will of God:

* Where the paging of a passage is noted in the text, the reference is to the *Globe* edition of Froissart's *Chronicles*. Where a passage referred to is not included in this abbreviated edition, the reference is by volume and page to the edition of Lord Berners's translation, published in London in 1814. This translation was that used in the *Globe* edition.

and also said that all knights ought to aid to their
power all ladies and damosels chased out of their own
countries, being without counsel or comfort ' (p. 8).
He told his brother that he would rather renounce
all that he had than that the good lady should
leave them without comfort and help.

The count gave him leave to go in the name of
God, kissing him and straining him by the hand,
in sign of great love, and the result of his enterprise is written in the history of England.

The occasion of sir John's next visit to England
was a happier one. Edward II. was dead and
his son reigned in his stead. He had not forgotten
his visit with his mother to the court of William
of Hainault, and the eight days spent there with
the good count and his countess Jean de Valois.
' Then this earl had four fair daughters, Margaret,
Philippa, Jean, and Isabel, among whom the
young Edward set most his love and company
on Philippa, and also the young lady in all honour
was more conversant with him than any other of
her sisters ' (p. 8). The young king—he was only
seventeen years of age—and his mother, with the
concurrence ' of all the barons of England and
by the advice of the king's council,' sent ambas-
sadors to sir John of Hainault praying him to be
a means to bring about a marriage between the
king and the count's daughter Philippa. The
count was well pleased, and the ' princess was
married by a sufficient procuration brought from
the king of England ' (p. 25). She was conducted
to London by sir John of Beaumont to the great
advantage of the king, of her adopted country,
and of a certain young Hainaulter, who was in

a few years to follow the princess to London and, in due course, to record for all time the virtues of good queen Philippa.

The chronicles of the ' right reverend discreet master John le Bel ' had a great fascination for Froissart. ' I took on me,' he says, ' as soon as I came from school to write and recite the said book' (p. 2). Froissart's writing of the chronicles was in verse, and this early effort became in time the foundation of his future success in life.

Valenciennes was at that time a flourishing commercial town, and Froissart appears to have been offered an opening in business, but he preferred the life of a learned clerk. Commencing poet, he became of sufficient account to obtain letters of recommendation from the king of Bohemia and the count of Hainault to queen Philippa. The queen, to the nobility of whose character Froissart bears affectionate testimony, took a lively interest in her fellow-countryman. He brought with him to London the volume that he had completed and presented it to the queen, who ' right amiably received it, to my great profit and advancement.'

The story of his ' single love adventure conducted on the well-known lines of conventional love,' and how it touched the heart of the queen is told by sir Walter Besant in his interesting memoir, printed in the eleventh edition of the *Encyclopædia Britannica*. There you may read how Froissart, at the suggestion and at the charges of his kind patron, spent some five years in travel, and returned to England in the year 1361, and how the queen made the young poet one of her secretaries, and he began to serve her with *beaux ditties et traites amoureux*.

He received another appointment which had an important result, when he became secretary to king John of France, who had been a prisoner in England since the battle of Poitiers in 1356.

It was at the court of Edward III. and in attendance on king John that Froissart for the first time ' followed and frequented the company of diverse nobles and great lords, as well in France, England, and Scotland as in diverse other countries, and had knowledge by them, and always to my power justly have enquired for the truth of the deeds of war and adventures that have fallen, especially sith the great battle of Poitiers, whereas the noble king John of France was taken prisoner, as before that time I was but of a young age and understanding.'

From the lips of combatants in that mighty battle Froissart heard the story of the feats of arms that were there done, so that, aided by his ' fertility of historical invention,' he writes of them as if he had himself borne a part in the fight. For in those days a war between England and France was waged after the manner of a chivalrous game, and if fair play were shown no angry feeling survived. When we read of heralds sent forth to arrange for a convenient day on which battle should be given, and of the combatants in a pitched battle staying their hands to witness with admiration a marvellous feat of arms between single combatants, we can understand how the deeds of valour done on either side during the great war, and especially on the field of Poitiers, would be discussed and appraised in the court of John; and how feats of arms were entrusted for commemoration to Froissart with full assurance that justice would be done and that his record would be an impartial one.

If warfare in the time of Froissart partook of the nature of a game, the great heraldic pastime of the tournament, although in course of time it had lost the deadly peril of its early days, was still the very image of war.*

In this society king John's secretary found it easy to obtain at first hand the information by which he was enabled to tell the story of the battle of Poitiers; of what had befallen the king in the field, and afterwards during his honourable confinement in England.

No one could give this information better than the comte de Tancarville, a great Norman noble-man who is often honourably mentioned in the chronicle, for he was taken prisoner when he was fighting near the king, and at the supper, when the Black Prince entertained the king and the captive chivalry of France, he sat at table with the king. It was from him, or from one like him, that Froissart learned how the king had borne him in the fight; how he ' with his own hands did that day marvels in arms; he had an axe in his hands wherewith he defended himself and fought in the breaking of the press' (p. 128), and how, when he was brought to the prince as prisoner, ' the prince made lowly reverence to the king and caused wine and spices to be brought

* Note A.: The Tournament in Froissart and in Scott.

forth, and himself served the king in sign of great love'; how at supper the king and his son, with de Tancarville and other great lords who had been taken, sat at a table and were served by the prince as humbly as he could; and how the prince bid the king be of good cheer: 'Surely the king my father shall bear you as much honour and amity as he may do, and shall accord with you so reasonably that ye shall ever be friends together after. And, sir, methink ye ought to rejoice, though the journey be not as ye would have had it, for this day ye have won the high renown of prowess, and have passed this day in valiantness all other of your party' (p. 131).

The king did not belie the promise of the prince. 'The French king rode through London on a white courser well apparelled, and the prince on a little black hobby by his side.' He and his household were lodged at the Savoy, where the king and queen often visited him and made him great feast and cheer. Presently they were removed to the castle of Windsor: king John there 'went a-hunting and a-hawking at his pleasure, and the lord Philip his son with him' (p. 135). They were afterwards joined by nobles of the realm of France, who came over as hostages; and among them was Guy, count of Blois, of whom we shall hear as lord of Beaumont; for it was at his instance that Froissart passed from the writing of verse to the composition in prose of chronicles founded on the work of John le Bel.

Of Froissart in the service of the king of France as secretary sir Walter Besant writes:

He probably acquired at this period that art, in which he has probably never been surpassed, of making people tell him all they knew. No newspaper correspondent, no American interviewer has ever equalled this mediæval collector of intelligence. From Queen Philippa, who confided to him the tender story of her youthful and lasting love for her great husband, down to the simplest knight—Froissart conversed with none beneath the rank of gentlemen—all united in telling this man what he wanted to know.

We gain some insight into his method from his account of a persistent but unsuccessful effort to induce a trusty knight of the household of Gaston Phœbus to divulge the secret of the death of his son. Froissart does not hesitate to record his failure, interesting, perhaps, because an event of rare occurrence; and his perseverance was rewarded by his discovery in the court of Orthez of an old squire who fell an easy victim.

From the cheerfulness of his pleasure-loving nature, and his readiness to impart as well as to receive information, he was a delightful companion. Disraeli found in his chronicles a most entertaining companion on a tiresome journey, and Gibbon writes: ' I would not complain of the labour of this work, if my materials were always derived from such books as the Chronicle of honest Froissart, who read little, inquired much, and believed all.' He finds the statement of facts in certain memoirs ' dry and deficient if compared with the pleasant garrulity of Froissart,' from whom he parts with evident regret.*

We may be sure that this ' pleasant garrulity '

* *Decline and Fall*, chap. lxiv.

was appreciated by his travelling companion
sir Espang de Lyon, and by the knights and
squires who had the good fortune to know him
in the flesh, from whom he would invite confidence
by holding out a prospect of immortality in the
chronicles which he promised to give to the world
on his return to his native country.

Happily devoid of all sense of the dignity of
history, he enterprised his book, ' to ordain for
pleasure and pastance, to the which always I have
been inclined '; and now and then he gives
assurance of the possession of a keen sense of
humour. In the Great Schism pope Urban of
Rome was supported by England against pope
Clement of Avignon. An attempt was made to
give practical effect to this support, in the first
instance by offers of absolution from sin, and
then by gathering together great riches for
Urban; ' he was certain that the nobles of England
for all his absolutions would not go out to war
without money, for warriors live not by pardons,
nor do they regard them but in time of death.'

He writes of the Great Schism in a spirit
becoming a churchman, but this was a topic
from which he was always glad to escape, and
to return to the main object of his work, which
was ' all noble hearts to encourage, and to show
them ensample and matter of honour' (p. 2). At
the end of a dull chapter of ecclesiastical history
he writes: ' Now let us leave speaking of these
popes, and return to other matters,' as who should
say—a plague on both your houses. The other
matters to which he gladly turns are—after a short
account of the taking of a castle—the celebrated

jousts at Inglevere in time of truce when three young
French knights maintained their challenge against
all comers, English or French, for thirty days.

But one thing Froissart lacked as an inter-
preter of the age in which he lived. If he had
been of Normandy, the home of venery, and not
of commercial and matter-of-fact Flanders, the
pleasant garrulity by which Gibbon was charmed
must have led him, from early recollections, to
digress from the main purpose of his work, and
to tell us something of the classics of the chase
that were written by famous masters while he
was closely associated with them. The opportunities which fell to his lot of furnishing matter
for these pages were so remarkable that his silence
must be attributed to absolute indifference to the
subject of field sports.

Gaston's great work was in full progress during
the twelve weeks which Froissart spent at the
court of Orthez. He writes of Gaston's love of
hunting, and gives a particular account of the
manner in which he spent his time; but of the
work to which much of it must have been devoted
he says no word. The earl may have forbidden
his literary occupation to be noised abroad in the
hall; but it could not have been a secret to the
four secretaries whom he employed. If it had
reached the ears of the talkative old squire from
whom Froissart extracted the secret of how
young Gaston met his death, or of the mysterious
squire with whom he gossiped in a dark corner
of the castle chapel, Froissart somehow failed to
acquire this particular piece of information; or if
he did attain to it, he did not regard it as of equal

interest with the question of the earl's relations
with the familiar spirit called Orthon.

It is still more remarkable that king John's
secretary has not a word to say about another
work undertaken by a fellow member of king
John's household, at his command. The secretary must have been aware that the king's first
chaplain, Gace de la Buigne, had been allowed
to accompany his master into captivity for the
purpose of instructing his son Philip in the art of
venery, and that by command of the king this
instruction was imparted in the form of a poem
of interest in the early history of the chase, and
also from the light which it throws on the kind
of education which formed part of the chivalry
of the Middle Ages.

Philip of France, afterwards duke of Burgundy,
was, while still a boy, an enthusiastic falconer,
and an apt pupil of his reverend instructor. The
account of the expenditure of the king his father,
kept by one Denys Collors in the years 1359 and
1350, bears witness to his devotion to the sport.
We find entries of money paid to ' Messire Gasse,
premier chappelain ' in respect of the falconry
of ' Mons. Philippe,' including the sum of XXs.
paid by the French king to the falconer of king
Edward III, who brought back a falcon that
Messire Gasse had lost (*Master of Game*).

This Messire Gasse was M. Gace de la Buigne,
a member of an ancient Norman family, who
filled the post of first chaplain to three successive
kings of France. It is, however, as the writer of
a book of sport, the *Romans des Déduits*, which
suggested to Gaston Phœbus the enterprising of

his more famous treatise; and as the instructor in woodcraft of Philip the Bold, to whom Gaston presented his work when completed as to the greatest living master of the craft, that he finds a place in these pages.

He tells us in this poem that the work was begun in the year 1359 at the commandment of the king, so that his son Philip, who was still young, might have a knowledge of sport, and avoid the sin of sloth (*la pechie doiseuse*), being well trained in good manners and in virtue. The book was not completed until after the year 1373. We shall see, later on, how it came into the hands of Gaston, and became the foundation of his more celebrated work.

Although Froissart took no note of the *Romans des Déduits* or of the *Roy Modus*—a famous work with which the name of another fellow-prisoner, the comte de Tancarville, was in some way connected —they have a close connection with the name which stands at the head of this chapter; for they were lying open before Gaston Phœbus when he was writing *La Chasse*, and he borrowed passages from them, in some instances with literal exactness.

Gace's poem is a strange medley of allegory, morality, and sporting lore, from which a fuller and truer conception of fourteenth-century ideas and modes of thought may be derived than from a bare record of historical fact, however accurate. It does not appear to have been ever printed separately, but a full account of this curious work is given by Mr. Baillie-Grohman, in the bibliography appended to his edition of the *Master of Game*.

The sport of falconry is the foundation of the

training of the young prince in good manners and virtue. The reverend author had been devoted to this sport from his earliest days, for at the age of nine he carried his hobby, and he could train a falcon at the age of twelve. It is interesting to learn that in the opinion of the first chaplain ' no alleluia has ever been sung in the chapel of the king that is so beautiful and gives so much pleasure as the music of hounds.'

The court of Edward was a famous school of Chivalry. This you may learn from the historians of the time. They tell us of the court of Chivalry, instituted by the king, of which the Lord High Constable and the Earl Marshal of England were judges. They also tell us of the great hunting establishment kept up by the king, and of the vast number of hounds and hawks by which he was accompanied in his wars in France. But it is left to a book of sport to introduce us to his court as a school of Venery, and to record among the excellences of the great king his profound knowledge of the learning of woodcraft: ' The king of England knows no master in the science of hunting, and cedes the place of honour to no one on the battlefield ' (*Romans des Déduits*). The court of Edward is the scene of a dispute imagined by Gace de la Buigne between a huntsman and a falconer, as to the relative merits of their favourite sports, in which de Tancarville is chosen as arbiter; being equally distinguished in both sports. The count is often honourably mentioned by the secretary in his chronicles, but if we would know something of him as an authority on field sports, we must have recourse to the reverend first chaplain.

The *Romans des Déduits* is of value to the inquirer into the history of education in the Middle Ages. There were then no public schools in which the cadets of noble and knightly houses could receive an education suitable to their position in life. There were famous schools in connection with some of the greater cathedrals, such as Chartres and Rheims, but these were mainly ecclesiastic in character, and were rarely resorted to except by young men destined to the life of a learned clerk.

Hallam writes of ' the regular scheme of education, according to which the sons of gentlemen from the age of seven years were brought up in the castles of superior lords, where they at once learned the whole discipline of their future profession, and imbibed its emulous and enthusiastic spirit ' (*Middle Ages*, chap. ix., part ii.).

With the management of arms, the art of horsemanship and an acquaintance with the science of woodcraft were necessary parts of the education of a gentleman. There was a graduation of service. To the poorer nobility it was, as Hallam points out, an inestimable advantage that their sons could acquire the accomplishments of their station, and become accustomed to obedience and courteous demeanour in the household of their feudal chief, who had, in his turn, the privilege of having his son trained in the service of the great nobleman under whom he held his estate.

Service thus rendered in household offices was not derogatory to honourable or noble birth. The service of the king was held in the highest honour; great houses—like that of Ormonde—

were proud to derive names and titles from household offices in which their ancestors had served their sovereign, and the same spirit inspired all the degrees of chivalry, and the instruction in virtue and good manners given to youth in every knightly household was, we may believe, not unlike that imparted by M. Gasse.*

For some reason that we do not know—it may have been at the instance of the queen—Froissart left England for the second time in the year 1366, in search of adventure. He continued to describe himself as in the service of the queen of England, and it is probable that he intended again to return, until the death of Philippa in 1369 led him to seek for another patron.

The story of his wanderings is told by sir Walter Besant:

'He repaired first to Brussels, whither were gathered together a great concourse of minstrels from all parts; from the courts of the kings of Denmark, Navarre, and Aragon; from those of the duke of Lancaster, Bavaria, and Brunswick. Hither came all who could *rimer et dicta*.'

What distinction Froissart gained is not stated; but that he received a gift of money appears from the account, ' uni Fritsardo, dictori, qui est cum regina Angliæ, dicto die VI mottones.'

We read of him in Brittany, and he accompanied the Black Prince to Dax. He formed part of the expedition which escorted Lionel, duke of

* The reproduction of the *Babee's Book*, and John Russell's *Book of Nurture* in the Mediæval Library under the general editorship of Sir Israel Gollancz, has thrown light on the course of instruction and discipline in the chivalric schools of manners in which children of gentle birth were educated.

Clarence, to Milan, to marry the daughter of Galeazzo Visconti. Here we find his name associated with the greatest in the literature of the age, for we read that Chaucer was one of the prince's suite, and that Petrarch was a guest at the wedding banquet, seated among the princes.

It was in Rome that he learned of the death of queen Philippa, of whom he writes:

> Propices li soit Diex a l'âme;
> J'en suis bien tenus de pryer,
> Et ses larghesces escuyer,
> Car elle me fist et créa.

In these simple words Froissart pays the debt of gratitude which he owed to the good queen, for it was to her encouragement of a humble fellow-countryman that his success in life was due; and years after he wrote in his chronicle 'of the death of the most gentle queen, most liberal and courteous that ever was queen in her days, the which was the fair lady Philippa of Hainault, queen of England and Ireland' (p. 195).

After some wanderings we find him, about the year 1574, settled in his native Beaumont, under the protection of Guy, count of Blois and lord of Beaumont, who, during his captivity in England as one of the hostages for king John, had become acquainted with the king's secretary. This Guy was grandson of the lord of Beaumont, at whose suggestion the chronicles of John le Bel were written, and it is to him that we owe the conversion of an indifferent rhymer into a famous historian.

We read of Froissart as curé of Lestines, canon and treasurer of Chimay, and chaplain to the count. He had written of feats of arms from his school-days, and what time could be spared from his clerical duties, which were probably not onerous, had been devoted to the composition of love songs and the *traites amoureux* in which the ladies of mediæval courts took delight.

During the years in which his literary powers were so employed he wrote no prose. It occurred to Guy of Blois that the literary ability which he had discerned in the king's secretary would be better employed in building a serious historical work on the foundation that had been laid by John le Bel than in versifying the old chronicles, or in the composition of occasional pieces for the amusement of lords and ladies of the court.

We are so much indebted to this count of Blois for the good advice given to his chaplain that we read with regret the story of his later years. He was unfortunate in his management of his great possessions; he sold Blois to France, and died so much in debt that his widow ' dared not take on her the administration of his testament, but returned to her dowry of the lands of Chimay and Beaumont.' Froissart, never ungrateful to his patrons, or forgetful of largesse, deals gently with his memory, and attributes his misfortunes to bad advisers: ' Consider what damage a lord or any other may do to his heir by giving credence to evil counsel; God forgive him.'

The widow of Guy of Blois was Mary, daughter of Robert of Namur, an actor in many of the events recorded in the chronicles. It was from him that Froissart learned the story of the siege of Calais, and of the queen's intercession on behalf of the six burgesses, for which he is our authority.

This Robert of Namur became in his turn the patron of Froissart, and it is to him that the prologue to the chronicles is addressed. He tells us how he came to enterprise the work ' at the request of the right high and mighty prince, my dear lord and master, Guy of Chatillon and of Blois. . . . I, John Froissart, chaplain to my said lord, and at that time treasurer and canon of Chimay and of Lille in Flanders, have enterprised this noble matter treating of the adventures and wars of France and England, and other countries conjoined and allied to them, as it may appear by the treaties they made unto the date of this present day: the which excellent matter, as long as I live, by the help of God I shall continue, for the more I follow and labour it the more it pleaseth me. As the noble knight or squire, loving feat of arms do persevere in the same and be thereby expert and made perfect, so in labouring of this noble matter I delight and take pleasure.'

In this is the secret of Froissart's charm; he loved his work, and his reader shares the pleasure and delight of the writer, when he reads of a famous tournament or a noble feat of arms.

Froissart had been living for years under the patronage of Guy de Blois. Starting with le Bel's chronicles, he had written two of the books into which his history is divided. From what he had learned from the lords and knights, English and French, with whom he was associated at the court of Edward, he was able to write of Crecy and Poitiers, and in the course of his wanderings he had been told of many noteworthy feats of arms,

9

but he felt that his life's work had not yet been accomplished.

He writes:

Considering in myself how there was no great deeds of arms likely toward in the parts of Picardy or Flanders, seeing the peace was made between the duke and them of Gaunt, and it greatly annoyed me to be idle; for I knew well that after my death this noble and high history should have his course, wherein divers noble men should have great pleasure and delight, and as yet, I thank God, I have understanding and remembrance of all things past, and my wit quick and sharp enough to conceive all things shewed unto me touching my principal matter, and my body as yet able to endure and to suffer pain, all things considered I thought I would not let to pursue my said first purpose; and to the intent to know the truth of deeds done in far countries, I found occasion to go to the high and mighty prince Gaston earl of Foix and of Bearn; for I knew well that if I might have that grace to come into his house, and to be there at leisure, I could not be so well informed to my purpose in none other place of the world; for thither resorted all manner of knights and strange squires, for the great nobleness of the said earl (p. 309).

Froissart's patron approved his project, and gave him letters of introduction to the earl of Foix. Provided with them and with a kind of passport without which he never approached the court of any high and mighty prince—a book of poetry—he left Hainault on the most memorable of his many adventures.

This Gaston of whom Froissart had heard so much was, of the princes of his age, the one who was most worthy of commemoration by a consummate artist who, conscious that after his death his work should have his course, spared no

pains to give us of his best. The portrait which
he presents of a great mediæval prince, in his daily
life, in the government of his people, in his inter-
course with visitors to his court, in his relations
with other powers, and in the state that he maintained, is complete in all its details, and it is
drawn with the consummate art which suggests
the absence of art.

It arrested the attention of Disraeli when
engaged in some work connected with the
chronicles, and although this work was not completed, or perhaps never seriously undertaken,
the portrait of Gaston, as limned by Froissart,
left an abiding impression on his mind (*ante*, p. 3).

. Gaston was fifty-seven years of age when
Froissart set forth to visit him at Orthez, in the
autumn of the year 1388. His life had been an
eventful one. He represented two independent
races of mediæval princes, whose strongly marked
characteristics can be recognised in their descen-
dant; and the man of whom Froissart wrote can
be best understood when the words of the
chronicler are read with some knowledge of his
history, and of the lords of Foix and Bearn from
whom he sprang.

The counts of Foix, a small territory in south-
eastern France, were at first feudatories of the
counts of Toulouse. Throwing off this yoke, they
were, during the thirteenth and fourteenth centuries, among the most powerful of the French
feudal nobles. They are described as acting as
the equals rather than as dependants of the kings
of France, a position which they owed to the
strong and independent spirit of the counts and

not to the importance of the territory over which they reigned.

The independent spirit of the counts brought them into frequent collision with Rome. The excommunication of count Peter who took part in the crusade of 1095 arose out of a dispute about ecclesiastical property which was afterwards satisfactorily arranged. In later years we find successive counts of Foix championing the cause of the Albigenses, one of whom, Raymond Roger, had accompanied Philip of France to Palestine, and distinguished himself at the capture of Acre. He had literary tastes, and was a patron of the Provençal poets.

Whatever obscurity may exist as to the tenets of the sect commonly known as the Albigenses, or the degree of enlightenment to which they had attained, there can be none as to the relentless cruelty with which it was persecuted to extinction.

Simon de Montfort, whose son holds an honourable record in the constitutional history of England, was the leader in the crusade. Languedoc was devastated and its inhabitants massacred in thousands. The territory of Raymond Roger was granted to de Montfort, but restored in 1223. His son of the same name, known as 'the great,' took an active part with Raymond, count of Toulouse, in supporting the Albigenses, and was twice excommunicated.

It was by the marriage of this distinguished member of the family with the daughter of Gaston, viscount of Bearn, that the principality of Bearn came to be united with the countship of Foix.

The viscountship of Bearn, now included in the department of Basses-Pyrenees, was in the early Middle Ages dependent on the dukes of Aquitaine, a link which was severed in the eleventh century, when its rulers asserted an independence which they maintained in opposition to successive kings of France and England. The French historian M. Benont writes in the *Encyclopædia Britannica* (tit. Bearn) of the Bearnais: ' From the eleventh century onward they were governed by their own special customs or dors. These were drawn up in the language of the country, a romance dialect, 1288 being the date of the most ancient written code.'

The story of the union of the two principalities, as told by Froissart, speaks for the sterling qualities which Gaston inherited from his ancestors of Foix and of Bearn (p. 328).

Gaston of Bearn had two daughters, of whom the elder married the count of Armagnac, and the younger the count of Foix. Gaston was at war with the king of Spain, who was invading Bearn with a great army, and he appealed to his sons-in-law to aid him. The earl of Foix, with a strong force, ' came into the country of Bearn to serve his father, who had of him great joy. They tarried for the earl of Armagnac three days, and on the fourth they received a message that he had nothing to do to bear arms for the county of Bearn.'

Gaston took him at his word, and treated him as having forfeited all right to a share in the county, all of which came to the earl of Foix, who had by himself won a great victory over

Spain, in which more than ten thousand Spaniards were killed, and the king's son and brother taken prisoners and sent to Gaston.

We are not surprised to find the counts of Foix maintaining the advantage which their ancestor had thus obtained in the hostilities that naturally ensued from the loss of a share in the inheritance of Bearn. Nothing need be said here of the unhappy far-off things and battles long ago which fill many pages of the chronicles. They resulted in a decisive battle in the year 1365, when Gaston Phœbus captured the count of Armagnac and exacted from him as ransom the sum of 250,000 livres, of which we shall hear something hereafter, for it was the occasion of a meeting between two of the great princes of the age, the Black Prince and Gaston of Foix, and Froissart's account of what was said and done at that meeting may well have been written in the words of Gaston.

Descended from these noteworthy ancestors, Gaston was born in 1338. In his early years he gave no promise of the qualities for which he was famous in after-life. He was so perverse and frivolous that his father and mother were ashamed of him, everyone saying that he would never be any good, and the country was unhappy of which he should be the ruler. So he says in the compositions in the form of prayers, sent many years after to his friend Philip the Bold, duke of Burgundy, which have a certain auto-biographical value.

His father died when Gaston was twelve years of age, leaving him under the pupilage of his

mother, Eleanor of Comminges, a princess re-
nowned for wisdom and virtue, to whose instruction we may attribute the strict orthodoxy
which—unlike the old counts of Foix—he professed. As he grew up the peoples of Foix and
of Bearn were troubled, for they lived in the midst
of turbulent neighbours, exposed to invasion
from France and from England, and to attacks
from the counts of Armagnac; and their youthful
prince, although endowed with great gifts of
mind and body, had given no promise of excellence in the art of war. ' Omnes gentes dicebant,
magna perditio tanti hominis, tam fortis et tam
sapientis qui nil valet in armis'; so he writes in
one of his ' Prayers.'

The occasion came, and Gaston proved himself
a man; the story of his life as a soldier is told by
M. Lavallée in the memoir prefixed to his admirable edition of La Chasse.

In 1257 we find him with the captal of Buch,
joining the knights of the Teutonic order in an
expedition against the pagan inhabitants of what
is now East Prussia. The Teutonic knights, one
of the three military and religious orders which
had their origin in the crusades, were at the
height of their glory in the middle of the fourteenth century. The work of the conquest and
' conversion' of the heathen tribes who inhabited
that district, undertaken by the order in the
preceding century, had been accomplished, but
on the borders of heathendom there was still a
place for knightly adventure. In the fourteenth
century ' it was the school of northern chivalry
engaged in unceasing struggle to defend and

extend Christianity against the heathen Lithu-
anians' (*Encyclopædia Britannica*, tit. Teutonic
Order).

Thither resorted from all parts of the world those
who would win their spurs in knightly adventure.
Chaucer's 'veray parfit gentil knight' had won so
high distinction in this field that he was awarded
the place of honour among those who sat at board:

> Full often time he had the bord begonne
> Above all nations in Pruce;
>
> (*Canterbury Tales*: Prologue.)

and as we shall see, an adventure with these
knights was not beneath the dignity of a knight
of the most noble order of the Garter.

Thither resorted Gaston with his cousin, the
captal of Buch, in the year 1357. Gaston had
fallen into disfavour with his feudal lord, the
king of France, and was for some time a prisoner
in the castle of Chateret, where one of his prayers
was composed. His liberation was attributed to
the reverse which king John had met with at
Poitiers. The result of this battle was also to
render it possible for the captal of Buch to take
part with his cousin in the expedition to Prussia.
He was a great nobleman of Aquitaine and a
knight of the Garter, who had fought with distinction under the Black Prince at Poitiers.
What we have been told of the captal—truly
typical of the fourteenth century—can be most
conveniently presented in the form of a note, save
when we find him associated with Gaston.*

Serious warfare had ended with the conquest
of the country by the knights: *Si on allait encore*

* Note B: The Captal de Buche.

*combattre dans leurs rangs, ce n'était plus pars
religion, mais par mode, ou par sentiment cheval-
eresque. On s'y rendait comme à une passe d'armes,
ou à une partie de plaisir.**

The expedition on which Gaston started with
his cousin was prompted by motives of religion,
of chivalry, and of sport, in a combination characteristic of the age. To Gaston each of these
motives appealed with power, and from his close
association with his cousin we may conclude that
he found in him a kindred spirit.

To Gaston the expedition offered a prospect
not only of knightly adventure, but of a kind of
field sport which could not be had at home. He
found time to cross the Baltic and to hunt the
reindeer in Sweden and in Norway. His chapter
in *La Chasse* on this sport is founded on experience, for of the ' rangier ' he writes: *J'en ai veu
en Nourveque et Xuedene.* This chapter was
intended as a record of the author's exploit; it
was of no practical value, for when it was written
the reindeer was no longer an object of interest
to sportsmen in southern Europe.

In the month of May, 1358, while Gaston and
his cousin were so engaged, an insurrection of
peasantry broke out in the Île de France and
about Beauvais. Few in number at the outset,
and unarmed save with staves and knives, they
rapidly gained strength. They chose as their
leader ' him that was the most ungraciousest of
all other, and they called him king Jaques Good-
man and so thereby they was called companions
of the Jaquery.' They laid the country waste

* Lavallée: *Vie de Gaston*, xi.

with fire and sword, committing outrages on
ladies and damosels, so horrible that Froissart
dared not to tell of them (pp. 136-8).

They were moved, not by any particular
grievance, but by the misery caused by the war,
for which they held the knights and squires
responsible. 'When they were demanded, why
they did so evil deeds, they would answer and
say that they could not tell, but they did as they
saw others do, thinking thereby to have destroyed
all the nobles and gentlemen of the world.'

As Gaston and the captal were returning to
France they heard of 'the great mischief that
fell among the noblemen by these unhappy
people: and in the city of Meaux was the duchess
of Orleans, and a three hundred other ladies and
damosels and the duke of Orleans also,' in peril
of nameless atrocities; 'then the two said knights
agreed to go and see these ladies and to comfort
them to their powers.'

When they of the Jaquerie scented the prey in
the city of Meaux they assembled from all quarters
to the number of nine thousand, and multitudes
resorted to them every day, while Gaston and
the captal had with them only three score spears,
but they were men of war well apparelled.

The noble ladies were lodged in a strong place
closed about with the river Marne, and the
knights and their companions 'issued from the
gate and set on those villains who were but evil
armed: with the earl of Foix's banner and the
duke of Orleans' and the captal's pennon.' The
insurgents fled in terror and soon became a dis-
organised mob.

The rescuers of the noble dames beat down their enemies 'by heaps, and slew them like beasts and chased them all out of the town, and slew so many that they were weary; and many of them by heaps to fly into the river.'* The slain were more than seven thousand. The insurrection was completely crushed by Charles the Bad, king of Navarre, in the month of June in the year in which it broke out, in a decisive battle followed by sanguinary reprisals.

Though the pursuit of arms was one of the three to which Gaston (as he tells us) devoted his life, he modestly disclaims any right to be regarded as an authority on the subject. Indeed, the service which won the affection and gratitude of his subjects was the foresight and skill with which he saved them from the disasters by which they would have been overwhelmed if their prince had taken an active part, on either side, in the great war between England and France: as Elizabeth won the title of 'Good queen Bess' by the statecraft which kept England outside the wars of religion in her day.

Gaston made neutrality safe for his peoples by the accumulation of wealth beyond that of any contemporary prince, and the knowledge that he was ready to expend it in safeguarding his principalities from harm. Some fighting there was— the hereditary feud with the counts of Armagnac rendered this inevitable—but no enemy put his foot on the soil of Foix or Bearn while Gaston was their lord.

Throughout this warfare, interrupted from time

* See Note C: Chivalry in Froissart.

to time by truces, Gaston had been uniformly successful; and when peace was finally concluded an attempt was made to extinguish the hostility between the two great houses, and thereby secure tranquillity to Languedoc, by a marriage between the only son of Gaston, of whose virtues Froissart writes, and Beatrix, daughter of count Jean of Armagnac, whose delightful character had won for her the name of *La Gaie*. The contract was signed and the betrothal solemnised on the 4th of April, 1379, and the result of the union of the two powerful houses, long at enmity, was the appointment of Gaston by Charles the Wise as his representative in Languedoc.

The tragic death of Gaston's son in 1381 put an end to the hopes which had been built on the union of the two contending houses, and the death of Charles the Wise a few days after his choice of Gaston as his lieutenant, followed by the appointment of the duc de Berri, brought trouble on Languedoc which Gaston tried in vain to avert.

In the year after the death of his son, 1382, an event occurred which had the double result of engaging Gaston in warfare for the last time, and leading to the composition of his great work on the chase.

Towards the end of the year 1382 the count of Flanders was driven out of Bruges by his rebellious subjects. In the war that followed, Philip the Bold, duke of Burgundy, had a deep interest, for he had married the daughter of the count and was his heir presumptive. The king of France, in accordance with his duty as sovereign lord, came to the assistance of his vassal against the rebels, leading his army in person, with the Oriflamme of France.

There was a difficulty about the oriflamme. It was 'a precious banner, and was sent first from heaven for a great mystery, the which was ever a great comfort to them that saw it,' and it was said that it was never before displayed against Christian men. Finally, divers reasons considered, it was determined to be displayed because the Flemings, being Urbanists, were to the French 'heretics and out of the true belief.'

Gaston, as we shall see hereafter, took a more liberal view of the consequences of a difference of opinion as to the validity of a pontifical election. But any scruples in the displaying of the precious banner must have been relieved when on this day 'it shewed some of his virtue, for all the morning there was a great thick mist, that one could scant see another, but as soon as it was displayed and lift up on high, the mist brake away and the sky was as clear as any time in the year before. The lords of France were greatly rejoiced when they saw the sun shine so clear that they might see all about them: this greatly did re-comfort them.' A dove also, a little time before they fought, 'sat down on one of the king's banners, the which every man took for a good token' (p. 289).

Gaston was under no feudal obligation to take part in the war, but he was bound to Philip in the closest ties of friendship, and he led to the assistance of the count a body of men-at-arms which contributed to his success in the victorious and conclusive battle of Rosebec.

When Burgundy and Flanders were united in his person, Philip became a prince little, if at all, inferior in power to his sovereign lord, and the terms on which the grandson of Philip, also known as 'the Bold,' treated with so able a monarch as Louis XI., are made manifest in the pages of *Quentin Durward*.

M. Lavallée writes of the battle of Rosebec:

Ce fut le denier des faits d'armes qui signarèrent la glorieuse carrière de Gaston. De retour dans ses Etats, il s'appliqua surtout à y faire régner L'ordre et la justice. Après les soins du gouvernment, la chasse et l'étude des lettres lui aidèrent à tromper le souvenir de ses chagrins. C'est probablement vers ce temps qu'il prit la résolution d'écrire son livre de vénerie (p. xxviii.).

Gaston was engaged in these peaceful pursuits when Froissart resolved to visit him in his court of Orthez. Starting from Hainault, well mounted, he met with no adventure worthy of notice until he arrived at Pamier, a principal city of Foix. Here his good fortune did not desert him, for ' on a day it so fortuned that thither came a knight of the earl of Foix from Avignon-ward, called sir Espang de Lyon, a valiant and an expert man of arms, about the age of fifty years; and so I gat me into his company, and he was greatly desirous to hear of the matters of France: and so we were a six days' journey or we came to Orthez, and this knight every day after he had said his prayers, most part all the day after, he took his pastime with me in demanding of tidings, and also when I demanded any thing of him he would answer me to my purpose ' (p. 313).

The position held by sir Espang in the court

at Orthez does not appear. But it must have
been a considerable one, for at a famous feast
held at the castle while Froissart was a guest
we find his name foremost among the 'chief
stewards of the hall.' We also learn that he
was present at the death of Gaston, and that
he was afterwards engaged in the settlement
of affairs of state.

The six days' ride to Orthez (pp. 313-329) was the
beginning of a friendship to which the chronicler
and his readers owe much. Most of the information about Gaston and his doings which he brought
with him to Orthez was imparted to him by sir
Espang, and his position at court enabled him to
render the service which is thus acknowledged;
' he caused me to be acquainted with knights and
squires such as could declare to me anything that
I could demand.' Froissart, who never forgot
a service rendered, would in after times and in
less congenial company look back on the happy
and instructful ride to Orthez in company with
sir Espang.

The road led through one of the most beautiful
parts of France, richly cultivated, watered by a
goodly river, and with the Pyrenees as a back-
ground. It led through busy towns—Tournay,
Tarves, and Montesquieu—and at each turn of the
road a strong castle came into sight, about which
sir Espang had a tale to tell of knightly adventure.

By now many of these strongholds must have
disappeared, and their memorial perished with
them. But to an archæologist there could be no
more interesting expedition than a ride from
Pamier to Orthez with Froissart as guide.

It is not likely that Disraeli brought with him on his journey to Scotland more than one of the quarto volumes in which lord Berners's translation of the chronicles was at that time read. It is certain that this volume was the third, which contains the account of the ride to Orthez and of Gaston and his court, for it was this part of the chronicles which made a lasting impression on his mind. Happily, the traveller of to-day can carry with him a *Froissart* no greater in bulk than an ordinary handbook, and with its aid trace the roads that were trodden more than six hundred years ago by the chronicler and his knightly guide.

The distance from Pamier to their destination, as the crow flies, is not many miles. But the road was a winding one, and the travellers had more regard for good company than for good speed; and so the days were spent in the pastime of demanding and giving of tidings, and ' every night as soon as we were at our lodgings I wrote over all that I had heard in the day, the better thereby to have them in remembrance, for writing is the best remembrancer.'

If the canon of Chimay had been travelling alone, his clerical habit might have ensured safety, but on more than one occasion the presence of an expert man of arms who knew the country through which they were to pass was an additional safeguard.

When they had left Mont-royal, ' a good strong town of the French king, the road lay through a great laund enduring a fifteen leagues called the Lande de Bouc, wherein were many dangerous passages for thieves and evil doers '; also the road between one large town and another would seem right strange; ' I thought myself but as lost there if I had not been in the company with that knight.'

On one occasion the travellers were saved when in imminent peril by sir Espang's resourcefulness and knowledge of the country. As they rode from Montesquieu to Palaminich it was necessary to cross the Garonne, but this, and a tributary river, were so swollen that the bridge, which was of wood, was broken. They had to return to Montesquieu, and ' the next day the knight had counsel to pass the river by boats to Caseres.' Thus they passed the Garonne ' with great pain and peril, for the boat that we were in was not very great, it could not take at one time but two horses and three keepers and they that ruled the boat.'

Moreover, the knight knew the hostelry in each town in which wayfarers might find comfortable lodging, with good cheer, and Froissart was a sharer in the attention that was paid to his companion.

' In the town of Tournay we lodged at the sign of the Star, and took our ease '; for Froissart, like another sir John, loved to take his ease at his inn. Here the presence of sir Espang brought to the travellers welcome attention. ' At supper the captain of Malvoisin, called sir Raymond of Lane, came to see us and supped with us, and brought with him four flagons of the best wine that I drank of in all my journey; these two knights talked long together,' and Froissart, we may be certain, sat discreetly apart.

The gentle sir Espang, finding in Froissart a
travelling companion as agreeable as his chronicles
were to Scott, took no pains to shorten their
journey; for when they had come to Artigat he
said, ' Sir, let us ride together fair and easily,
we have but two leages to ride to our lodging,'
which his companion was content to do; and a
good story would be prefaced by words like these:
' Then we rode forth fair and easily, and he began
to say as followeth.'

Many pages might be filled with the good
knight's stories, but as they were for the most
part of long-forgotten battles fought by counts
of Armagnac and Foix, those only have been
transferred to these pages which are directly
connected with Gaston, or appear to throw light
on the manners and modes of thought of the age.

The knight's recollection of an exploit of his
master was now and then revived, as the scene
of some famous event was passed. After the
travellers had succeeded in crossing the swollen
Garonne they rode to Caseres and abode there
all day, and when their supper was ' adressing '
the knight suggested that they should go and
see the town; passing through a gate, the knight
showed his companion a part of the wall and
said: ' Sir, see you yonder part of the wall which
is newer than all the remnant ?'

This was a reminder of a famous exploit. The
earl invested so closely the town, in which were
the ' best personages ' of Armagnac, that they
were compelled to come to terms: the terms were
that the besieged were to make ' a hole in the
wall and go out thereat, to come one by one

without armour, and so to yield them as prisoners. It behoved them to take this way, and so made a hole in the wall and issued out one by one, and there was the earl ready and all his people in order of battle to receive them as prisoners, . . . and a twenty of the best personages he led with him to Orthez, and or they departed he had of them two hundred thousand franks; and thus was the hole in the wall made' (p. 316).

A victory had a money value, especially when the best personages were among the prisoners, and this was duly appreciated and recorded by the chronicler.

All the next day they 'rode along by the river of Garonne, and, what on the one side and on the other, we saw many fair castles and fortresses: all that were on the left hand pertained to the earl of Foix, and the other side pertained to the earl of Armagnac.' Of many a fortress the site of which is no longer traceable, this knight had a tale to tell, and the traveller could enjoy the beauty of the scene and its associations; for 'then was the peace.'

A wayside cross of stone recorded a famous fight between men of Lourdes and members of French garrisons, in which the combatants fought with axes for more than two hours, 'giving each to other great and horrible strokes every man with his match . . . and when any of them had fought so long that they lacked breath they would fair and easily depart, and go sit down by a dike side that was full of water and put off their bassenets and refresh themselves, and when they were well refreshed they put on their bassenets

and returned again to fight.' Both the leaders
were slain; 'then ceased the battle by agreement
of both parties, for they were so weary that they
could scant hold their axes in their hands: . . .
and to the intent that this battle shold be had
in remembrance, whereas the two squires fought
there was set a cross of stone. "Behold, yonder
is the cross," and with those words we came to
the cross, and there we said for their souls a
Pater noster and an *Ave Maria*. "By my faith,
sir," quoth I, "I am glad I have heard this, for
this was a sharp business of so little people."'

The story calls to mind a yet sharper business
of still less people of which we have read in *The
Fair Maid of Perth*, enacted on the North Inch of
Perth, before the king, between but thirty of the
clan Quhale and the same number of the clan
Chattan, eight years after sir Espang and Froissart
had said a prayer by the cross of stone (1386).

All sir Espang's stories were not of this sanguinary kind. There was a merry tale of a great
deed done in sport by sir Ernaulton of Spain,
a mighty man of valour who did marvellous in
arms. 'He had an axe in his hand, whosoever
he strake therewith went to the earth, for he
was big and well made, and not overcharged with
flesh. . . . In all of Gascogne there is none like
him in strength of body, therefore the earl of
Foix hath him ever in his company.'

The famous deed was done at Christmastide
when the earl 'held a great feast of knights and
squires, and after dinner went up into a gallery
of twenty-four stairs of heighth where there was a
great chimney' and a small fire, 'for the earl loved

no great fire.' But on this occasion there was a
great frost and it was very cold, and the earl said
to the knights and squires about him, ' " Sirs,
this is but a small fire and the day so cold." ' In
the courtyard of the castle were a number of
asses laden with wood to serve the house. Sir
Ernaulton went down, and 'took one of the greatest
asses with all the wood, and laid him on his back,
and went up all the staires into the gallery, and
did cast down the ass with all the wood into the
chimney, and the ass's feet upwards; whereof
the earl of Foix had great joy, and so had all
they that were there and had marvel of his
strength ' (p. 322).

Froissart took great pleasure in this tale whereby
he thought his journey much the shorter, and he
had the satisfaction of meeting the hero of it,
an honoured guest, at the court of Orthez.

Another of the knight's stories pleased him not
so well, but it is worthy of note, for it may assist
us to a full understanding of the man of whom
it was told, and also of the spirit of Feudalism,
one of the most potent forces by which the lives
of men and the destinies of nations were ruled.

The fortress of Lourdes was held for the king
of England by sir Pier Ernaulton of Bearn. How
this had come about was told to Froissart when
on his way to Orthez he had passed by the country
of Bigorre, and had ' demanded and enquired of
the news of that country, such as I had not
known before; and it was shewed me how the
prince of Wales and of Aquitaine ' had been impressed by the strength and commanding position
of the castle of Lourdes, ' for the garrison there

might run well into the realm of Aragon, into Cataloyne, unto Barcelone.

'Then the prince called to him a knight of his household in whom he had great trust and loved him entirely, and he had served him truly and was called sir Pier Ernault of the county of Bearn, an expert man of arms, and cousin to the earl of Foix.' This man he instituted and made chatelain and captain of Lourdes and governor of Bigorre in these words: ' "Look well that ye keep this castle, see well that ye make a good account thereof to the king my father and to me." " Sir," quoth the knight, "I thank you, and I shall observe your commandment." There he did homage to the prince and the prince put him in possession.' The knight was true to the feudal obligation thus created, even unto death.

The duke of Anjou having failed to take the castle by force, attempted to acquire it by bribery. The knight who held it, ' who was of great valiantness, excused himself.' The castle was not his, it pertained to the heritage of the king of England, and if he were to sell it or give it up he would be a traitor, 'which in no wise he would be, but true to his natural lord during his life; and moreover said that when the castle was delivered him it was on a condition, which he swore solemnly by his faith in the prince of Wales' hand, that he should keep the castle of Lourdes against all men during his life, except it were against the king of England. The duke could never have other answer of him, for gift or promise that he could make ' (p. 323).

A neighbouring fortress held for England was a

constant source of trouble between Gaston and the French. The great object of his statesmanship was to keep his principality of Bearn from being involved in the war between the two great countries; accordingly he determined to make the fortress his own. Sir Pier was a man of Bearn and a kinsman, and so the earl sent a messenger with letters desiring him to come and speak with him at Orthez. The knight knew his kinsman well, and 'when he had read the earl's letters and saw his notable messenger, he had diverse imaginings, and wist not whether he might go or abide. All things considered, he said that he would go, because in no wise he would displease the earl.'

Before he went he said to his brother, John of Bearn, in the presence of all the companions of the garrison, that he feared that he should be required to give up the fortress of Lourdes. He knew not what treaty there might be between Gaston and the duke of Anjou, ' "but one thing I say plainly—as long as I live I shall never yield up the garrison but to mine own natural lord the king of England," and he made his brother swear to him by the faith of his gentleness to keep the castle as he did, and to fail not for life or death.'

When Pier arrived at Orthez the earl 'with great joy received him and made him sit at his board, and showed him as great semblant of love as he could.' On the third day Gaston, in the presence of lords, knights, and squires, commanded him as he would eschew his displeasure, and by the faith and lineage that he owed him, to yield into his hand the garrison of Lourdes.

Pier was 'sore abashed and studied a little,' but answered thus: '"Sir, true it is I owe to you faith and homage, for I am a poor knight of your blood and of your country; but as for the castle of Lourdes, I will not deliver it to you: ye have sent for me to do with me as ye list: I hold it for the king of England; he set me there, and to none other living will I deliver it" (p. 324).

'Gaston's blood chafed for ire when he heard this answer, and drawing his dagger he wounded Pier in five places, calling him traitor, and there was no knight or baron that durst step between them. Then the knight said, "Ah, sir, ye do me no gentlenesse, to send for me and slay me"; and yet, for all the strokes that he had with the dagger, the earl commanded to cast him in prison down into a deep dike, and so he was and there died, for his wounds were but evil looked unto.

'"Ah, Saint Mary," quoth I to the knight, "was not this a great cruelty?"

'"Whatsoever it was," quoth the knight, "thus it was," as who should say, "things are as they are." . . . "Sir," quoth I, "hath the earl of Foix made any amends for the death of that knight, or sorry for his death?" "Yes, truly, sir," quoth he, "he was right sorry for his death; but as for amends, I know of none, without it be by secret penance, masses or prayers. He hath with him the same knight's son, called John of Bearn, a gracious squire, and the earl loveth him right well"' (p. 325).

Crimes like that of Gaston are the natural consequence of absolute power, with no restraint on the indulgence of dominating passion, followed, in natures of the higher order, by expressions of repentance, equally strong. A great crime, committed at the bidding of overpowering passion and followed by repentance and penitential words, may be found recorded in the book of the chronicles of another nation. They were little regarded when the eyes of the chronicler were blinded by the brightness of the great and good virtues of the sinner, and we find the son of the murdered knight accepting service in the household of his father's murderer.

As Froissart drew near to Orthez instinct told him that there was something to be learned about Gaston which sir Espang, with all his frank communications, had left untold, and this he was determined to find out.

His curiosity had been excited by the casual remark that Gaston's cousin german, the viscount of Castleton, was his heir. '"Why, sir," quoth I, "hath the earl of Foix no children?" "No truly, sir," quoth he, "by any wife, but he hath two sons, knights, that be his bastards, whom ye shall see, and he loveth them as well as himself; they be called sir Yvan and sir Gracien." Then I demanded if ever he were married. "Yea truly," quoth he, "and is yet; but his wife is not with him." "Why, sir, where is she?" "Sir," quoth he, "she is in Navarre, for the king there is her cousin [brother]; she was daughter to king Louis of Navarre." Yet then I demanded if ever the earl had any children. "Yes, sir," quoth he, "he had a fair son who had the father's heart, and all the country loved him, for by him all the country of Bearn was in rest and peace, whereas it hath been sith in debate and strife;

for he had married [espoused] the sister of the earl of Armagnac." "Sir," quoth I, "what became of that son, an it may be known ?" "Sir," quoth he, "I shall show you but not now, for the matter is over long, and we are near the town, as ye see." Therewith I left the knight in peace. And so we came to Tarbes, and took our lodging at the Star, and there tarried all that day, for it was a town of great easement both for man and horse, with good hay and oats and a fair river.'

The knight was not to be left in peace so long as the curiosity which he had aroused remained unsatisfied. As the travellers were approaching Orthez, sir Espang told two more tales of battles between the counts of Bearn and of Armagnac, either of which might easily have led to a disclosure of the secret of what had befallen the earl's beloved son, but sir Espang gave no sign. An attempt was then made to unseal his lips with a promise of immortality. '"Ah, saint Mary, sir," quoth I, "how your words be to me right agreeable, for it hath done me great pleasure all that ye have shewed me, which shall not be lost, for it shall be put in remembrance and chronicled, if God will give me the grace to return to the town of Valenciennes whereat I was born; but, sir, I am sore displeased of one thing." "What is that ?" quoth he. "I shall shew you by faith: that so high and valiant a prince as the earl of Foix is, should be without lawful issue." "Sir," quoth the knight, "if he had one, as once he had, he should be the most joyous prince of the world, and so would be all the country."' But sir Espang was not to be tempted, even with a

promise of immortality. He gave no sign, and
passed on to the story of the origin of the warfare
between Bearn and Armagnac, which will be
found on another page.

The city was to be reached next day, and a
final effort must needs be made. ' " By my faith,
sir," then quoth I, " ye have well declared the
matter; I never heard it before, and now that I
know it I shall put it in perpetual memory, if God
give me the grace to return unto my country.
But, sir, if I durst I would fain demand of you
one thing: by what incident the earl of Foix's
son died." Then the knight studied a little and
said: " Sir, the manner of his death is right
piteous; I will not speak thereof; when ye come
to Orthez, ye shall find them that will shew you
if ye demand it." And then I held my peace.'

Sir Espang did justice to his companion's power
of extracting information, for he had no sooner
arrived at Orthez than he 'inquired how Gaston
the earl's son died, for sir Espang de Lyon would
not show me anything thereof; and so much I
inquired that an ancient squire and a notable
man showed the matter to me.'

And, perhaps, now is the point at which something of the right piteous tale told by the ancient
squire should be transferred to these pages, for
it is the event in the history of the great earl to
which his inclusion in the number of the Fathers
of the literature of sport is mainly due. The story
is marred in the telling when it is not told in
Froissart's words (pp. 330-334). But for our present
purpose it is enough to say that it had its origin
in a quarrel between Gaston and his wife's

brother, Charles the Bad, king of Navarre. Like many quarrels of the Middle Ages it arose out of default in payment of money due in respect of ransom. Charles had been accepted by Gaston as security for the payment of the ransom due to him by one count D'Albret. D'Albret made good the money and entrusted it to Charles for payment to Gaston. Charles, true to his name, appropriated the money, and refused to pay it to Gaston. During this dispute Gaston sent his wife to her brother's court, to try to bring about a settlement, but Charles could not be moved: he pretended to a right to keep the money as his sister's dower; ' " but as for the money, I will not depart from it, it pertaineth to me to keep it for you, but it should never go out of Navarre." ' The countess, as Froissart suggests, ought to have returned to Orthez when she had given her message. But she tarried in Navarre, and Gaston, ' when he saw the dealing of the king of Navarre, he began to hate his wife, and was evil content with her.' Whether from fear of the wroth of a husband ' who was cruel when he took displeasure,' or influenced by another motive for which we must look outside the pages of Froissart, she did not return. Meanwhile their son, Gaston, grew and waxed goodly, and was, to the great content of the people of Bearn, affianced to the daughter of the earl of Armagnac.

When between fifteen and sixteen years of age, in an evil hour he obtained leave to go to Navarre to see his mother and his uncle the king. As he was returning Charles gave his nephew a small packet containing a powder, a little of which he was to put secretly on his father's meat, and this, when eaten, was to cause his father, forgetting his anger, again to love his wife, which their son ought greatly to desire. This packet, which the boy wore at his breast, was seen by his beloved playfellow, Ivan. In a boyish quarrel young Gaston struck Ivan a blow which sent him crying into his father's chamber. He told his father of the packet carried by young Gaston, and how the poor boy had ' " said to me once or twice that my lady his mother should shortly be again in your grace and better beloved than ever she was." ' Gaston had no faith in a love potion sent by Charles the Bad, and finding the packet hanging at the boy's breast, opened it, ' and took of the powder and laid it on a trencher of bread and called to him a dog and gave it him to eat; and as soon as the dog had eaten the first morsel, he torned his eyen in his head and died incontinent.'

The father's first words were, ' " Ah, Gaston, traitor, for to increase thine heritage that should come to thee I have had war and hatred of the French king, of the king of England, of the king of Spain, and of the king of Navarre, and of the king of Aragon, and as yet I have borne all their malices; and now thou wouldst murder me. It cometh of an evil nature, but first thou shalst die with this stroke." '

He would have slain his son upon the spot, had he not been with difficulty restrained by the knights and squires assembled in the hall, kneeling before him in tears.

Gaston had no doubt that his death had been plotted by his son and that those who were about

his person were parties to the conspiracy.   Fifteen
young squires who had been his companions were
put to a cruel death.   The earl assembled all the
nobles and prelates of Foix and of Bearn, and told
them ' how he had found his son in this default,
for the which his intent was to put him to death,
as he had well deserved.'   When all the people
with one voice implored him to spare his only
son and heir, ' he somewhat refrained his ire.
Then he thought to chastise him in prison a
month or two and then to send him on some
voyage for two or three years, till he might somewhat forget his evil will and that the child might
be of greater age and of more knowledge.'
    The unhappy child was chastised by confine-
ment in a dark chamber in the tower of Orthez
for ten days, ' alone without any company, other
to counsel or comfort him.'   According to the
authorised account, current in the castle and
retailed to Froissart by the ancient squire, the
earl was sore displeased on being told that his
son refused all food, and opening the prison door,
thrust his hand to his son's throat, exclaiming:
' " Ah, traitor, why dost thou not eat thy meat ?"
In an evil hour he had the same time a little
knife in his hand to pare withal his nails . . . and
the point of the knife a little entered into a vein
of his throat, and so fell down suddenly and died '
(p. 333).
    M. Lavallée reproduces Froissart's account of
the tragedy, having given in the following words
what may be regarded as the historical version:

Au dire de quelqes auteurs, ce jeune homme ressent-
ait vivement l'injure faite à sa mère, et pour la venger,

lorsqu'il revint de ce voyage, il rapporta du poison qu'il voulait employer pour faire périr son père: mais son projet fut découvert: . . . quant au jeune comte, il fut renfermé dans une prison ou il périt par la main du bourreau (p. xxiv).

Gaston was overwhelmed with grief. ' " Ah, Gaston," he cried, "what a poor peradventure is this for thee and for me. In an evil hour thou wentest to Navarre to see thy mother. I shall never have the joy that I had before." ' There were the customary symbols of grief, ' and with much sore weeping the child was borne to the Friars in Orthez and there buried.'

M. Lavallée tells a sad tale which may not have reached the ears of an inquirer into deeds of valour. A young woman named Marguerite had lived for several years at the court. She was good, pious, and charitable, beloved by all, and but one fault could be laid to her charge: *De vivre maritalement avec Gaston Phœbus, lorsqu'il n'était pas possible à l'Église de consacrer leur union.* Deeply affected by the death of the poor boy, her conscience may have told her that she was not altogether without responsibility for the sad event. But for her, she may have thought, Gaston might not have kept his wife so strictly in banishment in Navarre. However this may be, one night when praying in her oratory she had a vision in which she heard the soul of young Gaston asking with sighs for prayers. Poor Marguerite was found by her maidens fainting at the-foot of her *prie-Dieu*, and did not long survive (p. xxvii).

The gloom in which the court of Orthez was involved by these tragic events had been dispelled before the arrival of Froissart. Gaston, with his friend, Philip of Burgundy, had brought to a successful close a campaign to which he owed the suggestion of a work which might, like the *Romans des Déduits*, at the same time afford a safeguard against sin and also instruction in the science of venery, and in the composition of which relief from sorrow might be found. Gaston found in religion, M. Lavallée writes, consolation in his grief; and to the time of his trouble he attributes the strict devotional observances noted by Froissart, and also the composition of Prayers of which, at the end of the manuscript of his work, a copy is preserved in the *Bibliothèque Nationale*.

Although the tragedy of his son's death had an enduring influence on the character of Gaston, the court of Orthez had regained its far-famed brilliance when Froissart reached the city on the 25th day of November in the year 1388, and ' alighted at the Moon, where dwelt a squire of the earl's, Ernaulton du Puy, who well received me, because I was of France.'

Sir Espang went to the castle and found the earl ' in his gallery, for he had but dined a little before; for the earl's usage was always that it was high noon or he arose out of his bed, and supped ever at midnight. The knight showed him how I was come thither, and incontinent I was sent for to my lodging, for he was the lord of all the world that most desired to speak with strangers, to hear tidings. When the earl saw me, he made me good cheer and retained me as of his house, where I was more than twelve weeks, and my horse, well entreated ' (p. 329).

Froissart was not disappointed in the man of whom he had heard so much, and to see whom he had travelled so far. He had seen in his time many knights, kings, princes, with others, but never one 'like him of personage, nor of so fair form or so well made.'

About fifty-nine years of age, he still retained, though in more manly form, the beauty for which he had been famed in youth. ' His visage fair, sanguine and smiling, his eyen gray and amourous, whereas he list to set his regard.' He adopted the tribute to the god-like beauty of his youth, describing himself in the prologue to his great work on venery as, *Gaston, par la grace de Dieu, surnommé Fébus conte de Foys, seigneur de Bearn ;* and by this name he was known to Jacques du Fouilloux, who often refers to *Phébus* as the supreme authority on the chase.

' In every thing he was so perfect that he cannot be praised too much: he loved that ought to be beloved, and hated that ought to be hated. He was a wise knight of high enterprise and of good counsel: he never had miscreant with him: he said many orisons every day, a nocturn of the psalter, matins of our Lady, of the Holy Ghost and of the cross, and dirige' (p. 329).

He was of good and easy acquaintance with every man, and amorously would speak to them. To the chronicler, his court was an ideal place of resort, for ' all manner of tidings of every realm and country there might be heard, for out of every country there was resort for the valiantness of this earl, . . . and so I was informed by them, and by the earl himself, of all things that I demanded.'

Froissart loved to tell of the 'estate' in which the earl lived, 'for of it there cannot be too much spoken nor praised.' In the daytime, when he was not occupied in the chase—he loved hounds of all beasts, and winter and summer he loved hunting (p. 330)—he was engaged in the transaction of business with his secretaries. 'He had four secretaries, and at his rising they must ever be ready at his hand, without any call,' to write in reply to the letters which the earl had received. Gaston was a strict man of business, 'short in counsel and answers' (p. 330). He conducted in person all affairs of state. He appointed twelve 'notable persons' to be receivers of his revenue, of whom the one he trusted most was controller, to whom the other receivers should account: 'and the controller should account to him by rolls and books written, and the accounts to remain still with the earl.'

Under this system, without chancellor of the exchequer or parliamentary discussion of estimates, the earl's treasury waxed fat, and his people were prosperous and contented. They were heavily taxed, but the burden was apportioned to the back by which it was borne—'the rich to bear out the poor'—and so the ruler gathered great riches, 'and the people payeth it with a marvellous good will, for by reason thereof there is nother English nor French, nor robbers, nor reivers that doth them any hurt to the value of one penny; and so his country is in safeguard and justice truly kept for in doing of justice he is right cruel, he is the most rightful lord that is now living' (p. 319).

These are the words of one of his household, but the testimony of sir Espang is borne out by fact. In time of war between England and France, the fortress of Lourdes was held for England, and bands of adventurers proceeding thence, sometimes 'thirty leagues off from their hold,' overran the lands of France; 'sometime they brought home so great plenty of beasts and prisoners that they wist not how to keep them. Thus they ransomed all the country except the earl of Foix's lands, for in his lands they durst not take a chicken, without they paid truly therefor; for if they had displeased the earl, they could not long have endured' (p. 312).

Gaston was liberal and at the same time discriminating in the bestowal of gifts, 'for he never loved . . . folly largess' (p. 330). The giving of five florins in small money at his gate to poor folks for the love of God is counted as one of his religious observances.

'He had certain coffers in his chamber, out of which ofttimes he would take money to give to lords, knights, and squires, such as came to him, for none should depart from him without some gift, and yet daily multiplied his treasure to resist the adventures and fortunes that he doubted.'

The crowd of minstrels and rhymers who travelled from city to city in search of entertainment and largesse was a noted feature of mediæval society. Gaston was liberal in the distribution of rewards such as Froissart had shared on his visit to Brussels (*ante*, p. 120). At the famous Christmas dinner in hall at Orthez

'there were many minstrels as well of his own
as of strangers, and each of them did their devoir
in their faculties.   The same day the earl of Foix
gave to heralds and minstrels the sum of five
hundred franks, and gave to the duke of Touraine's
minstrels gowns of cloth of gold furred with
ermines, valued at two hundred franks.'

It was part of the policy of Gaston to make
display of his wealth, not only in the ordering
of his court, but on such occasions as his visit
to the prince and princess of Wales at Tarves;
the marriage of his ward, the daughter of the
comte de Paris, to the duc de Berri; and his
attendance on his liege lord the king of France
at Toulouse; and the visit of the duke of Bourbon
to Orthez, which, as Froissart 'heard, cost the
earl of Foix ten thousand franks.'

So Gaston was princely in expenditure and
munificent in largesse, 'and yet daily multiplied
his treasure to resist the adventures and fortunes
that he doubted.'   When Froissart was told by
sir Espang in their ride to Orthez that the treasury
in the castle contained well to the number of
thirty times a hundred thousand florins—thinking
in millions was then unknown—he asked to what
intent so much money was kept by the earl.
Sir Espang explained that the earl's policy was
to maintain a position of neutrality between 'his
neighbours, the French king and the king of
England,' whom he would not willingly displease:
'for he hath always dissimuled between them during
all the war season unto this present time; for he
never armed himself for any of their parties, he hath
always been ever in good case with both parties.'

There was indeed at one time danger from the prince of Wales, ' who at that time was great and sore feared,' when he threatened to compel Gaston to admit that he held Bearn of him, as prince of Aquitaine. This was at the instigation of his envious and defeated neighbours, the earl of Armagnac and the lord d'Albret, ' who tittled the prince ever in his ear and enticed him to have made war against the earl of Foix.'

Gaston would have none of this, ' and said how his country of Bearn was so free a land, that it ought to do homage to no man of the world.' The prince was ' fierce and courageous,' but he had a wise adviser in sir John Chandos, ' chief of council with the prince,' who ' was against it that the prince should make any war to the earl' (p. 319).

In the battle of Poitiers Chandos had saved the life of the Black Prince, who was thenceforth his devoted friend.   This fine soldier and wise states-man won golden opinions from all sorts of people. ' The earl of Foix loved right well sir John Chandos and he him.'   His influence was always exerted in the interest of peace.   The king of France expressed great grief at the news of Chandos's death (January 1, 1369-70), and declared that ' Chandos alone could have made the peace permanent between England and France.'* The prince turned a deaf ear to the tittling of Armagnac and D'Albret, and followed the advice of Chandos, when he counselled him ' not to make any war to the earl.'

Chandos knew well that Gaston's florins could bring a force into the field which, combined with

* Sir Sidney Lee (*Dictionary of National Biography*).

that of France, would be irresistible. It was an
age in which the fighting forces of a nation which
happened to be at peace were at liberty to enter
the service of a foreign prince, sometimes against
the will of their sovereign lord.

The ' chief flower of chivalry ' of Bearn fought
at Aljubarrota in the pay of the king of Castile.
Gaston ' had at first in manner consented thereto,'
but when he came to realise the probable consequences of the undertaking, he was ' angry and
sorrowful departing, for he saw well that his
country was much enfeebled thereby.' He gave
the knights a farewell dinner at Orthez at which
he counselled them to ' let the king of Castile
and the king of Portugal make their war between
themselves, for you are not bound to render them
any assistance.' The knights replied that this
could not be, ' for they had, to the knowledge of
the earl, received wages and gifts from the king
of Castile,' for which they were bound to make
a return. Gaston did not refuse to let them go,
and the knights laughed at his gloomy forebodings
which were justified in the result, for the Spanish
forces were cut to pieces by king John with the
aid of a body of English archers.

They were not mercenaries like the Bearnais
knights, but English soldiers sent at the instance
of John of Gaunt (who was not without a private
concern in the matter) to support an ally, and
the manner of their fighting is thus described:
they ' shot so wholly together that their arrows
pierced men and horse, and when the horses
were full of arrows, they fell one upon another '
(p. 347).

Fighting men of all ranks were in the market; from the Genoese cross-bowmen who served France so ill in the battle of Crecy, to the knight or expert man of arms whose country was at peace. The captal of Buch, a great nobleman and a knight of the Garter, entered the service of the king of Navarre in time of truce between England and France. 'My master the captal,' says the bascot (bastard) of Mauleon, an expert man of arms, ' and I and other abode still with the king of Navarre, for his wages.'

Thus did sir Espang account for the accumulated florins of Gaston, confident that Froissart would approve his foresight: ' I say to you, and so ye shall say yourself, when ye have once knowledge of him and heard him speak, and once know the order and state of his house, ye shall see that he is at this day the most sage prince in the world.' Sir Espang was right in his forecast, for a few days after his arrival in Orthez the visitor wrote: ' To speak briefly and according to reason, the earl of Foix then was right perfect in all things, and as sage and as perceiving as any high prince in his days; there was none could compare with him in wit, honour, nor in largess.'

The twelve weeks of Froissart's stay at Orthez passed pleasantly, for there he was ' well entreated.' ' I had been,' he writes, ' in many courts of kings, dukes, princes, and great ladies, but I was never in any that so well liked me, nor was there none more rejoiced in deeds of war than the earl did: there was seen in his hall chamber and court, knights and squires of honour, going up and down and talking of arms and of armours;

all honour there was found, all manner of tidings of every realm and country there might be heard, for out of every country there was resort, for the valiantness of this earl ' (p. 330).

During the daytime Gaston would come from his chamber to converse with the knights and squires who resorted to his court; and so it was noted as a token of his sorrow when he thought of the suffering of his people in the battle of Aljubarrota that he was ' so sad of cheer that no man could hear a word of him, and all the same three days he would not issue out of his chamber nor speak to any man, though they were never so near about him ' (p. 352).

' It was high noon or he arose out of his bed,' and this was no marvel, for ' he supped at midnight.' It must be supposed that he broke his fast before he came from his chamber to the hall. ' In the daytime he did but little eat and drink,' but he would have dinner in the gallery of the castle in the afternoon, for when Froissart and sir Espang arrived at sunsetting, ' he had but dined a little before.'

The only meal of which the earl partook in public was supper in the hall at midnight. Then princely state was maintained. When the earl ' came out of his chamber into the hall to supper he had ever before him twelve torches burning, borne by twelve varlets standing before his table all supper. They gave a great light, and the hall ever full of knights and squires, and many other tables dressed to sup who would. There was none should speak to him at his table, but if he were called. . . . He had great pleasure in harmony of instruments; he could do it right well himself; he would have songs sung before him.

'His meat was lightly wild fowl, the legs and wings only, and in the day he did but little eat and drink. . . . He would gladly see conceits and fantasies at his table, and when he had seen it, then he would send it to the other tables' (p. 330).

Froissart had brought with him to Orthez a book of songs, ballads, rondeaux and virelays, called the *Meliador*, which the earl was glad to see, and from which Froissart read every night after supper; 'and while I read there was none durst speak any word, because he would I should be well understanded, wherein he took great solace, and when it came to any matter of question, then he would speak to me, not in Gascon, but in good and fair French' (p. 329).

'For the season that I was at Orthez . . . I saw and heard many things that turned me to great pleasure. I saw on a Christmas day sitting at his board four bishops of his country, two Clementines and two Urbanists, the bishop of Pamiers and the bishop of Lescar, Clementines, they sat highest, then the bishop of Aire and the bishop of Roy, on the frontiers of Bourdelois and Bayonne, Urbanists; then sat the earl of Foix.'

Froissart had good reason for the great pleasure which he saw at the table of the earl bishops, both Clementines and Urbanists, for this told him that Bearn, like his native Beaumont, stood neutral in the Great Schism (p. 339).

As a chronicler he tells the tale of the schism, but it was a topic from which he always turned with pleasure to the main purpose of his work.

The schism had its origin in the election of a successor to Gregory XI., who died in March, 1378, and it lasted until it was healed at the accession of Martin V. in 1417. The vacancy was filled by the election of an Italian archbishop, known as Urban VI. There was never any question as to the canonical regularity of the election of Urban, but a number of cardinals, including those of France, agreed to treat it as a nullity, and proceeded to elect one of their body, who took the name of Clement VII. They alleged that freedom of choice had been rendered impossible by the violence of the Roman populace; but personal considerations and national jealousy entered largely into the dispute. Urban was unpopular; he was a 'fumous man and melan-cholious,' proud and headstrong, 'and so they spake together and imagined how he was not well worthy to govern the world; wherefore they purposed to choose another pope, sage and discreet, by whom the Church should be well governed.'

France had for a long time exerted a predominant influence in church matters. Successive popes had lived in Avignon in the long years of the Babylonian captivity, following the accession of Clement V. in 1305. Charles V., a strong monarch, was a personal friend of Clement, and his desire to have a pope a nearer neighbour than one at Rome was shared by the French ecclesiastics, and by the people, who had become accustomed to think of the pope as French. Accordingly, France, with Spain, Savoy, Milan, Naples, and Scotland, were Clementine; while

England, with the greater part of Christendom, including the Empire, Hungary, Austria, and Flanders, supported Urban, the regularity of whose election is now admitted.

The question at issue was purely one of fact. Had the disturbances at Rome interfered with freedom of action to such an extent as to justify the opponents of the archbishop of Bari in treating the election as a nullity, and proceeding to a second choice ?   No question of theology or of canon law was involved.   Just as the *flendum schisma* by which Crescentius was exiled from Bologna degenerated into a faction fight between great houses warring under the names of Guelf and Ghibellin, so the greater schism by which Christendom was distracted had become a quarrel in which the great powers engaged called themselves Clementine or Urbanist, with little thought of the origin or merits of the dispute.

The count of Flanders was a strong Urbanist. We have seen how the sacred Oriflamme, never before unfurled against a Christian people, could be displayed at the battle of Rosebec, to the great comfort of the French army, because the Flemings as Urbanists were outside the Christian pale.

'But they of Hainault and the churches there, and the lord called Albert, abode as neuter and obeyed no more to one than to the other.'   Some of the lesser states remained neutral.   Sir Otho of Brunswick 'forbare a long season and dissimuled the matter, and took none of both parties.' He was ready to fight against Urban if he were paid by Clement, but when he went to Avignon to get money for the fight, he could get none;

' for the pope's chamber was so clean voided from
gold and silver that the cardinals could not have
the money that pertained to their hats.' He
was given a thousand francs, but ' he set little
thereby . . . and would in no wise meddle any
more in the pope's wars ' (p. 356).

Gaston's neutrality was prompted by a higher
motive, and it was made effective by strict observance of ecclesiastical law. If he ' dissimuled '
between pope and anti-pope, as he did between
the kings of France and England, this was to
secure to his peoples immunity from the troubles
of the Great Schism, as he had safeguarded them
from disturbance during the great war. His
success in the former endeavour was attested
by the presence at his table at the Christmas
feast of which Froissart wrote of Clementine
and Urbanist prelates ; and in the latter by
the inclusion in the number of his guests of two
French noblemen of high rank with ' a knight of
England of the duke of Lancaster's, who as then
lay at Lisbon; the duke had sent him thither, the
knight was called sir William Willoughby ' (p. 339).

That nothing should be wanting at the Christmas feast which ' endured four hours ' to promote
harmony among the guests of the earl, ' there
were many minstrels as well of his own as of
strangers, and each of them did their devoir in
their faculties,' and were richly rewarded.

That the states of Bearn and Foix were saved
from ecclesiastical disunion by Gaston's recognition
of the rights of the church appears from what
Froissart has written.

Pamiers was in Foix, and its bishop was Clemen-

tine; so was the bishop of Lescar, an ancient city
of Bearn now decayed, whither visitors are
attracted from the neighbouring town of Pau by
the ruins of a fine cathedral. Roy was in Bearn,
and so, probably, was Aire. It is evident that
the cathedral corporation of each city elected a
bishop of its choice, Urbanite or Clementine, and
the election of each bishop was confirmed by the
pope, at Rome or at Avignon, to which the bishop-
elect professed allegiance. All were alike recognised by Gaston as having ecclesiastical rank
and authority, but as the king of France, his
sovereign lord, was a supporter of the pope at
Avignon, precedence at his court was given to the
Clementine prelates.

Froissart had been much impressed by the
' solemnities that the earl of Foix kept ' at the
feast of saint Nicholas, when they sang ' as they
did on Christmas day, or Easter day, in the pope's
chapel or the French king's,' and there, he says,
' I heard as good playing at organs as ever I heard
in any place.' At this festival ' the bishop of
Pamiers sang the Mass,' and as Orthez was not in
his diocese, an additional proof was given of the
ecclesiastical goodwill that prevailed under the
impartial rule of the great earl.

From one of Froissart's digressions from the
main purpose of his work we may learn the secret
of Gaston's successful neutrality. The division
of Christendom was, in his opinion, ' a plague sent
from God for the clergy to advise and to consider
well their great estate and superfluity that they
were in.' Attempts to heal the breach had
failed, ' for they were so blinded with pride that

each one thought to be as good as another; wherefore it went evil, and if our faith had not been confirmed in the hands and grace of the Holy Ghost, who illumined the heart of them that were gone out of the right way and held them firm in unity, else our faith had been greatly deformed ' (p. 357).

Gaston was religious after the manner of his age. His composition of prayers dates from his captivity in the castle of Chateret; he was strict in his private religious observances, and also in the keeping of the great church festivals. He and all his land kept the feast of saint Nicholas in great solemnity, and we know something of ' the feasts of Christmas, which he kept ever right solemn.' With Froissart he recognised and maintained the essential unity in which Clementines and Urbanists were alike bound, notwithstanding a diversity of opinion as to the validity of a certain election. Moreover, Gaston acted in accordance with his strong common sense, regardless of interested suggestions, unlike the great lords whom Froissart had known as he went about in the world, who were given to favouritism, and were ruled by ' a marmoset, or of the clergy, or a boy of simple lineage mounted up to honour, except the earl of Foix, for he had never none such, for he was naturally sage, for his wisdom was better than any that could be given him ' (p. 357).

Of the many tales that were told to Froissart by the knights and squires with whom he had been made acquainted by the gentle sir Espang de Lyon, none were of more serious interest than the account of the decisive battle of Aljubarrota, by which

king John was established on the throne of
Portugal; from its result in the foundation of the
maritime empire of Portugal; its relation to the
affairs of England; and, it may be added, its
connection with the subject of these pages; for
John is one of the royal contributors to the
mediæval literature of the chase to whom reference
is made in the Introduction (*ante*, p. 5).

' I was informed,' he writes, ' of the business
of Portugal and of Castile, and what manner of
war they had made, and of the battles and
rencounters between those two kings and their
assisters, of which businesses I shall make just
report.'

The business of Portugal was a topic of painful
interest in the castle hall, for Gaston's gloomy
apprehensions, when he bade good-bye to the
flower of his chivalry, going forth to fight against
the king of Portugal, had been fully realised.

This John, a natural son of Pedro I. the Cruel,
grand master of the military order of St. Aviz,
had been unanimously chosen to be their king
by the cortes of the realm, by whom the crown
of Portugal had been declared to be elective.
Hostilities with Castile ensued.   John of Gaunt,
who claimed the crown of Castile through his
marriage with Constance, the elder of the two
daughters of Pedro the Cruel, saw the opportunity
of making good his claim with the assistance of
John of Portugal.   He still retained much of the
power which he had acquired during the last years
of his father's reign, as the consequence of the
failing health of Edward, also of the Black Prince,
and the death in 1368 of Lionel, duke of Clarence.

His brother, the earl of Cambridge, had married the younger daughter of Pedro, and had a like interest in supporting king John. The king sent an embassy to the brothers asking for assistance from England, and holding out an alluring prospect of the overrunning and conquest of 'the realm of Castile, for the inheritance pertaineth to you and to your wives, and to your children.' On the meeting of Parliament, 'the duke of Lancaster endeavoured to procure the command of a number of men of war and archers to go into Portugal,' alleging a solemn promise made when his nephew Richard was crowned. After a long debate, the substance of which is given by Froissart, 'it was determined that the duke of Lancaster should pass the sea with seven hundred spearmen and four thousand archers, all of whom were to receive a quarter of a year's pay in advance'; provided no untoward incident should occur touching the realm of England. John of Gaunt was detained in England, and with the assistance of an English force less than had been voted by Parliament, king John won the decisive battle of Aljubarrota on August 13, 1385 (pp. 340–348).

The intervention of England in a private quarrel at the instance of John of Gaunt had the happy result of creating an alliance which has continued unbroken to the present day, and it also brought good fortune to the house of Lancaster. Later on, king John was supported by a stronger force under the duke, and on May 9, 1386, the alliance between England and Portugal was placed on a firm foundation by the treaty of Windsor. Lancaster brought with him his wife and two daughters, of whom the elder, Philippa, marrying king John, became queen of Portugal; and the younger married Henry, son of John of Castile, and became queen of Castile.

From the marriage of king John of Portugal with an English princess sprang the rulers of the house of Aviz, under whom there came the age of discovery and colonisation, with the creation of a world-wide maritime empire, which placed Portugal in the forefront among the nations of Europe. The first place among the famous band of discoverers was held by prince Henry, third son of king John and Philippa of Lancaster, known in history as Henry the Navigator. ' To him the human race is indebted in large measure for the maritime exploration within one century (1420-1522) of more than half the globe, and especially of the great waterways from Europe to Asia, both by east and by west ' (Professor C. R. Beazley in *Encyclopædia Britannica*).

John I., the founder of the dynasty, has been called ' the Great ' and the ' Father of his country.' He was also one of the Fathers of the literature of sport. He holds a high place among the great men in history who wrote a Book of Sport, and we regret that the court of John and his English queen did not find a chronicler who would preserve the memories of a bright period in mediæval history by presenting to us pictures such as Froissart drew of a contemporary prince.

Froissart's promise to make ' good report ' of the information imparted to him by knights and squires concerning the war between Portugal and Castile, was fulfilled to the letter, and many

chapters of the chronicles are filled with details of
this warfare. These are the least interesting of
the pages which we owe to Froissart's visit to
Orthez, but they include a conversation with one
of these squires which is worthy of note, if we
would form a truthful picture of the world, as
it was understood by knights and clerks of the
fourteenth century.

' It is great marvel to consider one thing, the
which was shewed me in the earl of Foix's house
at Orthez of him that informed me of the business
at Juberoth (Aljubarrota). He shewed me one
thing that I have often times thought on sith,
and shall do as long as I live. As this squire
told me, that of truth the next day after the
battle was thus fought at Juberoth the earl knew
it, whereof I had great marvel ' (p. 353). It was
noted that for three days the earl was pensive
and sad, and ' would not issue out of his chamber
nor speak to any man, though they were never
so near him.' After ten days the truth of the
disaster that had befallen the chivalry of Bearn
was known at Orthez. ' Then the earl renewed
again his dolour, and all the country were in
sorrow, for they had lost their parents, brethren,
children and friends.'

' "Saint Mary," quoth I to the squire that
shewed me this tale, " how is it that the earl of
Foix could know on one day what was done one
within a day or two before, being so far off ?" '

The squire could not tell how it was done, but
people had their imaginings. ' "Show me your
imagining," said Froissart; " I will be discreet, and
never speak thereof as long as I am in this country."

"I pray you thereof," quoth the squire, "for I would not it should be known that I should speak thereof; but I shall show you as divers men speaketh secretly, when they be together as friends." ' Then he drew him apart into a corner of the chapel at Orthez, and began a tale on which the hearer pondered for the rest of his life (pp. 353-356).

Some twenty years before a knight, lord of the neighbouring town of Corasse, had a plea before the pope at Avignon, in which the curate of the town—a great clerk—claimed the dimes of the church, valued at a hundred florins by the year. The pope in consistory gave judgment for the clerk and condemned the knight, who was very wroth with the clerk, and in great indignation, regardless of letters and bulls of the pope, ordered him to go and get a benefice elsewhere, for no part of the lord's heritage should he have. The knight was ' a cruel man,' and the clerk prudently withdrew to Avignon, but as he departed he promised to send a champion of whom the lord should stand more in dread.

The lord made little of the threat, but the clerk forgot not his promise, and the advent of the champion was in this wise: ' About a three months after, as the knight lay on a night abed in the castle of Corasse with the lady his wife, there came to him messengers invisible and made a marvellous tempest and noise in the castle, that it seemed as though the castle should have fallen down, and great strokes at his chamber door, that the good lady his wife was sore afraid.' The lord made little of it, and when the servants

told him of the disturbance in the house 'and
how all the vessel in the kitchen was overturned,'
he began to laugh and said : ' " Yea, sirs, ye
dreamed; it was nothing but the wind." " In
the name of God," quoth the lady, " I heard
it well." '

Next night the disturbances were renewed, and
the spirit when challenged proclaimed himself
a messenger from the aggrieved clerk, Orthon
by name. ' " Orthon," quoth the knight, " the
service of a clerk is little profit for thee; he will
put thee to much pain if you believe him. Pray
thee leave him and come and serve me, and I shall
give thee good thank." ' Orthon was 'in amours
with the knight ' and readily entered his service.
' Oftentimes he would come and visit him while he
lay in his bed asleep, and other pull him by the
ear or else strike at his chamber door or window
to awake him,' when he would bring his master
tidings from England, Hungary, or some other
place (p. 354). At first 'the lady the knight's wife
would be sore affrayed, that her hair would stand
up, and hide herself under the clothes,' but after
a time she ' was so inured to hear Orthon that
she was no more affraid of him.' The lord of
Corasse shared the early and exclusive information which he thus obtained with ' the earl of
Foix, who had great joy thereof, for he was the
lord of the world that most desired to hear news
out of strange places.' Thus when the lord of
Corasse had lost the services of Orthon by a
strange mishap, it was reasonable to conclude
that the earl of Foix, whose knowledge of current
events was unaffected by the loss, had secured the

services of a spirit, so useful, and so ready to welcome promotion. This was the 'imagination' of which men spoke secretly when they met as friends. That it was accepted as the explanation of the rapidity with which the news of the disaster of Aljubarrota travelled to Orthez appears from the importance attached by both squire and chronicler to the tale of the communications of the spirit called Orthon, manifestations which differ from spiritual manifestations of the twentieth century mainly in the practical value of the information imparted by the unseen visitor. It was an age in which the supernatural was at once accepted as the probable explanation of an occurrence out of the everyday course of events; and in this sense the words whispered in the quiet corner of the castle chapel are to be understood. It never occurred to Froissart to question the truth of the squire's tale. The lord of Corasse was not an obedient son of the church, and he might easily have availed himself of forbidden agency; but the suggestion that the secret service of the great and good earl of Foix should be so conducted gave the canon of Chimay pause, and he thought thereon for the remainder of his life.

' " Lo, sir," quoth the squire, " thus I have shewed you the life of Orthon and how a season he served the lord of Corasse with new tidings." " It is true, sir," quoth I, " but now as to your first purpose: is the earl of Foix served with such a messenger ?" " Surely," quoth the squire, " it is the imagination of many that he hath such messengers; for there is nothing done in any place, but an he set his mind thereto, he will know it, and when men think least thereof; and so did he when the good knights and squires of this country were slain in Portugal at Juberoth. Some saith the knowledge of such things hath done him much profit, for an there be but the value of a spoon lost in his house, anon he will know where it is." '

The informants in the castle of Orthez, whose tales delighted Froissart, spoke with differing degrees of authority. The squire with whom the chronicler withdrew into a corner of the chapel may have been simply retailing the gossip of the hall, and his tale may have been lightly regarded at the moment, for the chronicler writes: ' I took leave of the squire and went to other company, but I bare well away his tale.'

More weight was attached to the story of the death of Gaston's son, for it was told by ' an ancient squire, and a notable one,' whom Froissart saw 'divers times in the earl's house, and talked oftentimes with him.' Still more authentic was the account which he received of the warfare between Portugal and Castile, for he had it from knights and squires amongst whom there must have been some who fought in the battle of Aljubarrota.

Above all, the great earl was ready to give information, when Froissart would apply to him, for he writes of the knights and squires of all nations whom he met at Gaston's court, ' I was informed by them and by the earl himself of all things that I demanded ' (p. 330); and to the earl we must attribute the information which enabled the chronicler to report with exact truthfulness what was said and done at the famous interview between Gaston Phœbus, the count of Armagnac, and the Black Prince with his princess, in the town of Tarbes.

The battle of Poitiers was won in the year 1356, and by the treaty of Bretigny (1360) Aquitaine and Gascony were ceded to England. Edward formed these provinces into a principality under the rule of the prince of Wales, who held them of the crown.

Among the territories acquired by England was the county of Bigorre, and the prince as ruler of this country had as neighbours the count of Armagnac, and Gaston, lord of Bearn. A year had passed since the prince, coming to Bordeaux, had taken possession of his principality, but he had not, as yet, visited Bigorre. Count John of Armagnac bethought him of a scheme by which he might regain by diplomacy some of the loss which he had suffered in war. In their descendants we may discern somewhat of the qualities of their ancestors, sons-in-law of Gaston of Bearn: the ready response which won for the husband of the younger daughter the inheritance forfeited by the unworthy default of Armagnac.

The prince and ' the princess were desired by the earl John of Armagnac that they would come into the country of Bigorre into the city of Tarbes to see cothat untry, which as then he had not seen before; and the earl of Armagnac thought that, if the prince and princess were in Bigorre, that the earl would come and see them, and whereas he did owe him for his ransom two hundred

and fifty thousand franks, he thought he would
desire the prince and princess to require the earl
of Foix to forgive him the same sum or part
thereof.   So much did the earl of Armagnac, that
at his instance the prince and princess came to the
city of Tarbes ' (p. 311).

The motive which made Armagnac so pressing
in his invitation to the prince and princess was
well known to Gaston, from whom nothing could
be kept secret.   It was not necessary to have
recourse to the imaginings of knights of his household to account for the prescience which made
him aware of the scheme of the count of Armagnac;
and he was ready to act.   He was prepared to
deal liberally with his worsted neighbour, and
thus secure the safety and tranquillity of his own
people, an object which seemed to be effectually
secured when a few years later he arranged a
marriage between his son and the daughter of
Armagnac.

So ' as soon as he knew the coming of the prince
and princess being at Tarbes he ordained to go
and see them in great estate with more than six
hundred horses and threescore knights in his
company; and of his coming to Tarbes was the
prince and princess right joyous and made him
good cheer.'

Froissart, when he wrote these words, had
pleasant memories of the town of Tarbes.   It lay
on the road from Pamiers to Orthez, and he had
tarried all day at the Star, for there he found
great easement for man and horse (p. 325).   There
he ' demanded and inquired of the news of that
country, such as I knew not before.'   There he

learned how the prince of Wales, when he visited Tarbes, struck by the strength of the neighbouring fortress of Lourdes, had entrusted the safekeeping of it for England to a right trusty knight of his household, sir Pier Ernault of Bearn, who justified the confidence of the prince by loyalty to his feudal lord, even unto death (*ante*, p. 146).

The chronicler's knowledge of the Black Prince and Gaston at Tarbes, and of what was said and done at their meeting, is not attributed by him to local inquiry, or to information given by his travelling companion, sir Espang. When he had been made welcome at the court of Orthez, Froissart could draw his information from the fountain-head. The earl was easy of access, and ready to inform his visitor of all things that he demanded.

That Froissart demanded of the earl information as to what had passed at his meeting with the Black Prince may be regarded as certain, and as equally certain that his request was granted. Of the Black Prince he wrote: ' For to say truth the prince himself was the chief flower of chivalry of all the world ' (p. 177); and these pages bear witness to his admiration of the great earl. Froissart let it be known that the information given to him would be recorded in a book to be written on his return to his native Valenciennes; and for this work an authentic narrative of a famous meeting of such men as the prince and the earl would be of great value; and a man of the sagacity of Gaston would welcome an assurance that what was said and done at the interview should be truthfully recorded.

The city of Tarbes ' is fair and standeth in a plain country among the fair vines, and it is a town, city and castle, closed with gates and walls and separated each from other. From the mountains of Bearn and Cataloyne cometh the fair river Lisse [Adour], which runneth through Tarbes and is as clear as a fountain: . . . and under the mountain a six leagues from Tarbes is the town of Pau, which [also] pertaineth to the said earl.' There the earl was ' building of a fair castle joining to the town without on the river of Gave,' known by his name to this day; and thence came Gaston with great estate to greet the prince and princess of Wales, on their visit to Bigorre.

' There was the earl of Armagnac and the lord of d'Albret,' by whom the meeting had been brought about, ' and they desired the prince to require the earl of Foix to forgive the earl of Armagnac all or else part of the sum of florins that he ought to have; and the prince, who was wise and sage, considering all things, thought that he might not do so, and said: '' Sir earl of Armagnac, ye were taken by arms in the journey of battle and ye did put my cousin the earl of Foix in adventure against you: and though fortune were favourable to him and against you, his valour ought not to be made less. By like deeds my father nor I would not be content that we should be content to leave that we have won by good adventure at the battle of Poitiers, whereof we thank God.''

' When the earl of Armagnac heard that he was abashed, for he failed to his intent; howbeit, he left not off so, but then he required the princess, who with a good heart desired the earl of Foix to give her a gift.'

Armagnac was happy in the intercessor to whom he applied. The princess of Wales—the fair maid of Kent—was famed for her beauty, and the kindliness of her nature was shown by her interposing as peacemaker in more than one of the quarrels of the time.

' " Madam," quoth the earl, " I am but a mean man, therefore I can give no great gifts: but, madam, if the thing that ye desire pass not the value of threescore thousand franks, I will give it you with a glad cheer." Yet the princess assayed again if she could cause him to grant her full desire; but the earl was sage and subtle and thought verily that her desire was to have him to forgive clearly the earl of Armagnac all his debt, and then he said again: " Madam, for a poor knight as I am, who buildeth towns and castles, the gift that I have granted you ought to suffice." The princess could bring him no farther, and when she saw that, she said: " Gentle earl of Foix, the request that I desire of you is to forgive clearly the earl of Armagnac."

' " Madam," quoth the earl, " to your request I ought well to condescend: I have said to you that if your desire pass not the value of threescore thousand franks, that I would grant it you; but, madam, the earl of Armagnac oweth me two hundred and fifty thousand franks, and at your request I forgive him thereof threescore thousand franks." Thus the matter stood in that case, and the earl of Armagnac at the request of the princess won the forgiving of threescore thousand

franks.   And anon after the earl of Foix returned
to his own country ' (p 311).

The story of the meeting of the Black Prince
and Gaston Phœbus is here given as it was written
by Froissart on the day when he received it from
the earl.   We know that he was wont to commit
to writing—the best remembrancer—all that he
had heard from sir Espang de Lyon in the day;
and nothing so told was of such interest as the
interview at Tarbes, either as regard the actors
in the scene, or the authority of him by whom the
tale was told to the chronicler.   The speeches have
an air of reality which distinguishes them from
traditional or imaginary utterances attributed to
characters in histories.   The dignified courtesy
with which the prince, putting Armagnac into his
true position, kept out of a matter with which he
was not personally concerned; the persistence of
Armagnac; the grace with which the princess
played the part allotted to her; and the playful
gallantry with which Gaston put aside an unreason-
able demand, present a picture worthy of such
an artist as Froissart.

For the twelve weeks of Froissart's stay at
Orthez he and his horse were retained by the earl
as of his house, but his lodging was at the sign
of the Moon, where dwelt a squire of the earl's,
Ernaulton du Puy.   The dulness of the long mid-
winter hours that intervened between the pastime
of converse with knights and squires in the hall and
a summons to supper at midnight were relieved
by converse with the notable men of all countries
who resorted to the court, and found a lodging
in a hostelry closely connected with the castle.

The arrival of a guest who proved a source of much curious information is thus recorded: On a day 'I saw the Bascot (bastard) of Mauleon, a man of a fifty year of age, an expert man of arms and a hardy by seeming. He alighted at my lodging. . . . He brought with him his somers (packhorses) and carriages, as though he had been a great baron, and was served, both he and his servants, in silver vessel ' (p. 336).

Froissart lost no time in finding out the name and condition of this pretentious Gascon, who was treated with a respect which did not accord with his apparent rank. The gentle sir Espang was at hand; he knew everybody, and the curiosity of the chronicler was soon satisfied. Moreover, it so happened that he was well acquainted with a cousin of the Gascon; and as the party were ' sitting by the fire abiding for midnight, that the earl should go to supper,' the talk was of deeds of arms; and the Gascon's cousin began to draw him out for the benefit of a chronicler who was of their company. He demanded of Froissart, and said: ' Sir John, have ye in your history any thing of this matter that I speak of ?' Froissart thereupon gives an example of a successful, as he had already of an unsuccessful, effort to obtain matter for his chronicles. He ' answered and said: " I could not tell till I hear them: show forth your matter, and I will gladly hear you, for peradventure I have heard somewhat, but not all." " That is true," quoth the squire,' and he began a tale of adventure which could not have been told in any other age.

' " The first time that I bare armour was under

the captal of Buch at the battle of Poitiers," when he had the good fortune to take prisoners " of whom I had one with another four hundred thousand franks."' His next service with the captal was not so profitable. It was with the Teutonic knights against the heathen in Prussia, and then came the rescue of the ladies and damosels besieged in Meaux, and the slaughter of more than six thousand of the Jaquerie (*ante*, p. 133).

'At that time it was truce between France and England, but the king of Navarre made war in his own quarrel against the French king and regent. The earl of Foix returned into his own country, "but my master the captal, and I and other abode still with the king of Navarre for his wages."' In his service the squire and his fellow soldiers ' made great war in France, and specially in Picardy, and took many towns and castles, . . . and conquered great finance.' Then, when the truce with France had ' failed,' came some regular warfare and a visit to England with his master the captal at the command of the king. But the interesting part of the Bascot's life begins with the conclusion of peace between England and France, ' when it was ordained that all men of war and companions should avoid and leave their fortresses and castles that they held.'

But the long war had brought into existence a great body of men of all classes who lived by war, and whose occupation was gone in time of peace. ' Here were captains of all nations, English, Gascons, Spaniards, Navarrois, Almains, Scots, and of all manner of nations, and there I was as a captain. They took counsel what they should do, and then they said: " Though these two kings have taken peace together, yet we must live." '

No other means of earning a living occurring to them, they proceeded to make war on their own account, and as ' Free Companions ' succeeded in holding to ransom the richest parts of France and Italy. The company of the Bascot was twelve thousand strong, ' and in the same company there were a three or four thousand of good and chosen men of war, and as subtle in all deeds of arms as might be and apt to advise a battle and to take their advantage, and as hardy to scale and assail town or castle.' The strength of the companies was proved in the battle of Birgnais,* in which the companies overthrew an army commanded by the constable of France: a victory that ' did great profit to the companions, for before they were but poor, and then they were all rich by reason of good prisoners, towns and castles that they won.'

The leaders amassed much wealth, and held a position among their fellows and in history which could not have been attained in like manner in any other age. It is easy to understand how, when the Bascot of Mauleon arrived at Orthez, Froissart ' saw the earl of Foix and every man do him so much honour,' for he and his master, the captal of Buch, had been closely associated with the earl in service with the Teutonic knights; in the rescue of the ladies and damosels besieged by the Jaquerie; and, beyond doubt, in the pursuit of the reindeer in Sweden. But it is somewhat

---

* This has been claimed as an English victory by historians who discredit the Bascot's account.

startling to find the exploits of two English knights, as free companions, extolled by the Bascot as he sat with the chronicler by the fire in the Moon, and also honourably recorded in the *Dictionary of National Biography*.

Sir Hugh Calveley, ' a distinguished soldier,' and sir John de Hawkwood, ' general,' had earned a title to be remembered among the most famous Englishmen of the fourteenth century, for they and another English knight, sir John Aymery, were amongst the most dreaded of the free lances by whom France was pillaged and held to ransom; and a study of their lives, with the tale told by the Bascot of Mauleon, will assist us in arriving at an understanding of the age in which they lived. These men passed easily from regular warfare to highway robbery on a heroic scale, and having laboured diligently in their vocation, made a good end. Indeed, the free companion was in some respects treated as a regular soldier; if he were made a prisoner, he was not executed as a criminal, but held to ransom in an amount which was instantly paid out of the funds of the company.

Sir Hugh Calveley is rightly called a distinguished soldier. He fought with distinction under sir John Chandos in the decisive battle of Auray. After the conclusion of the war he and some free lances entered the service of Henry of Trastamare in his struggle for the crown of Castile, but when he found that Pedro the Cruel was supported by the Black Prince, he changed sides, and in this loyalty to England he was followed by the squire of the captal of Buch (vol. iii., p. 152).

'We next hear of him as the leader of two thousand freebooters, making disastrous war in the territories of the earl of Armagnac.' In the later years of his life he was free from temptation to engage in enterprises of this kind, for 'the estate of Lea in Cheshire devolved upon him. . . . His paternal estate, the profits of his various offices, and the booty produced by the kind of warfare in which he was long engaged, must have resulted in great wealth. He devoted a portion of his plunder to works of piety. In conjunction with his supposed brother, sir Robert Knolles, and another famous free lance, sir John Hawkwood, he is said to have founded a college at Rome in 1380. Six years later he obtained a royal licence for appropriating the rectory of Bunbury, which he had purchased, for the foundation of a college with a master and six chaplains' (*Dict. Nat. Biog.*). So completely did the pious disposition of his wealth atone for the practices by which it had been acquired that he holds an honourable place in *The History of the Worthies of England Endeavoured by Thomas Fuller, D.D.* There we read of the tradition recorded by Camden that he 'would feed as much as two, and fight as much as ten men'; of the famous 'duel in France, when he was one of thirty English who encountered as many Bretons,' and of his 'most certain marriage' to a purely mythical queen of Aragon: in such honour was this famous free lance held.

Sir John Hawkwood, known to Froissart as 'sir John Hacoude, a valiant English knight,' was, in the opinion of Hallam, 'the first real general of modern times.' The story of his life

13

as told in the *Dictionary of National Biography*
illustrates the ideas and habits of the age.   We
read of him first as in command of a troop of
free lances, living by pillage, who took Pau by
storm, robbing the clergy, and letting the laity
alone.   Then we find him at the head of a formid-
able body known as the White Company, ' probably by reason of the splendour of their equip-
ment,' ready to enter the service of any state
that stood in need of their aid.   ' The genius for
organisation which enabled him to convert a
band of freebooters into something like a regular
army, his rude but effective strategy, his energy
and resource distinguish him from all his mediæval
predecessors.'   For several years before his death
in the year 1391 these great qualities were devoted
to the service of the Florentine republic.   Her
gratitude was testified in his lifetime by a liberal
pension, when he was ' much troubled by pecu-
niary embarrassment,' and after his death by a
public funeral, and by a monument in the Duomo,
which still perpetuates his memory.

The name of sir John Hawkwood is worthy to
be remembered as that of ' the first distinguished
commander who had appeared in Europe since the
destruction of the Roman Empire' (Hallam, *Middle
Ages*, chap. iii., part ii.).   The English knights of
gentle birth who won renown as free lances, and
ended their days as benefactors to holy church,
were characteristic of the age, in their combination
with freebooters whose only relation to virtue
was feudal loyalty, and a honour rooted in dis-
honour which sometimes limited the range of their
depredations.   The Bascot of Mauleon never forgot

his duty to the captal of Buch, a feudatory of England, as whose squire he wore armour for the first time in the battle of Poitiers; and he never fought against England. The baronial splendour of his retinue at Orthez does not suggest the devotion of his wealth to pious uses.

The Bascot told the tale of his life and adventures—interrupted only by a call for the good wine of the Moon—and at the conclusion Froissart assured him of a place in the noble chronicle on which the earl of Blois had set him to work.

In converse like this the hours were spent between a winter sunset and the midnight supper in hall. Froissart had no lack of company. On the night when the Gascon told his tale two other free lances—squires—who sat with him at the fire, wished him to record their lives, but there was 'then no leisure, for the watch of the castle sounded to assemble all men that were in the town to come up to the castle to sup with the earl of Foix. Then these two squires made ready, and lighted up torches and so went up to the castle, as did all other knights and squires that were lodged in the town' (vol. iii., pp. 145-158).

The splendid hospitality of the count was extended to those who won distinction in the arts of peace as well as of war, and it was noted as proof of the generosity of the earl's nature that he recognised merit which had failed to win success. *La valeur malheureuse était certaine de trouver dans ses Etats un généreux accueil* (Lavallée, p. xvi.). Henry of Trastamare, after his defeat in battle, was received with honour in the court of Orthez. The earl's interests

were varied. He had ever in his company
Ernaulton of Spain, of whose gigantic strength
a merry tale was told (p. 322); and minstrels
and poets of all nations resorted to his court
assured of a hearty welcome and largesse; not
'folle,' but princely. Every night after supper
Froissart would read from a book called the
Meliador songs, ballads, rondeaux or virelays,
' and while I read, there was none durst speak any
word, because he would I should be well understood' (p. 329).

Gaston fut d'ailleurs l'ami le procteur des lettres; lui-
même il les cultiva avec succes. Il composa beaucoup
de poésies dans la langue de ses montagnes, et parmi ces
vieux refrains populaires qui font retentir les vallées du
Béarn, s'il se trouve des couplets brillants de fraicheur,
de grâce et de naïveté, on les attribue encore au bon
comte de Foix. Les prières qu'il a laissées sont écrites
partie en francais, partie en latin. Elles portent l'em-
preinte de son caractère. On y retrouve le prince et
même le chasseur (Lavallée, p. xxxviii).

Gaston's ancestors had been for several generations patrons of the poets of Provence, in the
number of whom they loved to be included.
Gaston's fame as a poet must be left to the traditions of the peasantry of Bearn. The reputation
of the famous work which won for him the highest
place among the Fathers of the literature of the
chase rests on a more secure foundation. By
Jacques du Fouilloux, whose *La Vénerie* came
into general use, supplanting by the aid of the
printing-press the classics of the fourteenth
century, ' *Phébus* ' is referred to as an authority
beyond question, and Mr. Baillie-Grohman's
tribute to it has been already quoted (*ante*, p. 3).

M. de Chevreul, a high authority, classes *Le Livre du Roy Charles* with the *Roy Modus* and Gaston's *La Chasse* as the only original treatises on venery: *Car de Fouilloux, malgré la reputation et la popularité dont il jouit, ne fait le plus souvent que copier Phœbus,* and the earliest book on the chase in the English language is the *Master of Game,* by Edward, second duke of York, which is substantially a translation of Gaston's work (*ante,* p.6).

On the first day of May, 1387, Gaston began to write. In *Le Prologue du livre de Chasse que fist le conte Fébvs de Fous** the author tells the purpose with which his book was written: *Ce ai commencé à ceste fin.* This was to make known to his readers how much good may be had from the chase. The true sportsman makes the best of both worlds; this is the sum and substance of his philosophy. The avoidance of mortal sin and the salvation of his soul were to be attained by the instruction in the science of woodcraft imparted to Philip of France by Gace de la Buigne in his *Romans des Déduits,* begun during the imprisonment of his pupil in England, and completed shortly before the campaign in which, as duke of Burgundy, he was associated with his intimate friend, Gaston of Foix.

That Gaston came to know of the work of Gace through his association with Philip, to whom it had been presented on its completion, is probable; that he had it before him when he wrote his *La Chasse* is certain. Mr. Baillie-Grohman in the Bibliography appended to the *Master of Game*

* Pp. 1-9 in M. Lavallée's edition of *La Chasse,* to which reference is made in these pages.

has collected a number of passages in *La Livre de la Chasse* copied from the poem of Gace, in some instances with literal accuracy and exactness. He notes passages in which he has borrowéd only an idea, and one which he regards as a rendering in prose of Gace's description of the greyhound.

Gaston's belief in the moral value of his treatise is shown by the carefulness with which he explains how it is that idleness is the cause of sin. Every act, good or bad, small or great, is the result of *ymaginacion : ne se fist que premier ne fust ymaginée et pensée*. Men's *ymaginacions* are more often bad than good; this is the work of his three enemies, *c'est le diable, le monde et la char*, and other causes too many to mention. So it is that when one is idle and careless, his unoccupied mind is possessed by *ymaginacions* of the seven mortal sins. So powerful is imagination that a man may become ill by thinking himself ill. Gaston had much more which he might have written on the subject of ' imaginations,' but he prefers to appeal to the experience of his reader: *pouree que chascun qui a bonne rayson scet bien que c'est juste.*

Gaston begins his work with an invocation which accords with the seriousness of the motive by which it was prompted:

Au nom et en tout honneur de Dieu le créateur et seigneur de toutes choses et du benoist son fils Jésucrit et du saint Esperit et du toute la sainte Trinité et de la vierge Marie et de tous les saitz etsaintes qui sont en la grace de Dieu.

In a Prologue prefixed to the work by way of introduction, the author tells his readers of himself, of the contents of the book, and of the motive by which it was inspired.

In all his lifetime he took special delight in three things—in arms, in love, and in the chase. Of two of these pursuits, there had been greater masters than he; there had been many better knights; and in love, far better opportunities had fallen to the lot of many men than to him, therefore it would be foolish of him to speak of them. For another reason he puts aside the pursuits of arms and of love, for they who desire to follow them will learn more from experience than they could from any words of his, and so he is silent. But of the third pursuit, in which he acknowledges no master, he proposes to speak.

His subject is the *Chace*, and he proposes to tell, chapter by chapter, of the ordinary beasts of the chase, writing fully of the nature of each, its habits, and mode of life; *de toutes natures de bestes et de leurs manieres et vie.* Of out-of-the-way sports, such as the hunting of lions, he says nothing, for they fall to the lot of few. But of the beasts of chase, ordinarily pursued with hounds, he wishes to treat for the instruction of the many whose knowledge of woodcraft is not equal to their love of hunting.

He treats of each kind of hunting in connection with the natural history of each beast of chase, and this part of his work gives proof of careful study.

Having written of beasts of chase, he would then *par la grace de Dieu* treat of the nature of the hounds by which they are hunted and taken, and, finally, he would say something of certain qualities which the true sportsman ought to possess.

Before entering on the practical part of hi
treatise, Gaston states the object which he had
in view when he began to write his book, and here
the connection is apparent between his book and
the *Romans des Déduits*.   Gace's work was written
by command of king John the Good to provide
his son Philip with an acquaintance with field
sport by which he would be safeguarded from
the sins of idleness and sloth.   Gaston's intention
had a wider range: it included his readers of all
classes, and it imparted to them the secret of
how to make the best of both worlds.   The true
sportsman escapes from the seven mortal sins—a
proposition in support of which he has much to
say—and he thus states the sum and substance
of his moral philosophy : *Brief et court toutes
bonnes coutumes et meures en viennent, et la salvation de l'ame ; quar qui fuyt les sept pechies mortelz,
selon nostre foy, il doit estre saulvé : donc bon veneur
sera saulvé, et en ce monde aura assez de joye, de
liesse et de déduit,* provided always that he fails
not to do his duty to God and to man.

To establish his proposition that ' *le bon veneur* '
cannot be idle and thus is safeguarded from
' *mauvaises ymaginacions* ' and consequent evil
deeds, Gaston gives an interesting account of the
activities by which every hour of a huntsman's
day is so completely occupied as to leave no time
for the bad thoughts which lead to bad deeds,
and he ends with his favourite appeal to experience; for everyone *qui a bonne raison* knows well
that he speaks the truth.

If immortality was denied to Froissart by
reason of the language of which he was con-

demned to write, by a like decree of fate Gaston's
work is forbidden to rank as literature; it was not,
like his poems, written in his mother tongue. As
an excuse for the shortcomings of his *La Chasse*
he says that he was not as much at home in French
as in his own language: *et aussi ma langue n'est
si duite de parler le Fransois comme mon propre
lengaige* (p. 278). Gascon was his native language,
but when it came to any 'matters of question' in
his conversations with Froissart, the earl, he says,
'would speak to me, not in Gascon, but in good
and fair French' (p. 329).

Gaston's French served well for conversation
and for written descriptions of the nature and
hunting of beasts of chase. But it lacked finish,
and its purity was marred by the occurrence of
words and phrases, often of Spanish origin, calling
for the explanation which is found in M. Lavallée's
edition. Its inadequacy for literary purposes
must have been felt by Gaston in the composition
of his Prologue, more especially when he wrote
to prove that the true sportsman not only ensures
the salvation of his soul, but has also the best
of his present world.

He tells of the enjoyment of life which falls to
the lot of none but the hunter, from the moment
when he rises in the morning until, after a day
spent in happy sport, he lies down to rest in his
bed *en beaulx draps fraiz et linges et dormira bien
et sainement la nuyt sans penser de faire péchié.*
The freshness of the morning air, the melodious
love-songs of the birds, the dewdrops at sunrise
on the boughs and herbage, beautiful until dis-
solved in the light of the sun: all this rejoices the

hunter's heart. Then come the pleasures of the chase; the finding of a great hart; the uncoupling of the hounds; the hunter, mounted in hot haste to be with the hounds; the behaviour of the pack, and the gallop, cheering on the hounds in full cry— there is here no place for evil thoughts. *Lors al grant joye et grant plaisir et je vous promets qu'il ne pense lors à nul autre péchié ne mal.*

The hunter's pleasure does not end with the taking of the hart. The breaking up of the deer, and the making of the *curée*—for his lord has given him of his good wine *a boire a la cuyrée*— delight him, and his return homeward is joyous. *Donc dis je que veneurs s'en vont en paradis, quant ils meurent, et vivent en ce monde plus joyeusement que nulle autre gent.*

To this comfortable assurance it is to be added that the hunter's life is not only merry but also long. He drinks and eats less than others, and Hippocrates says that more are killed by over-eating than by the sword. Healthy sweat comes from their constant exercise; *et comme les veneurs mengent petit et suent touzjours, doivent ils vivre longuement et sains.*

Gaston writes of the hunting of the hart, but this does not fall to the lot of all, and his advice is addressed to all sorts and conditions of men— *gens de quelque estat qu'ilz soient*—let them love hounds, hunting, and sport with beasts of one kind or another, or falconry (*d'oysiaux*), for to live in idleness, without love of sport with hounds or hawks, is—so help him God—not wise in a man, however rich he may be.

The thought with which the Prologue concludes is worthy of reproduction in Gaston's words, and

his French, though not classical, is here intelligible.
The true sportsman is a gentleman, whatever his
rank in life may be, for there is no man who loves
to work with hounds and hawks *qui n'eust moult
de bonnes coustumes en soy ; quar celi vient de
droicte noblesce et gentillesce de cuer de quelque
estat que l'homme soit, ou grant seigneur ou petit,
ou povre ou riche.*

Next to the Prologue, in which Gaston declares
the motive with which his book was written, come
chapters on the natural history of beasts of chase.
They fill 75 of the 279 pages in M. Lavallée's
edition of the treatise, and the estimation in which
this part of the work was held is shown by the
fact that several of these chapters are reprinted
by Jacques du Fouilloux in his *La Vénerie.*

Little need be said of Gaston's exposition of the
science of woodcraft; it is evidently the outcome
of the lifelong experience of a lover of the chase,
written with a knowledge of the books that had
been then written on the subject. Gaston had
before him, not only the *Romans des Déduits* of
Gace de la Buigne, but the first of the great French
classics of the chase, for twenty references to the
Roy Modus have been noted in his work. The
importance of *La Chasse* is recognised by mediæval
writers and also by modern authorities, and it
was a welcome gift when received by Philip,
duke of Burgundy. That the book was written
at the suggestion of Philip is a supposition which
is supported by a passage at the end of *La Chasse,*
which fills the place of the modern dedication.
The author modestly offers excuses for deficiencies
in the work that he had undertaken; these were

due partly to the author not being a complete master of the craft, and also to the subject—so comprehensive that it was impossible to avoid omitting something. There are many reasons, apart from his exalted rank and noble character, why he sends his book to Philip of France, duke of Burgundy, for he is master of all of us who devote ourselves to woodcraft. He feels that he ought not to send his poor contribution to the science to one who has forgotten more than he himself ever knew; *quar il en a plus oublié que je n'en sceu oncques.* But because they cannot now meet, which he deeply regrets, he sends his book by way of remembrance of one who is a humble member of the same craft, and he begs him, of his courtesy, to supply what is wanting and to correct what is wrong. With the book he sent a prayer which he had composed at a time when he was out of favour with his sovereign lord, and he concludes with some pious advice and good wishes for his friend and himself, in this and in the other world.

Gaston was a lover of the dog. Ten chapters of *La Chasse* are devoted to this subject, of which the greater part treat of the hound, as employed in different kinds of sport; but of the dog, as the loving and faithful companion of man, he has much to say. In addition to his favourite appeal to experience—*ce scet bien; tout homme qui a bonne raison*—he tells two stories illustrative of the faithfulness of the dog to his master, even after death, which he found in trustworthy records. Dogs have this fault, *c'est que ils durent pou; quar a grant paine passent douze ans.*

Gaston's treatise did not find its way into print

until the year 1507. In the meantime, copies in MS., some with illustrations of great magnificence, were produced, forty-one of which are mentioned by Mr. Baillie-Grohman in the bibliography appended to his edition of the *Master of Game*. The earliest edition was printed in Paris by Antoine Verard. The *Romans des Déduits* of Gace de la Buigne was printed by him at the end of *La Chasse*, and attributed to the same author, for the title of the volume was *Phebus (Gaston) de deduix de la chasse des bestes sauuaiges et des oyseaux de praye*. Whether this came from a traditional connection between the two treatises, or from a desire on the part of M. Verard to present his readers with a complete book of sport, the result was that for several centuries Gace's poem on falconry was attributed to Gaston Phœbus.

While *La Chasse* was still in manuscript it came into the possession of Edward, second duke of York, who occupied himself, probably during his imprisonment in Pevensey, in producing a version of the work in English, adapted to the requirements of English sport. This book, entitled the *Master of Game*, has been already referred to as the earliest book of hunting written in the English language.

At the end of his twelve weeks' stay Froissart left Orthez, to return to Valenciennes, and to make good the many promises of immortality by which he won so much of the information on which his chronicles were founded. On the way he was present at the wedding, solemnised with mediæval splendour, of Joanna of Boulogne, who had lived for years in the castle of Orthez as the ward of Gaston. He had also witnessed the reception in Paris of Isabella of Bavaria, the bride of the ill-fated Charles VI. He tells of the extraordinary display of gold and of rich arras in the city, ' And I, sir John Froissart, author of this history, was present and saw all this and had marvel where such number of cloths of silver were gotten,' for the street was covered with them.

His recollection often went back to the days with the great earl, and he tells of his sudden death in the month of August, 1391, in the presence of the faithful sir Espang de Lyon, from whom, no doubt, the chronicler's information was derived (vol. iv., p. 209).

' On the day that he died, he had hunted and killed a boar, and by that time it was high noon.' He rode to dinner at the hospital of Rions, ' where he alighted and went into his chamber, which was strewed with green herbs, and the walls set full of green bows to refresh the chamber, for the air without was excessively hot, being in the month of May. When he felt the fresh air he said: "This freshness does me much good, for the weather has been very hot "; and so sat down in a chair, and conversed with sir Espang de Lyon of his hounds, which had run best.' Converse like this between a lord returning from hunting and his huntsman is thus recorded:

Saw'st thou not, boy, how Silver made it good
At the hedge-corner, in the coldest fault ?
I would not lose the dog for twenty pound.
    First Hun. Why, Belman is as good as he, my lord;
He cried upon it at the merest loss,
And twice to-day pick'd out the dullest scent:
Trust me, I take him for the better dog.

(*Taming of the Shrew*, Ind., 19-25.)

As the earl washed his hands before dinner, suddenly his heart failed him, and he fell down, and when he fell he said: " Ah, I am but dead; God have mercy upon me." He spoke not a word after, . . . and in less than half an hour he gently yielded up his breath, and died without a struggle. God of his pity have mercy on him.'

When the news of the earl's death reached Orthez ' every man, woman, and child cried and wept piteously . . . in the remembrance of his nobleness and puissant estate, his wit and prudence, his bravery and generosity, and the great prosperity that he lived in ; for there was neither French nor English that durst displease him ' (*ib.*, pp. 212, 213).

It may have been the consummate statesmanship that safeguarded his peoples from the troubles of the Hundred Years' War and the Great Schism that attracted the attention of Disraeli to a prince, whose great qualities as a ruler, if he had been given a wider scope for their exercise than the petty principalities of Foix and Bearn, would have won for him a great place in history.

Attempts had been made on behalf of France and of England to engage him in the war, but without success. Sir Lois of Saxerre, marshal of France, was sent to Orthez for this purpose; and as Froissart was there at the time, the earl was probably his authority for what occurred at the interview. ' " Sir," quoth the marshal, " the king intends to know plainly whether you will side with the French or English, for you have hitherto remained entirely neutral." " Ah, sir," quoth the earl, " I thank you for this information; for sir, I

have good cause for not arming against either
party; as for the war between England and
France, I have nothing to do therewith; I hold
my country of Bearn of no man—but of God and
the sword: why should I subject myself to one
king or other ? But I know my adversaries of
Armagnac have tried all they could to incense
both parties against me: for before the prince of
Wales went into Spain, by the information of the
earl of Armignac, the prince would have made
me war, but for the interference of sir John
Chandos: but thank God, I have always conducted myself as meekly and courteously as I
could, and so I will do as long as I live; and when
I am dead, let matters go as they will"' (vol. iv.,
p. 41).

A remarkable tribute to Gaston's wisdom as
a ruler was its recognition by neighbouring
powers. Charles the Wise made him his lieutenant
in Languedoc. The government of the dukes of
Berri and Boulogne, under the less wise successor
of Charles V., was so oppressive that the people
of Toulouse, 'great and puissant,' approached
Gaston, offering him a large monthly revenue if
he would take on him the governing of their city
and the surrounding country. Other towns made
the same request, desiring ' him, because they
knew him for a just man and a right wise in
justice, redoubted of his enemies and fortunate
in all his business; and also they of Toulouse
loved him, for he had been ever to them a good
neighbour.' Gaston undertook the charge and
cleared the country of the ' robbers and pillers '
by which it was infested, slaying and drowning

more than four hundred in one day. These drastic measures won for him 'great grace and honour' from the citizens of Toulouse and the other important towns, but envy and ill-will from the duke of Berri, the nominal ruler of the country, to whom the earl of Foix was 'the most presumptuous and proudest knight of all the world' (p. 326).

Gaston realised that the man-power of his small principalities would not suffice to safeguard their neutrality, or to support him in the leading part which he was asked to assume. He also understood the purchasing power of his accumulated wealth in an age when knights and squires, expert in war, were ready to accept his pay; and so, in the words of sir Espang, 'he lay still in his castle of Orthez by his florins' (p. 318).

Our estimate of the character of Gaston Phœbus should be formed with regard to the standard of his age, and also to the temptations which beset an absolute ruler, the violence of whose passions make themselves manifest in the pages of an admiring chronicler.

There is no reason why we should question the sincerity of the penitential prayers and religious exercises with which he sought to atone for such crimes as the murder of his kinsman, Pier of Bearne. Whatever be the truth as to the killing of his son, it left a black stain on his memory, but how little this was regarded by his contemporaries appears from the heading of the chapter in which Froissart tells the tale 'of the great virtuousness and largesse that was in the earl of Foix, and the manner of the piteous death of Gaston the earl's son.'

14

Froissart has painted an undying picture of chivalry at its best in which the principal figures are the Black Prince and the count of Foix, and the abiding impression left by his portraiture on admirers like Scott and Disraeli is due no less to interest in his subjects than to the genius of the artist.

If fate denied immortality to Froissart when she condemned him to write his chronicles in fourteenth-century French, she made amends when she decreed him to be englished by lord Berners, for thereby his work became an English classic. John lord Berners was born in 1467, fifty years after the date assigned to the death of Froissart, into a world not far removed in years or in spirit from that of which Froissart wrote; for the great movements of the sixteenth century had not as yet made themselves felt. Members of his family and of the houses with which it was allied find honourable mention in the chronicle, to which lord Berners was naturally attracted. Always a lover of 'books containing famous histories' and, in particular, of the four volumes of sir John Froissart (Lord Berners's *Preface*), it was a labour of love when he was moved at the 'high commandment' of his most redoubted sovereign lord to translate these volumes 'out of French into our maternal English tongue.'

Henry had not then belied the promise of his early manhood. In learning, capacity, and excellence in manly exercises he was before all other princes of the age; and it has been well said that if he had died before the raising of the question of the divorce, his loss would have been deplored as one of the heaviest misfortunes that had ever befallen his country (Froude, i., 875).   To his credit must be placed his friendship with lord Berners, and the instinct which discerned in him fitness for the task imposed on him, for his literary success as the translator of such chivalric romances as *Huon of Burdeux* and *The History of the most noble and valyant knight, Artheur of Lytell Brytaine*, came to him later in life.   In his early years he engaged to serve the king for a year in his wars beyond the sea with ' two speres.'   He helped to repress Perkin Welbeck's rebellion, and in 1523 we find him travelling in the king's retinue to Paris and Calais.   He was sent with the princess Mary to France as her chamberlain when she married Louis XII. (October 9, 1514).   In 1516 he became chancellor of the exchequer, in which office he was painted by Holbein.   It reads strangely now that he had obtained a grant of the reversion of the chancellorship in 1514, and succeeded to the office under the terms of the grant.

In 1520 lord Berners and his wife, a daughter of John Howard, duke of Norfolk, attended the king to the Field of the Cloth of Gold.   His relations to his sovereign were intimate.   We read in the *Dictionary of National Biography* of royal grants of land and loans of money, and of a gift of hawks sent to the king in return.

It was probably by command of the king that lord Berners forwarded to the privy council an account of the ceremonial for which he received their thanks on July 2, 1520.

This literary employment led naturally to the

royal command to which we are indebted for Berners's translation of the chronicles of Froissart, the first volume of which was published in 1523, after an interval which sufficed for the preparation of the work.

The story of this famous meeting is part of the history of modern Europe, but the scene and the actors are borrowed from the Middle Ages. Berners's account of the gorgeous pageant and of the famous jousts that followed has been lost, but the story fills many pages of a chronicle written by another eyewitness, the literary quality of which has not been sufficiently recognised.* When Hall tells us how the two noble kings went together arm-in-arm into ' the riche tente of clothe of golde that there was set on the grounde '; how the king of England ' shewed himself the most goodliest Prince that had ever reigned over the realm,' and Francis ' was a goodly Prince, stately of countenance, and mery of cheer '; how in the days when courses were run and spears broken in the presence of queens, though ' dukes, marqueses, knights, esquiers, and others ran as fast as ever they might . . .' the two kings surmounted all the ' reste in prowesse and valiantness,' we can understand how Berners, an eyewitness and chronicler of these scenes, approached his task of translator in 'the spirit of his author, who loved to write of gorgeous pageantry and lavish display of gold.

The first part of Berners's translation was

---

* *Hall's Chronicle*, ed. 1809, pp. 608-620. ' His literary merits are of a high order. Hall has scarcely yet met with due recognition ' (*Dict. Nat. Biog.* [Bishop Creighton]).

printed in 1523. The English language had not
as yet attained to full maturity and strength,
but in its youthful vigour and energy, and even
in its irregularities and defects, it was well fitted
to chronicle the feats of arms and chivalric doings
of an age which had but lately emerged from
barbarism. It was a great language, as the age
of chivalry was a great age, though destined to
give birth to a greater, for it was the language
in which Tyndale wrote his translation of the
Bible: an immortal work, inasmuch as it is the
foundation of the Authorised Version, of which
some of our most familiar passages are, in the words
of Tyndale, reverently preserved by revisers who
worked in a great literary age. A more accurate
and scholarly rendering of the French might have
won for the translator praise such as that which
Partridge bestowed on the actor who played the
king in *Hamlet*, for anyone would know that he
was a translator, but lord Berners's glory is that
he forbids us to think of him as other than an
original writer.

CHAPTER VI

THE BOOK OF ST. ALBANS AND ENGLISH WRITERS

'WE have practically no original literature of the chase until the eighteenth century, and it is idle to pretend that we have.' These words, written by the Hon. J. W. Fortescue in his contribution to *Shakespeare's England*, cannot be gainsaid. There was no lack of books. Burton exclaims at the ' world of bookes ' not alone on arts and sciences, but on ' riding of horses, fencing, swimming, gardening, planting, great tomes of husbandry, cookery, faulconry, hunting, fishing, fowling, and with exquisite pictures of all sports, games, and what not ? '* a reference to the beauty of the illustrations of the books of sport of his day which suggests a hope that our good friend Burton knew nothing of them beyond the titles.

In this crowd of books not one can be found of literary importance or interesting from the character of its author, and yet they have a historical value which is absent from works of the kind produced in other countries.

Their woodcraft is borrowed from the great French classics, and the books on falconry are little more than translations of well-known French and Italian treatises. But in the long series, from the Norman-French treatise of Twici, in

* *Anatomy of Melancholy,* part ii., 2 memb. 4.

the early years of the fourteenth century, to the popular writings of Gervais Markham in the sixteenth, traces can be clearly discerned of the making of England, brought about by a union of the descendants of the invader with the older inhabitants of the island; and we can understand how it came to pass that the pastime of the Norman conqueror became, in the course of centuries, the national sport of England.

The *Book of St. Albans* is not the earliest of the books of sport written in England, but as it was the first to appear in print, and also the best-known and most important, it is placed at the head of this chapter.

The earliest known treatise written in England was entitled *Le Art de Vénerie le quel Mestre Guyllame Twici, venœur le Roy d'Engletere fist*. Twici was the huntsman of Edward II., and the book is in Norman French, written about the year 1328. It remained in MS. until 1840, when the text without notes was printed by sir Henry Dryden. It was reprinted in 1843 with learned notes, and a further edition, with interesting additions, was published in 1908 by Miss Alice Dryden, daughter of sir Henry.

As Latin was the language of learned clerks, so Norman French was for centuries after the conquest the language of venery. Survivals of the ancient order are found in the use of the Latin language at the conferring of degrees in the old universities; and in the hunting-field, although the master of hounds may rebuke his field in the vulgar tongue, the terms of his art are borrowed from the French.

Twici's little treatise, like many other ancient books on sport, is in the form of a dialogue between the master of hounds and a disciple. The language is more archaic than that of the *Roy Modus*, written at about the same time, and it may represent an Anglo-Norman dialect, as spoken in the hunting-field. The terms of art proper to venery are explained, but as a treatise on woodcraft the work compares unfavourably with its French contemporary.

Next in date is the *Master of Game*, the earliest book on hunting in the English language, written at some time between the years 1406 and 1413, by Edward, second duke of York, who fell in the battle of Agincourt (1415). It is a translation of the *Livre de Chasse* of Gaston Phœbus, adapted by the translator to the use of an English master of hounds. It remained in manuscript until the year 1904, when it was printed in a sumptuous volume, edited by Mr. and Mrs. Baillie-Grohman, with reproductions in photogravure of the fine illuminations and miniatures with which a famous MS. of the *Livre de Chasse* is adorned. The notes, and the bibliography appended to this volume, constitute a mine of interesting and accurate information on old-world sport to which the writer of these pages has often had recourse; for which, and for helpfulness shown to one interested in similar studies by the late Mr. Baillie-Grohman, he desires to record his gratitude.

The neglect of the *Master of Game* in the age of printing was due to the popularity of the *Book of St. Albans*. Between the publication of this work in 1486 and the death of Shakespeare in

1616 it was reprinted in whole or in part, more or less altered, no fewer than twenty-two times. ' Its circulation for a long time vied with, and perhaps exceeded that, of every other contemporary production of the press of lesser eminence than Holy Writ.'*

Although the *Master of Game* did not find its way into print, it was an important and well-known work widely circulated in MS. No fewer than nineteen extant copies were found as the result of the individual researches of the editors.

The *Boke of Saint Albans* (1486) is the earliest book on field sports printed in England; it is also worthy of note, for before its publication no work attributed to a woman had issued from an English printing-press. The printer is described in the second edition (1496) by Wynkin de Worde as ' one sumtyme scole mayster if Seynt Albon's, upon whose soule God have mercy '; and the personality of neither author nor printer can be discerned through the mists of over four centuries.

The edition of 1486 consists of four parts. The first is a practical treatise on falconry, written in prose, for the instruction of ' gentill men and honest persones,' with particular note of the ' termys of plesure belongyng to gentill men hauing delite therin.' The second part explains to ' sych gentill persons the maner of huntyng for all maner of beestys.' It is a sort of rhyming primer, in which the traditional teaching of a mythical Sir Tristram is conveyed to a disciple:

Wheresoeuere ye fare by fryth or by fell,
My dere chylde take hede how Tristram dooth you tell.

---

* Hazlewood, reprint of the ed. of 1486, p. 21.

Then follow some moral maxims and useful information, especially as regards 'dew termys,' from which we learn that we should say that 'an Esquyer lodgeth,' and a 'yoman beddeth.'

The colophon runs thus: 'Explicit Dam Julyans Barnes in her boke of huntyng.' In the edition of 1496 the colophon is, 'explicit dame Julyans Bernes doctryne in her boke of huntynge.'

In the third part is 'determyned the lynage of coote armuris; and how gentilmen shall be knowyn from ungentillmen.' The lineage of coat armour is traced back to 'orderis of aungelis' before the creation of Adam. Abel was a gentleman, and Cain a churl. 'Of the offspring of the gentleman Jafeth come Abraham, Moyses, Aron, and the profettys, and also the kyng of ye right lyne of mary, of whom that gentilman Jhesus was borne, very god and man: after his manhode kyng of the londe of Judea of Jues, gentleman by is modre mary prynce of cote armure.'

The fourth treatise is a continuation of the third. The colophon is, 'now endyth the boke of blasyng of armys translatyt and compylyt togedyr at Seynt albons the yere from thincarnacion of owr lorde Jhû Crist. M.CCCC.lxxxvi.'

In the early editions of the *Book of St. Albans* the only part attributed to Dame Juliana Barnes, or Bernes, is the Book of Hunting, but in the course of the succeeding century she came to be regarded as the author of the whole volume. In a popular edition published in 1595 by Gervais Markham the work is described as 'containing three most exact and excellent Bookes: the first of Hawking, the second of all the proper termes

of Hunting, and the last of Armorie: all compiled
by Juliana Barnes, in the yere from the incarna-
tion of Christ, 1486.'   In the *Dictionary of National
Biography*, with a warning that ' the historic and
the legendary Dame Juliana Berners are very
different persons,' the lady is described as
' BERNERS, BERNES, or BARNES, JULIANA
(*b.* 1388 ?), a writer on hawking, hunting, and
heraldry,' possessed of a ' biography which is
more or less mythical, and which is due to conjecture, inference, and perhaps not a little to
imagination.'

The legendary dame is presented in her most
attractive form in the introduction and notes
to Hazlewood's reprint of the edition of 1496,
while Blades, in his introduction to the reproduction in facsimile of the first edition, carries
destructive criticism so far as to reduce Juliana
to the humble position of one who ' possibly
compiled from existing MSS. some rhymes on
hunting.'

Mr. Baillie-Grohman's summing up of the controversy will suffice for these pages.   ' This is not
the place to discuss at length the authorship of
the *Book of St. Albans.*   Blades has shown us on
how slight a fabric the biographers of Dame
Juliana built up their theories, the culminating
point of this fiction having been reached by
Joseph Hazlewood in his reprint of 1810, where
he makes her a daughter of sir James Berners,
and Prioress of Sopwell nunnery in Hertford-
shire.   There is nothing but the name to connect
the compiler of the verses on hunting with the
sir J. Berners alluded to, nor is there in the records

of Sopwell a prioress of the name of Barnes, or of any name remotely like it' (*Master of Game,* p. 244).

But when the authorship of this ancient book of hunting has been stripped of all adornments and accretions due to legend or imagination, the dame remains an interesting reality. The word 'dame' in the fifteenth century was used in the sense of 'housewife,' and as Blades points out, did not imply any connection with a titled family. Bernes is, most likely, Berners writ short, and Juliana, from her intimate acquaintance with the language of woodcraft, was probably of gentle birth. Our knowledge of her is scanty, but it is enough to secure for her immortality as the author of the earliest book on hunting written in the English language, and the English-woman who first gave her writing to the world in print.

The publication of the *Book of St. Albans* marks an epoch in the social history of England, for in it we find the earliest recognition of a class which grew in importance throughout the succeeding centuries.

There had come into existence a kind of ' gentle-men whose ancestors are not knowen to come in with William duke of Normandie (for of the Saxon races yet remaining we now make none accompt, much lesse of the British issue).' Harrison tells how such a man takes his beginning in England, and how when he is able to ' beare the port, charge and countenance of a gentleman, he shall for monie haue a cote and armes bestowed vpon him by heralds (who in the charter of the same doo of custome pretend antiquitie and seruice, and manie gaie things).' He is then called master, which is the title that ' men giue to Esquiers and gentle men, and reputed for a gentleman euer after.'*

But if the *novus homo* (called by plainspoken Master Stubbes ' a dunghill gentle man, or gentleman of the first head '—*Anatomie of Abuses*, 1583) is to pass muster as a gentleman, something more must be done than the obtaining for money of a coat-of-arms. He must learn to speak the language of the caste to which he has been admitted; and the literature of the sixteenth and seventeenth centuries teems with references to his endeavours to reach this standard with the aid of a book of sport.

The best-known one is in Ben Jonson's *Every Man in his Humour* :

STEPHEN: Uncle, afore I go in, can you tell me an we have e'er a book of the sciences of hawking and hunting, I would fain borrow it.

KNOWELL: Why, I hope you will not a hawking now, will you ?

STEP.: No, wusse; but I'll practise against next year, uncle; I have bought me a hawk and a hood and bells, and all; I lack nothing but a book to keep it by.

KNOW.: O most ridiculous !

STEP.: Nay, look you, now you are angry, uncle; why you an a man have not skill in the hawking and hunting languages nowadays, I'll not give a rush for him; they are more studied than the Greek or the Latin. He is for no Gallant's company without them.—(Act i., Sc. 1).

' Nothing so frequent,' Burton writes, as hawking, ' a great art and many bookes written of it ';

* Harrison's *Description of England*, i., 129 (reprint by New Shakespeare Society). The grant of arms to Shakespeare's father was made for valiant service pretended to have been rendered by his ancestors to king Henry VII.

and he quotes a writer who taxes the English nobility with their devotion to field sports 'as if they had no other meanes but hawking and hunting to approve themselves gentlemen with' (*Anatomy of Melancholy*, part ii.), and in this they were imitated by the *novus homo*, with the aid of the book of sport.

The great popularity of the *Book of St. Albans* was largely due to the assistance which it gave to the growing class of those gentry who were, in Ben Jonson's words, 'in the cradle of their gentry.'

In his *Speech according to Horace*, from which these words are taken, the old nobility, the 'Beauchamps and Nevills, Clifford Audleys bold,' ask—

> Why are we rich, or great, except to show
> All licence in our lives? What need we know
> More than to praise a dog or horse? Or speak
> The hawking language?

This, their gentle language, must needs be learned by study, as a foreign tongue, by the

> Hodges, and those newer men,
> As Stiles, Dike, Ditchfield, Millar, Crips, and Fen;

a difficult task, even to rare Ben Jonson, as we shall presently see.

But it must be undertaken by the would-be gentleman of the Tudor Age, for it would have been as difficult for one living in that age to be regarded as a learned clerk without knowledge of Latin as to pass muster as a gentleman without acquaintance with a mode of speech derived from the Norman French of the Conqueror.

I have elsewhere noted the difficulties with which the learner of this language had to contend, and his obligation to the *Book of St. Albans* and its successors. ' To him the Book of Sport served as grammar, dictionary, and exercise-book in one. The task was no trifling one. There was a separate word for every conceivable act done by, or to, each beast of venery or of the chase, and for every incident of sport; with an endless array of appropriate verbs, nouns, and adjectives, the misapplication of any one of which stamped the offender as no gentleman. . . . Many of these terms have survived to the present day, and lingering traces may yet be discerned of the old-world ideas associated with them. We still speak of a herd of deer, a bevy of ladies, a congregation of people, a host of men, a flight of pigeons, a brace and leash of greyhounds, a couple of hounds, a litter of whelps, a covey of partridges, a swarm of bees, a cast of hawks, a flight of swallows, a stud of mares, a drove of cattle, and a flock of sheep. Few of us are conscious that in so speaking we are correctly using the gentle terms appropriated by the *Booke of St. Albans* to the various " compaynys of beestys and fowlys." And even now—so inveterate are ideas wrought into our blood—while the misuse of scientific terms suggests nothing more than ignorance, we can hardly avoid associating the idea of vulgarity with a man who would speak of a flight of partridges, a flock of grouse, or a pair of hounds ' (*Diary of Master William Silence*).

Shakespeare's sporting vocabulary is as accurate and copious as that of any author of a Book of Sport; and reminiscences of Arden and of Cotswold are scattered throughout his works. In the book from which the foregoing words are taken more than two hundred and forty words and phrases relating to woodcraft or falconry are noted, employed by Shakespeare with an aptness and accuracy attainable only by personal experience.

Ben Jonson, city born and bred, had no such experience to appeal to, and when he would write of sport he must needs have recourse to the Book of Sport. How he fared is told in the interesting article on hunting, contributed to *Shakespeare's England* by the Hon. J. W. Fortescue, the historian of the British Army. The writer had in early life a practical acquaintance with the hunting of the hart, in the manner which has survived from the Middle Ages and is still carried on with a famous pack of hounds, of which his brother was at one time master.

Taking as his text a series of passages in Ben Jonson's *Sad Shepherd*, in which he finds a number of technical terms of woodcraft, for the most part misapplied, not one of which is to be found in the sporting sense anywhere in Shakespeare, Mr. Fortescue asks: 'Are we then to infer that rare Ben Jonson knew more of hunting than did Shakespeare? Just the contrary. Jonson knew nothing of woodcraft, and must have copied the whole of the words out of a book of sport, probably *The Noble Arte of Venerie*,' possibly, I would suggest, borrowed from his fellow, Shakespeare. 'It is probably nearer to the truth that in all ages good sportsmen, like good men, are rarer than bad; but good there must have been in all times, and among the best of the sixteenth century we must certainly rank William Shakespeare.'

Shakespeare had no need of the Book of Sport to teach him the hunting language, but that he had the love of a true sportsman for what was written about sport, and that he read it with an understanding to which the reader was a stranger who looked it over to pick up terms of art, by the use of which he might qualify for his newly won condition of gentleman, we may learn from what he has written in a passage quoted in another page (*ante*, p. 27). The collection of old-world books on outdoor sports by which these pages were suggested had its origin in an attempt to gain from them something by which light might be thrown on Shakespeare's modes of thought and forms of expression.

How was it that the language of the Beauchamps and Nevills, which Ben Jonson failed to acquire by study of the Book of Sport, was to Shakespeare as familiar as his mother tongue, for neither was he to the manner born? Shakespeare picked up the language of sport as he acquired a knowledge of his mother tongue, by hearing it spoken by the huntsmen and falconers among whom his young days were spent; and admission to this society would be easy to a young man whose knowledge of woodcraft entitled him to rank among the best sportsmen of his time.

A curious and interesting pamphlet printed in the year 1579 contains a dialogue between Vincent, the country gentleman, and Valentine, the courtier, in which Vincent explains how he manages to have

15

'many proper pleasures and honest exercises,' even though he lived in the country. This was attained by calling in neighbours, yeomen of the country, and good honest neighbours to take part in his amusements. This, the courtier says, is unbecoming in a gentleman, 'for as their resort unto your house will give them occasion to learne some point of civility and courtesy,' he fears that their entertainer might taste of their bluntness and rusticity. There were many country gentlemen not far from Stratford, lower in degree than the courtly Lucys, in whose houses points of civility might be learned, to which a knowledge of woodcraft would be the best recommendation— for Arden and Cotswold were famous as sporting countries; and so it was that the son of a Stratford yeoman wrote of sport like an English gentleman, without the aid of the Book of Sport.

The extreme rarity of the early editions of the *Book of St. Albans* places it beyond the reach of the collector of moderate means, who may regard himself as fortunate if he should become possessor of the popular edition, or, rather, version of the work published by Gervais Markham in 1595. But it is more easy for the student to attain to an exact knowledge of this work than of any other of the famous mediæval books of sport. The edition of 1486, printed in facsimile by Elliot Stock (1881), presents an absolute counterfeit presentment of the original, with an introduction by W. Blades, in which the question of authorship is discussed in a scholarly mànner. A handsome reprint of the edition of 1496, in black letter, was brought out in 1810 by Joseph Hazlewood, valuable from the research with which the editor has collected information regarding the sports and pastimes of the time, with tributes to the character of Dame Juliana Berners, including Bayles, who writes in his *Dictionary* of ' this heroic woman ' as ' an illustrious female, eminently endowed with superior qualities both mental and personal.'

The work undertaken by dame Juliana of making the hunting language known to ' honest persones ' ('You know, sir,' says Fag to captain Absolute, ' one says honest to one's inferiors ') was completed by Gervais Markham, interesting as a link connecting mediæval sport with the ' country contentments ' of the yeoman farmer.

Beginning with an edition of the *Book of St. Albans*, entitled *The Gentleman's Academy*, he proceeded to a number of popular works on sport, horses, and farming, addressed, not to the would-be gentleman, aping the manners of those of Norman descent, but to the honest countryman, with an Englishman's love of horses and of sport.

In an interesting account of his life contributed to the *Dictionary of National Biography* by the late sir Clements R. Markham, K.C.B., F.R.S., forty works are attributed to him dealing with subjects so various as poetry, the drama, field sports, horsemanship, cock-fighting, and military discipline. In the words of sir Clements Markham, ' his industry was prodigious, and as a compiler for the bookseller on an exceptionally large scale, he has been called the earliest English hackney writer.'

His essays in high-class literature were not well received, for Ben Jonson, in his *Conversations with Drummond*, says that ' he was not of the number of the Faithful, but a base fellow.' His habits of writing several works on the same subject under different titles and of re-issuing unsold copies under new titles brought upon him the wrath of the booksellers, who obtained from him a written promise to write no more books on a favourite subject—the diseases of horses and cattle.

Although Ben Jonson did not welcome Markham to the number of the faithful, a collection of his writings on country life and horsemanship bears witness to the reality of his desire to be of service to a class which was growing in importance—the yeoman farmers of England. He translated into English the *Maison Rustique* of Liebault and Estienne, which had gone through more than one hundred and six editions in French before the end of the seventeenth century, and was translated into German and Italian, and he wrote on such practical subjects as *Cheap and Good Husbandry* (1614), and *The Enrichment of the Weald of Kent* (1625), which was also often reprinted.

His *Discourse on Horsemanshippe* was published in 1593 when he was only twenty-five years old. It was followed by several works on horses and farriery, and although he was restrained by a promise exacted by his publishers from printing any more works on this subject, his pen refused to be kept idle, for sir Clements Markham writes: ' Finally, "Le Marescale, or the Horse Marshall, containing those secrets which I practise but never imparted to any man," is still in manuscript, and belongs to the writer of this article.'

But to the lover of the horse Markham is of interest, not on account of his long-forgotten

writings, but by reason of the part which he took
in a famous controversy, on which immortality
was conferred by Shakespeare's reference to it in
his earliest play, *Love's Labour's Lost*, i., 2, 57.

When Moth propounds to his master, Don
Adriano de Armado, a fantastical arithmetical
problem, he adds, ' the dancing horse will tell you.'
This dancing horse was the property of one Banks,
' a famous showman, to whose " dancing horse "
allusion is made by all the best-known authors of
his day ' (Sir Sidney Lee, *Dictionary of National
Biography*, tit. Banks). Dancing was the least
marvellous, as many horsemen can testify, among
the accomplishments of this famous horse, one
of which, the counting of money, was noted by
Shakespeare.

We learn from *Tarlton's Jests* (1699) that Banks
exhibited his horse ' of strange qualities . . . at
the Crosse Keyes in Gracious-streete' before 1588.
In the years of obscurity between Shakespeare's
coming to London, about the year 1585, and the
writing of *Love's Labour's Lost*, a young man from
Stratford, a lover of the horse, took such delight
in the strange qualities of a horse that so en-
livened his visits to the Crosskeys in Gracechurch
street as to cause them to find their way into a
play that he was then writing.

But there were those who took a more serious
view of the performances of Banks and his curtal,
and if they believed in ' his most famous but
hardly creditable exploit—that of climbing the
steeple of St. Paul's,' when, according to the
Owles Almanach (1618), ' the dancing horse stood
on the top of Powles, while a number of asses

stood braying below,' we are not astonished to learn ' that it was a general opinion, and euen some of good wisedome haue maintained the assertion, that it was not possible to bee done by a Horse, that which that Curtall did, but by the assistance of the Deuill' (*Cavalarice*, viii., p. 26).

In 1601 Banks exhibited Morocco in Paris, where the magistrates suspected that the tricks were done by magic, and imprisoned Banks and his horse, until satisfied that the horse was guided by signs. At Orleans, according to Bishop Morton (*Direct Answer unto the Scandalous Exceptions of Theophilus Higgins*, 1609), suspicion was allayed when Morocco, at his master's command, sought out ' one in the preasse of the people who had a crucifix on his hat : which done, he bid him kneele downe unto it, and not this onely, but also to rise up againe and to kisse it.' According to the legend Banks and his curtal venturing into Italy were both burned at Rome ' by the commandment of the pope'; but this is certainly untrue, for Sir Sidney Lee finds Banks in 1662 a prosperous vintner in Cheapside, who was said to have ' taught his horse to dance, and shooed him with silver.'

Markham believed Banks to be exceeding honest, and he knew the horse to be ' a beast of a most excellent understanding and pure sence then anie other beast whatsoever,' and he was satisfied ' by most assured tryals that there was no one tricke which that curtall did, which I will almost make any Horse do in lesse than a month's practise' (*Cavalarice*, p. 27).

In a chapter entitled ' How a Horse may be

taught to doe any tricke, done by Bankes his
curtall,' Markham's method is explained. The
showman and the horseman aim at the production
of different results, but the processes by which they
are brought about have this in common—they
are founded on a study of the character and disposition of the horse. Markham's exposition of
his method, how he became ' demi-natured with
the brave beast ' and made it submit his will
to that of his master, is interesting, but too long
to be admitted to these pages. The showman's
secret is that of the horseman, and the word
' witchcraft,' spoken in deadly earnest by the
common people and ' even some of good wisdom,'
who resorted to the Crosskeys when the dancing
horse was performing his tricks, was used by one
of the company years after, when he would write
of horsemanship in witchery excelling any tricks
which his memory or imagination could suggest,

> this gallant
> Had witchcraft in 't; he grew into his seat;
> And to such wondrous doing brought his horse,
> As had he been incorpsed and demi-natured
> With the brave beast; so far he topped my thought,
> That I in forgery of shapes and tricks,
> Come short of what he did.   (*Hamlet*, iv., 7, 86.)

CHAPTER VII

THE EMPEROR FREDERICK II. AND FALCONRY

THE emperor Frederick, known in history as Barbarossa, and his grandson, Frederick II., are among the most illustrious wearers of the iron crown of Italy, and titular rulers of the Holy Roman Empire. Their proper place is in European history, but as they were the parents of a field sport, once popular, they cannot escape notice in these pages, but no attempt is made to form an estimate of their genius, or to expound the mysteries of the sport with which their names are associated. On the former subject a few words may be quoted which illustrate the truth, that among the lovers of the field sports of any age the brightest intellects of the age may be found.

Of Frederick I. (1123-1190) Carlyle writes: 'No king so furnished out with apparatus and arms, with personal faculty to rule and scene to do it in, has appeared elsewhere. A magnificent, magnanimous man; holding the reins of the world, not quite in the imaginary sense; scourging anarchy down, and urging noble effort up, really on a grand scale. A terror to evil-doers and a praise to well-doers in this world, probably beyond what was ever seen since.'

The oft-quoted words written of Frederick II. by Matthew Paris—a contemporary English his-

torian—quoted at p. 2, express the amazement
of his world in the contemplation of gifts so
great and so varied, and ideas for the acceptance
for which the age in which he lived was not
prepared.

This marvellous man left unfinished a work on
falconry on which he is said to have spent his
leisure hours for thirty years. The manuscript
passed to his son, prince Manfred, by whom the
work was completed, with notes and additions
from his father's papers. The emperor died in
1250, and the manuscript was neglected until the
sixteenth century, when it came into the hands
of Joachim Camerarius, the learned doctor of
Nuremberg. From it the edition of 1596 was
printed, along with the work of Albertus Magnus,
De Falconibus, Asturibus et Accipitribus, in a
small volume which betokens the devotion of the
greatest intellects of a great age to a bygone
sport, which, though dead, yet lives for ever in
the literature of a still greater age.

Falconry, in the sense of taking game by means
of birds of prey, trained to hunt in concert with
their masters, was a kind of sport unknown in
Greece or Rome. The *aucupium* in which the
opulent Roman found occupation (Cicero, *De Fin.*,
118) was simply bird-catching, in nets, or with
the humble device of bird-lime.

As a field sport, falconry was practised from
the remotest antiquity by many nations of Asia.
Evidence of the practice of the sport in Anglo-
Saxon times will be found in Mr. Harting's in-
valuable *Bibliotheca Accipitraria*, and there is a
tradition of its introduction into Italy by Frederick

Barbarossa. Some knowledge of the sport was probably brought to Europe from the East by crusaders, but the great days of falconry begin with the emperor Frederick II. He brought from the East great numbers of trained hawks of all kinds, and spent thirty years in writing a treatise which is still an authority on the sport.

The Hohenstaufen emperors were dukes of Suabia, and among those on whom the newly imported Oriental sport cast its spell was the youthful son of a Suabian nobleman, Albert, destined to be known as the Great. In devotion to falconry we find a link connecting the famous philosopher with the great emperor, for each wrote a treatise on falconry which was in use during many centuries; and Albert may have had his first lesson in the sport from the falconer of the emperor, of whom he writes as a high authority.

The influence of falconry on letters is without a parallel, for it outlived the sport which was its source, and it was manifested in the creation, not of a literature, but of a language.

The treatises of the fathers of the sport are interesting from the greatness of their authors, but they have no claim to rank as literature, and the works collected and noted in Mr. Harting's *Bibliotheca Accipitraria* do not rise above what was written of other sports, but the ' hawking language ' becomes literature, by adoption, when it is chosen by poet or dramatist as the form in which his thoughts are expressed, and redeemed from the vulgarity of a passport to good society.

The tercel-gentle was the noblest hawk of the male sex, and when Juliet would recall Romeo the

hawking language was that in which her love
found expression:

> Hist ! Romeo, hist ! O, for a falconer's voice,
> To lure this tassel-gentle back again !
>
> > (*Romeo and Juliet*, ii., 2, 159.)

Of least consideration was the male of the
sparrow-hawk, when taken from the eyrie, and
Mistress Ford, in a different mood, thus addresses
Falstaff's little page:

> How now, my eyas-musket! What news with you ?
>
> > (*Merry Wives*, iii., 3, 22.)

Shakespeare was never at a loss for an apt word
or phrase from this language; of which eighty
have been found in his writings.   Petruchio found
in the hawking language words to tell ' how to
tame a shrew ':

> My falcon now is sharp, and passing empty;
> And, till she stoop, she must not be full-gorg'd,
> For then she never looks upon her lure.
> Another way I have to man my haggard,
> To make her come, and know her keeper's call,
> That is, to watch her, as we watch these kites
> That bate, and beat, and will not be obedient.
>
> > (*Taming of the Shrew*, iv., 1, 193.)

Shakespeare's love of falconry, and his adoption
of the hawking language, were noted by his fellow-
dramatists.

Ben Jonson, town bred, to whom the sport was
unknown, could not understand the devotion to
it of one so wise, until he had experienced the
fascination of falconry. This was when he visited
in Warwickshire sir Henry Goodyere, the friend
and patron of Drayton, whom Camden describes

as a 'knight memorable for his virtues,' to whom
he writes:

> Goodyere, I'm glad, and grateful to report
> Myself a witness of thy few days' sport;
> Where I both learn'd why wise men hawking follow,
> And why that bird was sacred to Apollo:
> She doth instruct men by her gallant flight,
> That they to knowledge so should tower upright,
> And never stoop but to strike ignorance;
> Which if they miss yet they should re-advance
> To former height, and there in circle tarry
> Till they be sure to make the fool their quarry

Fletcher paid to Petruchio's hawking language
the tribute of imitation in a comedy in which the
wife is the tamer and the husband the tamed. 'The
comedy is avowedly an imitation and continuation
of Shakespeare's *Taming of the Shrew*' (Introduction to the play in Weber's edition).   The wife's
plan of campaign, in the hawking language, will
be found in act i., scene 2.

Falconry was at an early date firmly established
in the British Isles as a popular sport.   Indeed,
it was the most popular of all the sports of the
field, for every man, however humble, had a recognised right to his place in the commonwealth of
sport.   The *Book of St. Albans* tells us that the
falcon gentle, the noblest of hawks, is for a prince,
and the degrees of duke, earl, baron, knight, and
squire are represented, each by a separate hawk.
All of these are of the class which had a share
in the duties and honours of chivalry, but the
yeoman had an honoured place, for to him was
allotted the goshawk, first of short-winged hawks,
and the 'powere man' was not forgotten, for he
too had his proper hawk—the tercel.   The clergy

had a place, though not an exalted one, in this commonwealth, for we read: 'Ther is a spare-hawke, and he is an hawke for a prest, Ther is a Muskyte, and he is for an holiwater clerke.'

Sudden and complete was the downfall of a sport which, though not a native growth, seemed to have struck its roots so deeply in the national life of England. In the early years of the seventeenth century falconry was a national sport; its language was adopted by men of letters, and the manner in which it was affected by the vulgar was a favourite topic with the satirist. In less than a century—in 1718—a book entitled *The Compleat Sportsman* was published by Giles Jacob, in which he says that he took no notice of the diversion of hawking because it was so much disused in his time, 'especially since sportsmen are arrived at such perfection in shooting.'

The use of the shot-gun was only one of the causes which led to the disuse of falconry; with other sports and pastimes it had declined during the years of the Civil War and the Commonwealth, and it never regained its former position. 'Hedge-rows and enclosures have taken part with gun and dog in the extinction of falconry, and though there never has been a time when hawks were not flown by lovers of the sport in some part of the British Isles, it cannot be said to have ranked among our national sports during the last two centuries.'

I have written elsewhere: 'Although the falcon and the gentle art to which she gave her name are too picturesque in their accessories and lend themselves too readily to poetic treatment to lose their place in literature, they hold it with a difference. Dryden is the latest English classic who writes the hawking language with the accuracy of Chaucer, Spenser, and Shakespeare . . . It is worth noting that the hawking language, once spoken by the card with absolute accuracy, is the only dead language of antiquity which it is considered allowable to write without any regard to the meaning of the words—an indulgence which authors are tempted to allow themselves, partly from consciousness of the ignorance of their readers, and partly by reason of the vague, pleasurable ideas of mediæval sport and gallantry associated with its terminology, however recklessly misapplied ' (*Diary of Master William Silence*).

In the age of falconry a writer of the Elizabethan age would as soon have written of a bull as ' she ' as of a falcon as ' he,' but even the greatest of their successors have not hesitated to unsex the noble bird and to degrade her to the level of her tercel. Illustrious examples in letters, including Dr. Johnson, may be quoted for the solecism. Tennyson published a poem entitled ' The Falcon,' in which the noble bird is the central figure, and always a male. In a poem by William Morris bearing the same title the falcon is likewise unsexed.

From Scott, a lover of nature, a sportsman, and an antiquary, more chivalrous treatment was her due, but to him in *The Abbot, Ivanhoe*, and *Rob Roy* the falcon is ' he.'

Scott had, in common with Homer and with Shakespeare, an intense love of nature and of country life, a sentiment which is, according to him, a common feature of genius (*Life of Swift*). He was a sportsman, too, though less catholic in his tastes than Shakespeare. When, therefore, we find his goshawks soaring high and hovering, after the fashion of a long-winged falcon towering in her pride of place, and when we note that his ' falcons ' are often male, we need no further evidence that falconry was unknown in his day, and from this and other tokens we may learn that he was less attracted by the sports and pastimes of antiquity than by other features of those bygone times which he has reproduced with such life-like reality—a unique example of letters of an antiquary inspired by the creative genius of a poet.

CHAPTER VIII

CLASSICAL WRITERS AND THEIR IMITATORS

A CHAPTER of mediæval history devoted to the literature of field sport and horses ought not to leave unnoticed the writers of the classical age. In the literatures of Greece and of Rome we can trace the steps by which mankind ascended from the taking of wild animals for food to the stately ritual of *La Grande Chasse*, and from the subjection of the horse as a beast of burden to the elaborate exercises of *La Haute École*.

Moreover, there is a literature of the chase, once highly esteemed, but now forgotten, which forms a chain of many links, connecting the Augustan age with mediæval and sixteenth-century Latinists. It consists of treatises on hunting and falconry in hexameter verse, after the manner of the *Georgics* of Virgil. These efforts, some of which attained great popularity, and were often reprinted, edited with scholarly care, ought not to be overlooked in a review of the sporting literature of the age in which they were written. They conclude with a curious work by a professor in the University of Laon, who finds an equivalent in the Latin classics for every term of art in the woodcraft of his day, and weaves the whole into a treatise in very readable hexameters.

Virgil's *Georgics* contain no poem on the sports of the field; no such imposition had lightened the *haud mollia jussa* of Mæcenas. But he has left us in no doubt that they were dear to his heart, for they often revisited his memory and kindled his imagination, when in undying lines he tells the story of their birth.

Man's love of sport has been called a primeval instinct. This is not so. Primeval man was prompted by instinct to take and eat any animal suitable for food that came to hand. Further than this instinct did not go, and in the devising of methods by which animals that did not come to hand might be taken, we may discover the earliest exercise of reason, by which man is distinguished from other animals: for without some contrivance, due, not to instinct, but to reason, neither the beasts of the field nor the fowls of the air could have been brought to his larder.

It is difficult to draw a line of separation between the faculty to which we give the name of Reason and the sagacity and intelligence with which the higher orders of animals are endowed. But, without essaying the dangerous task of definition, certain acts of mankind may be reasonably placed on one side or the other of a rather indefinite line of demarcation.

The cave-man who first thought of digging a pit where he found tracks of passing deer, and of concealing it with boughs broken from trees, was a pioneer; and his delight when, on revisiting his pitfall, he found that it contained a hart in pride of grease, was, in a rudimentary form, an instance of the pleasure which the sportsman, as a reasoning being, enjoys in contemplating the success of some device that he has thought out.

Then came the invention of the bow with its arrows and ' bird bolts,' and long afterwards someone bethought him of calling in aid of the reasoning power of which he became conscious, the courage and sagacity of a creature that had attached itself to man for the sake of the crumbs that fell from his table, in the form of bones and offal of captured beasts. This great unknown was the true father of woodcraft, and in the record of his success which he painted on the wall of his cave the literature of field sport had its origin.

As the ages went on, and as the association between man and hound in the pursuit and killing of game became closer, the dog, from the humble follower, became the companion and friend of man. But from the eagerness of the hound in pursuit of the quarry the thought of the reward was never absent; and in the mediæval book of sport the *curée*, or reward of the hounds, is a subject of careful treatment; the *droit de limier*, the special reward of the liam hound, to whose harbouring of the hart the day's sport is due, being religiously observed.

Later on, the horse was admitted to a share in his master's enjoyment of the chase, and of the keen delight which it brought him no one can doubt who has witnessed the eager desire of a veteran to whose ears the cry of hounds, or the music of the horn, has brought back the memory of bygone gallops with the hounds. And into this ' most mutual entertainment ' of man and horse there enters no thought of reward at the finish.

We know from observation of living races that are still in an early stage of development that the wit of man was exercised in the taking of animals *feræ naturæ* before he conceived the idea of adding to his supply of fruits and herbs of the field by cultivation of the soil. Man excavated a pitfall before he digged a garden; and the persistence of a love of field sport in even the greatest, of whose soul it has once taken possession, is best understood when we bear in mind the story of its place in the development of the human race. Thus it was that Shakespeare was visited by irrelevant memories of Arden and of Cotswold when writing his greatest dramas, and Albert the Great, when instructing his pupil Thomas of Aquin, bethought him of youthful works on falconry and horsekeeping and introduced them into a philosophical treatise on natural history.

Virgil has told us the tale of the invention of the sports of the field.

There was a time when life was easy, for the earth, unasked, brought forth all that was needed for the use of man. But this ignoble ease, by the Father's decree, gave place to an age in which the wit of man was sharpened by anxious toil, in a struggle with the forces of nature, no longer friendly. Then it was that man found out the use of snares and bird-lime in the taking of beasts and birds; and with the aid of the dog enclosed the quarry within the limits of a toil:

Tum laqueis captare feras et fallere visco
Inventum, et magnos canibus circumdare saltus.

(*Georg.*, i., 139.)

No treatise on sport or horsemanship in Latin prose has come down to us from the classical age. If Rome had produced works comparable to the *Cynegeticus* or the *Hippike* of Xenophon, it is probable that they would have survived or that references to them would have been found in the writings of extant authors. Such knowledge as we possess of field sports among the Romans of the Augustan age is derived from the poets, and they would have been but scanty had not Virgil, including within the range of his genius everything of human interest, and inspired from his youth by a love of country life, given us the power of entering into the spirit of a solemn chase in the time of Augustus as fully as we can reproduce, from what has been written by Shakespeare, a royal chase when Elizabeth was queen.

The *Venator* of Horace had not advanced beyond the chase in which the stag, viewed by trusty hounds, is driven into toils which proved too fine to hold the Marsian boar; and yet this primitive sport had charm enough to lead the sportsman, mindless of domestic joys, to spend the night under a wintry sky:

> Manet sub Jove frigido
> Venator, teneræ conjugis immemor;
> Seu visa est catulis cerva fidelibus,
> Seu rupit teretes Marsus aper plagas.
>
> (HOR.: *Odes*, i., 1, 25.)

Horace is not in sympathy with his *Venator*. A man about town with literary tastes and ambitions, he cannot understand how a sensible man can forgo the comforts of his home for a pursuit which may end in failure at the moment when success seemed certain; such a man, however, should be noted as a type.

Horace gives us a picture of the town life of his time. Of country life he knew nothing beyond the bounds of his Sabine farm; and to him field sports were a useful part of manly education, not a source of enjoyment.*

Horses and hounds entered into the life of the Roman youth, in a certain sense. Terence's Simo speaks of them among the different pursuits to which the young men of his time might be devoted (*Andria*, i., 1, 30), and it would be easy to collect references of this kind from writings of the Augustan age. The populace of Rome understood by the word *venatio* the indiscriminate slaughter in the arena of beasts of venery and of prey, as part of the triumph of a successful general. No *noble arte of venerie* was known, and the word *venator* was degraded by its application to the slaughterer of beasts in the arena.

If field sport had played an important part in the life of the Augustan age we should find it occupying a corresponding place in literature. We should not expect to find much on the subject in the works of one eminent as a statesman, advocate, and philosopher; or in his correspondence with his friends. Cicero approves those who live in elegant refinement, *optimis coquis, pistoribus, piscatu, aucupio, venatione* (*De Finibus*, ii., 8), and he contrasts true liberality with lavish

---

* References to the chase may be found in the writings of Horace, but none of them betoken a sportsman's interest in the pursuit: *Odes*, iii., 11, 12; *Satires*, i., 2, 105; *Epistles*, i., 6, 57-61; *ibid*, 18, 39-52.

expenditure on the *venatio* of the arena (*ib.*, ii., 16), but the subject does not interest him.

When Cicero wrote of old age, his most comfortable words took the form of a discourse by Cato the Censor, spoken at the request of friends grateful for what he had already written, by which they were aided in bearing the burden of advancing years. This was the famous *De Re Rustica* of Cato (236-149 B.C.), in which there is no hint at enjoyment to be derived from any form of sport; the dog being to the Censor simply a watchdog, to be kept shut up all day (poor thing!), to be more watchful and keen at night (cap. cxxiv.).

Cicero, in his *Cato Major, de Senectute Liber*, advises a study of the works of Xenophon, for they treat of much that is of practical utility; and, particularly, his *Œconomicus*, which treats of everyday life, and in which much is said of the cultivation of the soil.

Xenophon, the friend of Socrates—famous as a general and as a historian—was the writer of two books of more account with sportsmen of the Middle Ages than with Cicero. His *Cynegeticus* is a practical treatise on the chase; especially on the hunting of the hare, with running hounds.

' The hare is the kynge of alle venery, for al blowyng and the fair termys of huntyng commen of the seckyng and fyndyng of the hare for certayn it is the merveiloist beest that is.' Of this opinion is Dame Juliana Bernes, and a yet older authority, Twici, counts among the marvels of the hare that she is at one time male and at another female, whereby the huntsman is embarrassed, for he cannot blow the 'menee' of it as of other beasts: and, later on, Gervais Markham could say, ' The hunting of the hare is every honest man's and good man's chase.'

Two thousand years after the death of Xenophon, who loved hare-hunting, we find his Book of Sport, to which an excellent translator, Mr. H. G. Dakyns, gives the appropriate title of *The Sportsman's Manual*, referred to as an authority by Jacques du Fouilloux, the author of a handbook of venery as famous in its day as Xenophon's in the golden age of Greece (*La Venerie et Fauconnerie*, p. 96, ed. 1585). Xenophon's treatise on the kindred subject of horsemanship was famous throughout the Middle Ages, and it was regarded as of sufficient permanent value to be included in an important work on horsemanship published in the year 1771 by Richard Berenger, Gentleman of the Horse to king George III.*

It is natural that Xenophon's *Cynegeticus* should have been unnoticed by Cicero, for polite society in the time of Augustus took no interest in the sports of the field, and this work, in the purest Attic prose, was written by a sportsman for sportsmen.

The hunting of the hare is the oldest kind of sport which had any claim to be called ' the noble art of venery,' and it has suffered little change in the course of more than two millenniums. The master of harriers of the twentieth century can read with interest Xenophon's account of the working of his hounds, and of their differing dispositions; ' the swift, the slow, the subtle'

* Note D: Greek Writers on the Chase.

(*Macbeth*, iii., 1, 96), and the overtopping hound by which

> We may outrun
> By violent swiftness that which we run at,
> And lose by overrunning.
>
> (*Henry VIII.*, i., 1, 141.)

and as he read of the many windings of the hunted hare, he would understand how they were the same in the eyes of a keen observer of the Periclean or of the Tudor age, and how it is that certain lines of *Venus and Adonis* read like a poetical version of Xenophon's words:

> By this poor Wat, far off upon a hill,
> Stands on his hinder legs with listening ear,
> To hearken if his foes pursue him still.*
>
> (*Venus and Adonis*, 697.)

His disappointment when he reads of the importance of the work of the net-keeper will be diminished when he finds it to be very much that of the earth-stopper in fox-hunting. His business is to fix the nets about such places as brooks, dry torrents; resort to which by the hare would prevent a good run. The finish is sometimes the taking of the hunted hare in a net, but what the master intends is a run in which he can enjoy the working of the hounds, calling them by their names, with such words of encouragement as ' to her, to her ' ('Ιὼ κύνες, ἰὼ καλῶς, σαφῶς γε ὦ κύνες, καλῶς γε ὦ κύνες—vi., 17).

Minute directions are given for the making of the fine nets used in hare-hunting; and when the author comes to treat of the capture of the wild

---

* Προλαμβάνοντες δὲ τὰς κύνας ἐφίστανται καὶ ἀνακαθίζοντες ἐπαίρουσιν αὑτοὺς καὶ ἐπακούουσιν, ἔι που πλήσιον κλαγγὴ ἢ ψόφος τῶν κυνῶν (*Cynegeticus*, v., 19).

boar, he describes a net of very different strength. If Horace's *Venator* had known his *Cynegeticus*, his sport would not have been spoiled by the escape of the Marsian boar which his hounds had succeeded in driving into toils which should have been used only in hunting the hare.

When Xenophon passes from hare-hunting to other pursuits, we feel that he has lost all interest in his work; but something must be said of other modes of taking wild beasts with the aid of hounds to justify the title given to his work.

Fawns may be run down and taken even without the help of hounds. Deer are to be coursed until they are brought within the range of the javelins with which they are despatched. In hot weather this can be done without the aid of the foot-trap, which seems to have been generally used. This gin, set in the run of the deer, had attached to it a wooden clog which the hunted deer dragged with it in its flight. Having told of this ignoble hunting, after a spirited description of the killing of the wild boar, driven into a toil, Xenophon discourses of the value of field sports in the training of youth in a manner worthy of a friend of Socrates.

To the sophists, whom he denounces, this was foolishness, as was the love of field sport and of horses which Albert the Great brought with him from the forests of Suabia to his lecture-room in Cologne to the sophists of scholasticism (*ante*, p. 34). The age of Xenophon had not much in common with the age of Albert, but we find in each a philosopher who did not disdain to be known as the writer of a book of sport.

Xenophon is at one with mediæval writers on field sports in awarding the highest place to the hunting of the hare.

This hunting fills twenty-eight pages of Mr. Dakyns's translation; twelve sufficing for the deer, the wild boar, ' lions, leopards, lynxes, panthers, bears, and all other such game as are to be captured in foreign countries.' They treat of the practical work of taking game for food, and of the killing of wild beasts for the protection of the farmer and his flocks. This was the *venatio* of the Latin classics. Youthful and adventurous countrymen took delight in this exercise, and townsmen approved, for it strengthened both mind and body; but it was devoid of the idea of woodcraft as understood by mediæval sportsmen. This idea had descended from Carolingian time upon the mixed peoples by whom what we now call France was inhabited, and it owed nothing to the ideas or the literature of Rome; Italian, indeed, is the only Romance language which has not produced a mediæval book of sport comparable with the famous French classics. How this came to be is pointed out on another page.

No surer proof of the indifference of the learned world of Rome to the sports of the field could be found than the silence of the satirists. If some historian in a future age would inquire of the sports and pastimes to which the youth of the Victorian period was devoted, he would find an answer in the numbers of *Punch ;* for the range of the writers and artists is as wide as that claimed for the satirist.

Quidquid agunt homines, votum, timor, ira, voluptas,
Gaudia, discursus, nostri est farrago libelli.
(JUVENAL: *Sat.*, i., 85.)

But no trace of real interest in sportsmen or
their pursuits can be found in the satires of Horace
or Juvenal.

Sallust, when he retired from public life, would
not spend his time in idleness or devote himself
to pursuits fit only for servants—agriculture and
hunting: ' neque vero, agrum colendo aut venando,
servilibus officiis intentum ætatem agere '; and so
he returned to a former design, from which he
had been unhappily diverted by ambition, of
writing of the history of Rome (*Bellum Catil.*).

It could not be expected that an occupation of
so little account should fill an important place
in the correspondence of men such as Cicero or
Pliny. There was, indeed, one among the correspondents of Cicero at whose hands an account
of the sports of the field might have been looked
for, and this was baulked.

Varro was the author of a famous work on
country life which was popular during the Middle
Ages (*ante*, p. 95). He writes of hares, and of
the *leporarium* in which they are confined
(*lib.* iii., cap. 10), and of the watchdog without
which no country house would be quite safe
(*lib.* i., cap. 21); but the idea of interest in the
exercise of intelligence in the chase by both
hare and hounds—which is of the essence of all
true sport—was strange to the Roman mind, to
which the words *aucupium* and *venatio* suggest
nothing beyond the capture or the killing of the
quarry.

Although we cannot give the name of 'sport,' as understood by Xenophon or Gaston Phœbus, to the Roman *venatio*, it was a manly exercise, accompanied, in the hunting of the bear or boar, with the degree of danger which endeared it to adventurous youth.

To Virgil the sports of the field were something more than a healthy exercise; to his power of poetic interpretation they were inspiration. 'It is not Linnæus,' Matthew Arnold writes (*Essays in Criticism*), 'who gives us the true sense of plants; who seizes their secret for us, who makes us participate in their life; it is Shakespeare with his

> Daffodils
> That come before the swallow dares, and take
> The winds of March with beauty.

> (*Winter's Tale*, iv., 4, 118.)

From Shakespeare we get the true sense of a hare hunt as Xenophon could never give it; and Virgil, by throwing around the hunting of his day ' the consecration and the poet's dream,' has let us into the secret of its influence on the poet's mind in a manner that would have been denied to Varro, had he condescended to introduce so humble a topic into a work intended to be presented to the best literary society in Rome.

Virgil, born into the class of yeoman farmers, drank in with his mother's milk a love of the country and of country pursuits. The preservation of his father's farm, threatened with seizure to satisfy the claims of veteran soldiers, was the object dearest to his heart, and it was effected through his influence.

In this he was aided by C. Asinius Pollio, governor of Cis-Alpine Gaul, a scholar and a poet, his intimate friend, to whom he dedicated his earliest eclogues. Pollio introduced Virgil to Octavian; and to his friendship was due, not only the restoration of his father's farm, but the inclusion of the poet in the literary circle which Mæcenas had gathered around him in his mansion on the Esquiline. The eclogue which he placed at the head of the collection is an expression of gratitude to Octavian; the god, for to him he would always be a god who had restored the beloved farm to its owner and saved it from desecration:

> Impius hæc tam culta novalia miles habebit ?
> Barbarus has segetes ?
>
> *(Ec.*, i., 70, 2.)

Pollio introduced to the great world of Rome, and to the literary society of which it was the centre, the youthful poet who was once foolish enough to think that the Rome of which he heard was another Mantua, grown larger indeed, but of the same kind as the goat is greater than the kid (*ib.*, 19).

Into this refined and artificial life Virgil came, and with him a sense of country life and of fresh breezes blown from the rich pastures washed by the winding Mincio. Mæcenas, whose patronage of letters was directed to serious ends, both as regarding the poets in whom he was interested and also affairs of state, with his rare insight into character saw in Virgil one who could be brought to aid the policy of Octavian of building the empire on the foundation of healthy rural life.

A true poet, and this he discerned in Virgil, whose ideal life was that of the yeoman farmer, might, if he were to endow this life and its pursuits with the charm of poetical associations, raise it to a higher level in popular estimation, and by enhancing its dignity add to its attractions.

The poet's dream had been a great work in which the glories of Augustus should be celebrated, not by hackneyed allusions to Grecian mythology, but in a truly national poem; one which would exalt its author above the crowd, and win for him far-reaching fame. To this he looked forward if life were granted for its accomplishment; but meanwhile he is bound to forests, haunted by Dryads and glades unmarked by human foot-print, by the task—no light one—imposed on him by Mæcenas.

> What makes a plenteous harvest, when to turn
> The fruitful soil, and when to sow the corn?
> The care of sheep, of oxen, and of kine,
> And how to raise on elms the teeming vine;
> The birth and genius of the frugal bee,
> I sing Mæcenas, and I sing to thee.
>
> (DRYDEN.)

Virgil's regret for the postponement of the great epic might have been lessened if Mæcenas' mandate had included a poem on the chase. Without him nothing lofty can be essayed.

> A time will come when my maturer muse
> In Cæsar's wars a nobler theme shall chuse;

but now,

> I brook no dull delay;
> Cithæron loudly calls me to my way;
> Thy hounds, Tayg'tus, open, and pursue their prey;

High Epidaurus urges on my speed,
Famed for his hills, and for his horses' breed:
From hills and dales the cheerful cries rebound;
For Echo hunts along, and propagates the sound.*

Virgil, like Shakespeare, had often noted the effect of echo in redoubling the cry of hounds. Theseus brings Hippolyta to the mountain-top to hear the music of the hounds, and—

> mark the musical confusion
> Of hounds and echo in conjunction.
> . . . for besides the groves,
> The skies, the fountains, every region near
> Seemed all one mutual cry: I never heard
> So musical a discord, such sweet thunder.
> (*Midsummer Night's Dream*, iv., 1, 115;
> cf. *Titus Andronicus*, ii., 3, 17.)

Awakened from idle dreams by the memory of this much-loved music, Virgil applied himself to the task that had been set him, and by the way he sings songs unbidden of the rural sports that were nearest to his heart.

The blessings of a country life, not quite realised by those to whose lot they had fallen, were told in what was to Tennyson ' the stateliest measure ever moulded by the lips of man.' There, a hunting country where the quarry could be found in the thicket and hunted through the glades, gave scope to the energy and hardihood of youth:

> illic saltus ac lustra ferarum.
> (*Georg.*, ii., 471.)

---

* Rumpe moras; vocat ingenti clamore Cithæron
Taygetique canes domitrixque Epidaurus equorum,
Et vox adsensu nemorum ingeminata remugit.
(*ib.*, iii., 43.)

Winter is an inactive time for the farmer, but snares may be set for birds (*ib.*, i., 271); this is time to set springs for cranes and to track the hare in snow: does may be stricken by bolts slung from the Balearic sling.

> Tum gruibus pedicas et retia ponere cervis,
> Auritosque sequi lepores; tum figere dammas
> Stupea torquentem Balearis verbera fundæ,
> Cum nix alta jacet.
>
> <div align="right">(<i>ib.</i>, 307.)</div>

Very different from sport like this is the slaughter of deer collected in a stupefied crowd under the weight of a Scythian snowdrift, above which the tips of their antlers are barely seen. No hounds are uncoupled, nor are the deer driven into toils by fear of fluttering crimson plumes, but as they press in vain against the opposing mass of snow the natives stab them with the sword, close at hand, regardless of their piteous cries, and bear them off in triumph, with loud acclamation (*ib.*, iii., 369-375).

To Varro the dog was useful in a country farm as a protection to the country house and to the shepherds' flocks: but there was yet another use for him:

> With cries of hounds, thou may'st pursue the fear
> Of flying hares, and chase the fallow deer,
> Rouse from their desert dens the bristled rage
> Of boars, and beamy stags in toils engage.
>
> (DRYDEN.)

The woodcraft of Xenophon and of *La Grande Chasse*, the employment of the hound hunting by scent in finding and chasing hare or deer, had no place in Roman life, but the sport of taking them in toils with the aid of trained hounds, though of little account with Roman society, was to a country-bred poet a manly rural pastime worthy of celebration in verse, and when the poet approached the work of his life, the realisation of his early dreams, a great national epic in which praise of Augustus should be raised from the level of personal adulation to glorification of the great empire of which he was the ruler, he brought with him the delights that had become part of his nature. But the hunting of the hart had, with the poet's art, suffered a change. From the countryman's recreation it had become the sport of kings; and an incident in the hunting-field was the turning-point in the fortunes of the unhappy Dido.

What was in later ages called a general hunting was proclaimed by Dido in honour of her guest.

> Venatum Æneas unaque miserrima Dido
> In nemus ire parant, ubi primos crastinus ortus,
> Extulerit Titan, radiisque retexerit orbem.
>
> (*Æneid*, iv., 117.)

To Virgil, as to Shakespeare, the chase suggests the glories of the dawn:

> I with the Morning's Love have oft made sport;
> And, like a forester, the groves may tread,
> Even till the eastern gate, all fiery red,
> Opening on Neptune with fair blessed beams,
> Turns into yellow gold his salt-green streams.
>
> (*Midsummer Night's Dream*, iii., 2, 389.)

At daybreak preparation for the chase began Youths selected for the task leave the city at the earliest dawn, when the deer will have left the thickets to feed in the open lawns. To prevent

17

their return to cover when chased by the hounds the glades must be enclosed and the forest passes stopped with encircling nets, in which at intervals bunches of bright feathers, fluttering in the breeze, deterred the startled deer from attempting to break through the nets:

> It portis iubare exorto delecta iuventus:
> Retia rara, plagæ, lato venabula ferro.
> (*Æneid*, iv., 130.)

Saturnia knew well what business was in hand,

> Dum trepidant alæ saltusque indagine cingunt,
> (*ib.*, 121.)

and she devised a scheme so transparent that Cytherea smiled.

The youths who carried the nets and hunting-spears are followed by the mounted sportsmen— the prickers of Elizabethan hunting—and a pack of hounds, keen of scent—

> Massylique ruunt equites, et odora canum vis.

The queen may remain in her bower until all preparations for the chase are complete. The nobles of both nations await her, with Iulus, in boyish delight, and her richly caparisoned steed impatiently champs the foaming bit. They are joined by Æneas, goodliest of all (*ib.*, 143-5).

> Like fair Apollo, when he leaves the frost
> Of wintry Xanthus, and the Lycian coast,
> When to his native Delos he resorts,
> Ordains the dances and renews the sports.
> (DRYDEN.)

Dido's attire is not suggestive of the hunting-field, but a golden quiver shows that she intends

to take part in the sport, and, like another royal
Elissa of happier fate,* to shoot the deer as they
are driven by her stand.

When the hunting-party have come to the tract-
less coverts on the hills they see wild goats dis-
lodged from the highest peaks running down the
rocks, and on the other side herds of deer, huddled
together and dusty in their flight, run over the
open country and leave the uplands.

> The glad Ascanius, as his courser guides,
> Spurs through the vale, and these and those outrides,
> His horse's flanks and sides are forced to feel
> The clanking lash, and goring of the steel.
> Impatiently he views the feeble prey,
> Wishing some nobler beast to cross his way,
> And rather would the tusky boar attend,
> Or see the tawny lion downward bend.
>
> (DRYDEN.)

The gathering thunderstorm which scattered the
hunting-party, and brought Dido with Æneas to
find refuge in the fateful cave, compels us to turn
from the story of their love if we would learn from
Virgil how a sportsman should bear himself in
the killing of the driven deer.

Here Virgil is at one with Shakespeare. The
true woodman strikes home and kills outright, for

> Mercy goes to kill,
> And shooting well is then accounted ill.
> Thus will I save my credit in the shoot;
> Not wounding, pity would not let me do't.
>
> (*Love's Labour's Lost*, iv., 1, 24.)

---

* Elizabeth on one day, at Cowdray, saw 'sixteen bucks
all having fayre lawe, pulled downe with greyhounds in a
launde or lawn' (*Nichols's Progresses*).

Virgil had deplored the agony of some woodland hind fatally wounded by a stray shot and trying in vain to be free of the deadly shaft, and he wrote of Dido:

> Qualis conjecta cerva sagitta,
> Quam procul incautam nemora inter Cresia fixit
> Pastor agens telis, liquitque volatile ferrum
> Nescius: illa fuga silvas saltusque peragrat
> Dictæos; hæret lateri letalis harundo.
>
> (*Æneid*, iv., 69-73.)

> The stricken deer go weep
> (*Hamlet*, iii., 2, 282),

so wrote a poet-sportsman of a later age who, with Virgil, was often moved to pity by the fate of the

> poor sequester'd stag
> That from the hunter's aim had ta'en a hurt,
> . . . and the big round tears
> Coursed one another down his innocent nose
> In piteous chase.
>
> (*As You Like It*, ii., 1-32.)

The pious Æneas had skill,

> Culling the principal of all the deer
> (3 *Henry VI.*, iii., 1, 4)

to lay low the antlered leaders of a herd,

> Ductoresque ipsos primum, capita alta ferentes
> Cornibus arboreis, sternit.
>
> (*Æneid*, i., 189.)

The well-directed and deadly aim of the pious Æneas differs widely from the rash and ineffective shooting of the young Ascanius on another day; and Juno, when she would frustrate the hope of a peaceful settlement of the storm-tossed Trojans

in the promised land, found in him an uncon-
scious ally.

His killing of the royal hart, *forma præstanti
et cornibus ingens*, tame and so obedient to his
mistress Sylvia, daughter to king Latinus' steward,
that he would stray through the forest by day
and never fail to return at night, is told in lines
of surpassing beauty.

While Ascanius was hunting along the coast, his
hounds hitting on a burning scent, the device of
the fury Allecto, inspired by Juno, chased the hart
to the river, and as he swam with the stream he
became an easy prey. Ascanius, fired by the
prospect of rare distinction (*eximiæ laudis suc-
census amore*) aimed at the hart. His feebly
directed shaft would have missed the mark had
not Allecto helped (*nec dextræ erranti deus afuit*),
and it had strength to wound but not to kill.
To his well-known shelter the much-loved hart—

> That from the hunter's aim had ta'en a hurt,
> Did come to languish, and . . .
> The wretched animal heaved forth such groans
> That their discharge did stretch his leathern coat
>   almost to bursting.
>
> (*As You Like It*, ii., 1-34.)

These words of one who had often deplored the
result of an unsportsmanlike shot may stand as
a version of Virgil's:

> Saucius at quadrupes nota intra tecta refugit,
> Successitque gemens stabulis, questuque cruentus
> Atque imploranti similis tectum omne replebat.
>
> (*Æneid*, vii., 500.)

In the sorrow of the gentle Sylvia and in the
wrath of her father's sturdy labourers to whom

she appealed, Allecto found fuel for the flame that she fanned into a widespread conflagration. In the wars that followed we lose sight of the boy-sportsman to find in Ascanius a noted warrior:

> Tum primum bello celerem intendisse sagittam
> Dicitur, ante feras solitus terrere fugaces,
> Ascanius.
>
> (*Æneid*, ix., 590.)

His successful valour is applauded by the Trojans, and Apollo, who chanced to witness the feat from the cloud on which he sat, addressed the victor in undying words (*ib.*, 641):

> macte nova virtute, puer; sic itur ad astra.

Strengthened in body and in mind by the exercises and lessons of the hunting-field, Ascanius took his place among the heroes of his race; and Mæcenas was taught that a poet could find in country life something that went to the building up of a healthy and war-like people which had escaped the notice of the learned and industrious Varro.

In Virgil's fourth *Eclogue* the coming is foretold of an infant of divine birth, who was to bring back to a labouring world the blessings of the golden age.

The early Christians saw in this a prophecy of the coming of Christ, and Virgil was honoured as a saint, endowed with prophetic insight. To Dante, he was the master by whom he was guided in his visit to the world beyond the grave. To the vulgar of the Middle Ages he was a magician, and marvellous tales were told of his skill. At the Renaissance we find his poems bearing a certain relation to field sports, when with the study of the ancient classics a literature came into being in which the glories of the chase were sung in Virgilian verse.

Meanwhile, Books of Sport were written in Greek and Latin hexameters. The first edition of the collected works of Latin poets on field sports was printed in Venice *in ædibus heredum Aldi Manutii*, 1534, under the title *Poetæ tres egregii nunc primum in lucem editi*. The three poets were Grattius Faliscus, M. Aurelius Olympius Nemesianus, and T. Calpurnius.

Grattius Faliscus was a contemporary of Ovid. His *Cynegeticon Liber* is thus referred to by him:

> Tityrus antiquas et erat qui pasceret herbas,
> Aptaque venanti Grattius arma dabat.

This is an apt description of his work, for his lines contain a full explanation of nets, plumes, and other accessories of the chase, in the form of poetry, but without its inspiration.

Nemesianus, according to *Smith's Classical Dictionary*, flourished at the court of the emperor Carus (A.D. 283), and carried off the prize in all the poetical contests of the day. He appears to have been the ' author of poems upon fishing, hunting, and aquatics; all of which have perished, with the exception of a fragment of the *Cynegetica*, extending to 325 hexameter lines, which, insofar as neatness and purity of expression are concerned, in some degree justifies the admiration of his contemporaries.' Admiration of Nemesianus was not limited to contemporaries. His *Cynegetica* was often reprinted, usually with the poem of Calpurnius, and sometimes with learned and elaborate notes. It was translated into French, and a rendering into that language, in verse, appeared in 1849 (Souhart).

Oppianus, who wrote a treatise on hunting in Greek hexameter verse about the year 206, succeeded in pleasing classical scholars during many centuries. J. C. Scalinger is quoted for a comparison of Oppian with Virgil in the elegance and harmony of his style. His *Cynegetica*, with another poem, the authorship of which is uncertain, was greatly esteemed by continental scholars. Nineteen editions are noted by Souhart. They were translated into French and Italian, and edited with the carefulness usually reserved for writers of the golden age. Another poet of the same name, of earlier date, who wrote on a kindred subject in Greek hexameters, has sometimes been mistaken for this writer.

After a silence of more than twelve centuries we again meet with writers on the chase, in Latin hexameter verse. But they are not the successors of the silver age, nor is the sport of which they write the *aucupium* and *venatio* of the Roman empire.

The woodcraft of the Middle Ages was the creation of the barbarians by whom the Roman empire was overthrown, and in the time of Charlemagne and the Frankish kings of the Carolingian dynasty the chase became one of the principal institutions in the state. The kings of the house of Capet and the dukes of Normandy were devoted to the hunting of the red deer, a kind of sport which, with its laws and observances of almost religious obligation, became in time *La Grande Chasse* of the great French classics of the fourteenth century.

Meanwhile, a kind of sport unknown to classical antiquity had been introduced into Italy, and speedily became popular throughout Christendom. The emperor Frederick I., known as Barbarossa, is said to have introduced falconry into Italy from the East, and famous treatises on the sport were written: one by his grandson, Frederick II., and another by Albert the Great. As the sport was not of native origin these early works were written, not in the vernacular, but in Latin (chap. vii.).

The great movement of the fifteenth century to which we give the name of the Renaissance, brought, with an understanding and love of the ancient classics, a real danger to the vulgar tongues of Europe, now capable of literary expression in prose and in verse. ' There were some who despaired of the French language altogether, who thought it naturally incapable of the fulness and elegance of Greek and Latin—*cette élégance et copie qui est en la langue Grecque et Romaine*— that science could be adequately discussed, and poetry nobly written, only in the dead languages ' (*The Renaissance*, by Walter Pater.-Joachim du Bellay). Happily the battle was won by those who would have the spirit of the great writers of Greece and Rome embodied in the language understanded of the people; and Milton wrote *Paradise Lost* in the vulgar tongue.

The literature of the chase had attained sufficient importance to be involved in this struggle. Francis I. of France, from his devotion to the chase and also to letters, has been well called the king of the Renaissance. Guillaume Budé, a famous humanist, better known by his Latinised name Budæus, ' beyond question the best Greek scholar of his day in Europe,' after spending three years in the University of Orleans, is accused of losing time, ' for he spent his days in hunting and in the pleasures of youth' (Bayle). He had an influence with the king, to whose court he was attached for many years, which he exerted in the interests of the new learning. His *Traitté de la Vénerie*, written in the form of a dialogue between Francis and the author, was the response to a challenge addressed to Budæus as ' *protecteur tant de la langue Latine que de la Grecque sa parente,*' in which he was invited to show that the Latin tongue is suitable for use by sportsmen who would speak of the mysteries of woodcraft. How far Budæus was successful in the main object of his work it is impossible to say, for the original is now lost, and his work survives in a translation made at the instance of another king of France, Charles IX., when he was collecting materials for his treatise on stag-hunting: it was a time when kings took pride in the association of their names with Books of Sport.

If the humanists of the early years of the sixteenth century had any serious thought of founding a literature of the chase written in Latin prose it came to naught, and men wrote of field sports and of horses in the vulgar tongues of the European countries. With Latin verse the result was different, and the sixteenth century saw the birth and death of a literature of which the subject-matter was supplied by the barbarian and the form by Virgil. The offspring of a union so unnatural could not be long-lived, and versifiers are now forgotten whose poems, carefully annotated, went through many editions.

' The glory of the Renaissance was marred by a spirit of imitation, and the century after the deaths of Petrarch and Bocace was filled with a crowd of Latin imitators, who decently repose on our shelves ' (Gibbon, chap. lxvi.). A considerable space on these shelves is filled with poems on hunting and on falconry written in discipleship to Virgil.

In 1551 a small book, entitled *Natalis Comitum Veneti De Venatione, Libri* IIII. *Hieronymi scholiis brevissimis illustrati,* was published by *Aldi Filii* at Venice; the estimation in which the poem was held is shown by the facts that it was edited with scholarly care, and that fifteen editions of the author's works of which it formed part appeared between from 1551 and 1553 (Souhart).

Jacques du Fouilloux in his *La Vénerie* includes among ancient and modern writers on the chase in the Latin language *Le Pape Adrian Sixiesme* (96 *f.*, v. ed. 1585), and in a volume printed in Frankfort in 1582 we find among various poems on the chase and falconry *Hadriani Cardinalis s. Chrysogoni, qui deinde Pontifex Maximus factus est, carmen elegans de Venatione Aulica.*

The mediæval writers on field sports include kings, poets, and philosophers, but no pope.

' Hadrian, cardinal priest of the title of Chrysogonus,' was, according to Bayle, ' a native of

Cornetto in Tuscany. . . . This cardinal's life was a scene of odd changes the end whereof was far from being honourable. He narrowly escaped on the day on which Alexander VI. poisoned himself by a mistake.' Getting into trouble with Julius II. and afterwards with Leo X., ' he made his escape by night, and it was never certainly known what became of him.' He certainly did not find his way to the Vatican; and by a curious mistake the *De Venatione* of this somewhat erratic priest was attributed to another cardinal of the same name but of different character and tastes, Adrian VI. (1522-1523). Jacques du Fouilloux cared little for succession to the popedom; also an error which would not have been possible in the days of Gaston de Foix was not apparent to the eyes of a writer in the year 1582, in a city so far removed from Rome as Frankfort.*

The most distinguished of the contributors to this literature was the historian who wrote under the name Thuanus a poem in Latin hexameters entitled *Hieracoscophion, sive De Re Accipitraria, Libri* III. The author, Jacques Auguste de Thou, was born in Paris in 1553, and attained the position of president of the parliament and privy councillor to Henry III. and Henry IV., kings of France. His history of his own times—1546-1608 —was highly esteemed by Voltaire, who ranks him with Hume, and Dr. Johnson thought so highly of his work that in his seventy-seventh

---

* *Venatio et Aucupium: Iconibus artificiosis ad vivum expressa, et suscinctis versibus illustrata.* Frankfort, 1582. One of the poets is Hadrian, Cardinal, *qui deinde Pontifex Max. factus est.*

year 'he seriously entertained the thought of translating "Thuanus." He often talked with me on the subject' (*Life of Johnson*, æt. 76). The *Hieracoscophion* was often reprinted—in 1735 in quarto with an Italian translation in parallel columns with the Latin original.

The *De Aucupio* of Pietrus Angeli ' da Barga,' commonly called ' Il Bargeo,' described as public professor in Pisa, was ' happily rendered in Italian verse, and annotated by Professor Gio. Pietro Bergantini of the Academy of Pisa' (Harting), and the *Cynegetica* of the same author was famous in its day. But these scholarly endeavours to apply Virgilian verse to the uses of mediæval sport may now be allowed to repose on the shelf to which they are consigned by Gibbon.

NOTE A

The Tournament in Froissart and in Scott

The reader whose idea of a tournament is that of the gentle and joyous passage of arms of Ashby, will read with some disappointment Froissart's tale of the famous ' deeds of arms at St. Ingilbert, continuing thirty days, against all comers of the realm of England and other countries, every man three courses' (vol. iv., pp. 109-121).

The memorable field of Ashby de la Zouche was ' one of the most gallantly contested tournaments of that age, for although only four knights including one who was smothered by the heat of his armour, had died upon the field, yet upwards of thirty were desperately wounded, four or five of whom never recovered. Several more were disabled for life; and those who escaped best carried the marks of the conflict with them to the grave '; the victor was conducted to the foot of prince John's throne, ' through a field slippery with blood, and encumbered with broken armour and the bodies of slain and wounded horses' (*Ivanhoe*).

The tournament at Ashby was over in two days. At St. Inglebert after four days the English knights ' and all other knights that had jousted in the course of those four days with the French knights thanked them kindly for their pastime,' and left the three knights in the field, where they remained until the thirty days were completed.

Each course during the four days for which the jousts continued is recorded with the careful accuracy of the reporter at a test cricket match : spears were broken, knights were unhelmed and compelled to leave the field, but no serious accident occurred, and it is evident that none was expected. One ' Sir Boucequant was unhelmed with such violence that the blood ran out at his nose, and so he returned to his pavilion, and ran no more that day, for it was near night.' In another course the knights met together with such force that they ' were in danger of receiving some injury, but they passed by and came to their places.' Of another it is said 'this was a good and dangerous course, but the combatants received no injury; their spears broke close to their hands, and the heads still stuck in their shields; every man feared they had been hurt.' A course between a noble knight of Hainault, ' brought up in the court of the noble King Edward of England ' and a French knight ' was run so furiously that it was a wonder they escaped unhurt,' but so it was.

Scott, poet and antiquarian, was able to give vitality and reality to his presentation of the events and the ideas of bygone ages, and his story of the tournament of Ashby is as true to life as the chronicler's report of the deeds of arms at St. Inglebert. At the time of Richard's return to England and for many years after, in the words of M. Jusserand, *La seule différence avec la vraie guerre était qu'on se battait sans haine et que la lutte ne se terminait pas par des cessions de provinces.**

At a famous tournament at Neuss, near Cologne, in the year 1249, sixty knights were killed. Popes and monarchs endeavoured in vain. The savagery of this pastime called down ' countless prohibitions of popes and kings.'†

The passion for this barbarous pastime was indulged, notwithstanding all efforts to suppress it. *Le goût pour ces jeux était trop puissant ; c'était une vraie passion, un de ces états d'âme ou tout sentiment de règle, d'obligation morale, de danger disparaît* (Jusserand).

By degrees the tournament gave way to the joust and passage of arms, the result of advancing civilisation with a consequent regard for human life and suffering. The joust, a conflict between two mounted combatants who, carrying lances, encountered each other at full gallop, was the counterpart of the duel, as the tournament was of the battle. By the violence of the ' shock ' lances were broken, knights were unhelmed, and sometimes unhorsed, but more serious injuries were probably rarer than in the modern steeplechase.

The joust grew in popularity, *malgré le dedain des anciens tournoyeurs pour les ' plaideries.'* The jousts

---

* *Les Sports et Jeux d'Exercice dans l'Ancienne France,* by J. J. Jusserand.

† *History of the Tournament in England and in France,* by Francis Henry Cripps-Day.

were an important part of the celebration of events of public interest, such as coronations, royal marriages, and entries into capital cities. At the meeting of Henry VIII. of England and Francis I. of France at the Field of the Cloth of Gold, the kings rode with distinction in the lists.

The tragic death of Henry II. of France, following a fatal misadventure at the entrance into Paris of Francis I., brought upon the jousts the disfavour that had proved fatal to the tournament. But it died hard. *Le vieux Pluvinel, modèle des ecuyers, déplore, a chaque page du beau traité qu'il ecrivit pour son maître, le jeune roi Louis XIII., l'adoucissement des mœurs et la perte des anciens usages* (Jusserand).

A sport or pastime which is not altogether without danger has a special attraction for adventurous youth. The jousts were a means of displaying skill in horsemanship in a scene associated with chivalry and romance. Sir Philip Sidney, among whose many accomplishments was skill in horsemanship, tells how he carried off the prize at the jousts:

> Having this day, my horse, my hand, my lance,
> Guided so well, that I obtained the prize,
> Both by the judgement of the English eyes,
> And of some sent by that sweet enemie, France.
>
> (*Astrophel and Stella*.)

The jousts as a display of horsemanship were succeeded by the exercises of the *manège*, and as public entertainments by the *carousel*, of which illustrations are given in M. Perrault's *Courses de Testes et de Bague, faites par le Roy et par les princes et Seigneurs de sa Cour en l'année*, 1662; but old-world masters of horsemanship and of the joust looked back with regret on the more robust pastimes of their early days.

Pluvinel's famous work, published in 1623, is in the form of instruction given to his master, the young king, Louis XIII. Although he instructs his pupil in the exercises of the jousts, this was then a moribund art. In the fine illustrations by Crispin de Pas, which render the volume a treasure to the collector, we can realise the pastime of the jousts, and also the exercises of the *manège* by which they were succeeded.

The passage of arms—*pas d'armes*—as described by

M. Jusserand, approached more nearly to a warlike game than the tournament or the joust. It matters nothing by what name a production of nature or of art is called. If Scott could have had the guidance of M. Jusserand, of which he would have gladly availed himself, he would not have called the tournament of Ashby a passage of arms. What really matters is that he was at pains by the study of contemporary writers to get at the reality of things. To ' the delightful pages of the gallant Froissart, although he flourished at a period so much more remote from the date of my history ' than some obscure chroniclers, Scott, like Gibbon, did ' gladly fly for relief.' But the fascination of Froissart did not blind him to the fact that the feat of arms at St. Inglebert differed widely from the tournament of some three centuries earlier, and so it came to pass that Scott's tournament and Froissart's jousts are each equally true to the time of which the account was written.

No better proof could be given of the *entente* between the chivalry of England and their ' sweet enemies ' of France than the international combats in which, during the Hundred Years' War, they delighted, in times of truce. One of these deeds of arms was done ' at Bordeaux, before the duke of Lancaster, by five Englishmen of his own house, and five Frenchmen . . . their arms were three courses with a spear, three strokes with a sword, three with an axe, and three with a dagger, and all on horseback: and this they did in three days, and none of all ten hurt ' (vol. iv., p. 41). Even in the midst of active operations of war, the leaders looked on with pleasure at a joust between a squire of France and an English squire, who accepted his challenge to joust with him (vol. ii., p. 338).

Very different from ceremonial and friendly jousts was the ' jousting at utterance ' held under an order of the *parlement* of Paris, the supreme court of judicature, for the determination of a plea by wager of battle.

Froissart never approached more nearly to Herodotus in ' simplicity, liveliness, and power over the heart ' (*ante*, p. 105), than when he told the story of the lady of Carogne and the vindication of her honour, in the presence of the king and barons and knights of France and other countries (vol. iii., pp. 339-344).

A squire called Jacques le Gris and a knight called John of Carogne were both of the land and household of the

18

earl Peter of Alençon, and well beloved by their lord.
Sir John, when he carried out a long-intended enterprise
and went over the sea for the advancement of his honour,
left his wife in charge of his castle. The squire, Jacques,
took advantage of the knight's absence: he rode over to
his castle, where he was hospitably entertained. The
servants made him good cheer, because their master
and he were companions together, and the lady suspect-
ing no harm in him, received him kindly, leading him
into her chamber, and informing him of some of her
affairs. The squire ' desired the lady to allow him to
see the dungeon, for he said that one chief reason of his
coming was to see that. The lady readily granted him
his desire; and so she and he went thither alone, for the
lady had no suspicion of his having a design against her
honour.' The squire, having shut the door by which
they had entered, had the lady at his mercy, and carried
out his purpose by violence. The lady added to her bitter
reproach these words, ' the blame shall not rest on me,
but on you, if God permits my husband to return.'

The lady told no one until her husband's return. The
knight could not at first believe her lamentable tale;
' but the lady said so much as induced him to credit it;
and he said: " Certainly, lady, since the matter is so as
you shew me, I pardon you; but the squire shall die for
his deed, by the advice and counsel of my friends and
yours: and if your words be found untrue, you shall never
come into my company." '

The friends of husband and wife, assembled in his castle
of Argenteuil, advised the knight to go to his lord, the
earl of Alençon, and show him all the matter: and so he
did. The earl appointed a day for the parties to appear
before him, with the lady who had impeached Jacques
le Gris. She attended ' with a great number of her
lineage: so the pleading was great and long in the earl's
presence.'

The squire ' proved by them of the house of the earl of
Alençon, that on the same day at four o'clock in the
morning he was seen there in his master's castle; and his
master said and affirmed that at nine o'clock he was with
him at his up-rising, wherefore the earl said it was not
possible for him to go and come a distance of twenty-
three leagues and to do that deed in four hours and a half;
wherefore the earl said to the lady that she did but dream

it; wherefore he would maintain his squire, and commanded the lady to speak no more of the matter: but the
knight, who was of great courage, and well trusted and
believed his wife, would not agree to that opinion, but so
went to Paris and stated the matter there before the
parliament, and there appealed Jacques le Gris, who
appeared and answered to his appeal, and there laid in
pledges to accomplish the ordinance of the parliament.'

The affair had gained great publicity, wherewith
the earl of Alençon was much displeased with the poor
knight, and oftentimes could have had him slain, but
that the matter was in the parliament.' The plea continued more than a year and a half, and ' so long their
plea endured that the parliament determined, because the
lady could bring no proof against Jacques le Gris but her
own assertions, that there should be battle at utterance
between them.'

We can well understand how it was that the *parlement* failed to come to a conclusion on the plea. The
earl's statement that Jacques was with him at his up-
rising was, no doubt, true; but that he had been seen in
the castle at four o'clock was ' proved by them of the
house of the earl,' who was prepared to go any length in
maintaining the cause of his favourite squire, and some
sage and experienced member may well have advised the
parlement of the certain result in a conflict between regard
for truth and fear of the disfavour of a merciless lord and
master. It does not appear that the lady's servants testified to the presence of the squire at the castle of Argenteuil;
but any evidence given by the lady's servants might
fairly be set off against the statement of the household
of the earl, and so the knight and his wife and the squire
being present, ' judgment was given that on the following
Monday mortal battle should take place between the
knight and the squire.'

Trial by battle in which, it was believed, God was the
judge remained part of the judicial system of France,
notwithstanding the attempt of Saint Louis to abolish it.
' That incomparable prince, unable to overthrow the
judicial combat, confined himself to discourage it by the
example of a wiser jurisprudence. It was abolished
throughout the royal domains ' (Hallam, *Middle Ages*,
chap. ii., pt. ii.). In the year 1387, like the sanguinary
tournament of an earlier age, it was moribund; and the

king and great lords of France ' had a great desire to see that battle.' So by command of the king the battle was postponed until his arrival in Paris with his uncles and the constable of France.

The crowd of people at the place where the lists were made were so great that it was marvellous to behold: ' and on the one side of the lists there were made great scaffolds, that the lords might the better see the battle of the two champions.'

We do not read of seats being provided from which ladies and damosels might witness a judicial combat in which the honour of a lady and the life of her champion were at stake, from which we may conclude that enjoyment by them of scenes of this kind is of later date than the age of chivalry.

On the appointed day each of them, John of Carogne, supported by the earl of St. Poule, and Jacques le Gris, accompanied by the earl of Alençon, were each seated in a chair. The lady ' was there sitting in a chair, covered with black . . . much dejected, for her own life was in great danger: for, according to the sentence that had been passed, if her husband should have been discomfited, she was judged to be burnt, and her husband hanged.'

When the knight entered the field he said to his wife, ' Dame, by your information, and in your cause, I do put my life in adventure, in fighting with Jacques le Gris: you know whether the cause be just and true.' ' Sir,' said the lady, ' it is as I have said: wherefore you may fight with confidence, the cause is good and true.' With those words the knight kissed the lady, and took her by the hand, and then blessed himself, and entered into the field, while the lady sat still in humble prayer that the victory should be sent to her husband, according to the justice of the cause he was engaged in.

The tale of the combat is shortly told. The champions jousted on horseback, but neither of them received any injury: and after the jousts, they alighted from their horses to perform their battle, when after a valiant fight the knight slew his adversary on the field. The king called for the victor; awarded him one thousand franks, ' and retained him to be of his chamber, with a pension of two hundred pounds a year during the term of his life,' and the knight and his wife did not forget a grateful offering in the church of Our Lady in Paris.

NOTE B

THE CAPTAL DE BUCHE

' JOHN, captal of Buch, was the chief of the Savoyard family of Grilly, or Graïlly, which settled down in the Landes of Bordeaux to produce the Gascon family of the Graïllys, whose chief, the captal de Buch of Edward III.'s reign, was by far the most eminent among the Gascon generals in that king's service ' (*France and England : Their Relations in the Middle Ages and Now*, by T. F. Tout, p. 91). The title of captal appears to have been originally equivalent to that of count, ' and ‚marked even superiority, as the word " *capitalis* " announces principal chief. . . . Towards the end of the fourteenth century, there were no more than two captals acknowledged, that of Buch and that of Franc.' (Note to Johnes's *Froissart*, quoting *Gloss., du cange, ad verb., ' capitalis.'*)

The captal de Buche of Froissart stood so high in the estimation of Edward III. that we find his name enrolled among the original members of the noble order of the Garter in the year 1344. At the battle of Poitiers, in 1356, he distinguished himself, taking prisoner James de Bourbon, whose ransom was fixed at 25,000 florins. In 1357 he embarked with the Black Prince and took part in the triumphal entry into London. You may read in the *Globe* edition of *Froissart* of his taking part with Gaston in his expedition with the Teutonic knights, and in the overthrow of the Jacquerie (p. 138) ; and also of the manner in which he was captured by the French in the battle of Cocherel (p. 147). The lords of France were a long time in council. The Gascon enemies of the captal said to them, ' Sirs, we know well that the captal is as worthy a knight as can be found in any land, for as long as he is able to fight, he shall do us great damage. Let us ordain thirty a-horseback of the best men of arms that be in our company, and let the thirty take heed to nothing but to address themselves to the captal. . . . They took heed to nothing else but to the executing of the enterprise that they had in charge ; so all together came upon the captal, whereas he was fighting with a great axe in his hand and gave therewith so great strokes that none durst approach near him, but these thirty by force of their horses brake the press, and came on the captal and by clean force they took him ' (p. 150).

It is to be regretted that the needful work of abridgment has deprived the reader of the *Globe* edition of the remainder of Froissart's account of the captal, for it is deserving of note by the student of the age. Peace was shortly afterwards concluded between ' the French king and the king of Navarre, by the aid and wisdom of the lord captal de Buche, who did all that he could to conclude that peace, and thereby he was liberated from prison; and, indeed, the French king showed him many great tokens of love '; one of which might have led to a breach with England. The French king gave the captal the good castle of Nemours, with ample revenue, ' and so the captal became liege-man to the French king whose homage was received by the king with great joy, for he loved well the service of such a knight as the captal was in his time; but that service endured no great length of time.' He went to the Black Prince, his feudal lord, and informed him of the case as it stood. The prince blamed him for accepting lands in France, saying that ' he could not acquit himself truly in serving two lords.' When the captal realised the position ' and how much he had offended the prince, his natural lord . . . he renounced all that the king had given him; and he himself remained still with the prince, for he was acquitted of his imprisonment by the composition of the peace made between the French king and the king of Navarre ' (vol. i., p. 541).

' Sir John de Greilly, captal de Buche, constable of Aquitaine,'—so he is styled by Froissart—was taken prisoner again, fighting before Soubise against the French for his natural lord, and this capture was a fair one. ' There advanced forth a hardy squire of Vernandois called Peter Danvilliers, and he approached so near to the captal de Buche that he took him prisoner by feat of arms; which captal was then the knight who of all others, either of England or Gascony, that the French king and his subjects were most anxious to take, because he was a good captain and a valiant man ' (vol. ii., p. 112).

After this battle a ' treaty was agreed unto, and then the knights of France returned to Paris, and thither was brought the captal de Buche, and put in prison under safe custody, in a tower in the temple; and the king, who was much pleased at his being taken, caused twelve thousand franks to be delivered to the squire who took him.'

King Edward and the Black Prince were not forgetful of the captal. ' There was much intercession made for his release at the council at Bruges, and there were offered for him in exchange the young earl of St. Poule and three or four other knights; but the French king and his council would not agree thereto; however, the king caused him to be informed by the prior who had him under his charge, that if he would swear never to bear arms against the crown of France, that then he would condescend to his deliverance. The captal answered that he would never make such an oath even though he should remain a prisoner all his life: so he continued in prison under a strict guard for the space of five years, with but little comfort, for he possessed but little patience to bear his imprisonment: and so long did he remain in captivity that at last he died in prison. The French king caused him to be interred with great solemnity, and there were many barons, knights, and prelates of France who attended his funeral' (*ib.*, p. 162).

The captal de Buche became the founder of the second line of the Foix dynasty, for he married Isabelle de Castelbon, the cousin-german and only surviving relation of Gaston de Foix (*Master of Game*, xxxi.). It may be association with Froissart's Gaston that won for the sixteenth century Gaston de Foix, who fell in command of the French in the battle of Ravenna at the age of sixteen, inclusion in a famous passage of *Coningsby*, among more noteworthy instances of the truth that ' genius when young is divine.'

Froissart's sketch of the captal de Buche does not rest in the memory like his finished portrait of Gaston, for it is to be found in fragmentary notices scattered through many chapters, but when collected they enable us to realise the character of a great mediæval nobleman—strong, brave, and loyal even unto death—a worthy knight of the most noble order of the Garter; and at his funeral the king and nobles of France acted in the same spirit of courtesy as was displayed, by English and French, after the battle of Poitiers.

NOTE C

Chivalry in Froissart

IT must be remembered that, in the words of Freeman, ' the chivalrous spirit is above all things a class spirit. The good knight is above all bound to courtesy towards men, and more towards women, of a certain rank: he may treat all below that rank with any degree of scorn and cruelty' (*Norman Conquest*, vol. v., chap. xxiv.).

The truth of this statement is often borne in upon the student of Froissart: he there finds a defeated army divided by the conqueror into two classes—those who can pay and those who cannot: the latter are mercilessly butchered, and the former courteously ransomed.

When through some mischance prisoners were killed who were ready to come to ransom, the loss was deplored; not so much of the lives as of the ransom. At the battle of Aljubarrota the victorious Portuguese under king John I. had taken as prisoners a number of ' lords, knights, and squires '; when, under the belief that the king of Castile was coming up with a great army, and that ' it was better to slay than to be slain,' orders were given to kill the prisoners. ' Lo, behold the great evil adventure that fell that Saturday, for they slew as many good prisoners as would well have been worth, one with another, four hundred thousand franks ' (p. 349). In the battle of Poitiers many who would have come to ransom were sacrificed—earls, knights, and squires—for the arrows of the English yeomen were no respecters of persons, and ' the archers shot so wholly together that none durst come in their dangers: they slew many a man that could not come to ransom ' (p. 126).

That mercy should be shown to a conquered foe who was under the degree of knight or unable to come to ransom, was no part of the code of chivalry. Gaston Phœbus and his kinsman, the captal of Buch, did a gallant act when, on their return from aiding the Teutonic knights in their warfare against the heathens of Prussia, they turned aside to rescue ' the duchess of Normandy, and the duchess of Orleans, and a three hundred other ladies and damosels, and the duke of Orleans also,' who had taken refuge in a strong place of the city of Meaux from the fury of the Jaquery.   Gaston and the captal had with them but threescore lances, but they were men of war well apparelled, while the Jaquery, numbering over nine thousand, were ' without any armour saving with staves and knives.'

These two knights and their company ' with the earl of Foix's banner and the duke of Orleans,' and the captal's pennon made a gallant show as they galloped through the town and ' entered in among their enemies and beat them down by heaps and slew them like beasts, and chased them all out of the town.'   Thus the rescue was made good; and a massacre followed of enemies not one of whom had means to come to ransom.   ' Briefly, that day they slew of them more than seven thousand, and none had scaped, if they would a followed the chase any farther ' (p. 138).

The Black Prince ' was the chief flower of chivalry of all the world ' (p. 177), and the measure meted out by him to the city of Limoges was in accordance with the law of war.   The city had turned French, and the prince was enraged by the conduct of the rulers, and especially of the bishop, ' who was his gossip.'   He sat down before the city, and in the end it was mined and taken by storm (p. 201).

Froissart was moved to pity for the unoffending inhabitants—' men, women, and children, that kneeled down on their knees before the prince for mercy,' but in vain, ' for more than three thousand men, women, and children were slain and beheaded that day.   God have mercy on their souls, for I trow they were martyrs.'

' Now let us speak of the knights that were within the city; as sir John of Villemur, sir Hugh de la Roche, Roger Beaufort, son to the earl of Beaufort, captains of the city.'

The captains of the city and the bishop, who had caused the defection of the city, met with a different fate.   The bishop was delivered to the duke of Lancaster, to do with him at his pleasure.   ' Then the pope with sweet words entreated the duke of Lancaster to deliver to him the said bishop.   The duke would not deny the pope, but granted him and sent him to Avignon, whereof the pope was right glad.'

The knights found salvation in the spirit of chivalry, as the bishop through religion, both characteristic of the Middle Ages.   Time did not permit of the formal admission of Roger Beaufort to knighthood, but he was dealt with as one of the order, and ' they assembled them together in a place against an old wall and there displayed their banners.'

Then followed knightly combats: ' The duke of Lancaster himself fought long hand to hand against sir John Villemur, who was a strong knight and a hardy, and the earl of Cambridge fought against sir Hugh de la Roche, and the earl of Pembroke against Roger Beaufort, who was as then but a squire. These three Frenchmen did many feats of arms: their men were occupied otherwise. The prince in his chariot came by them and appeased himself in beholding of them.'

The appeasing of the prince went no further than the receiving as prisoners of the three noble knights who had delighted him with ' many feats of arms ' before yielding their swords to their conquerors: and the unoffending citizens, unprotected by chivalry or religion, were put to the sword.

The chivalry of which the Black Prince was the brightest ornament, with its merits and its defaults, is a memory of the past; but the name survives in the higher sense of ' the brave, honourable, and courteous character attributed to the ideal knight ' (*New English Dictionary*), and in this sense, as Scott tells us (*Essay on Chivalry*), it is regardless of rank or position in society.

The mediæval knight too often fought for gain, not glory, and peoples as well as individuals acted as they were prompted by a prospect of gaining wealth by ransom. The Gascons, Froissart tells us, ' still love the English better than the French; and the chief reason for this is, because the war against France was more profitable to them than that against England.' The lord d'Albret, when asked how he liked to be French, spoke with regret of the good times when he and his men ' always found some rich merchant, either of Toulouse, Condon, or Bergerac; there was scarcely a day passed but we got some rich booty. Then we were brisk and jovial, and now we are in a manner dead ' (vol. iii., p. 212).

When we read of a knight of the Garter entering the service of the king of Navarre when he was not required to fight for England, we realise the stain which the mercenary spirit of the fourteenth century casts upon the chivalry which shone so brightly when regarded from afar.

NOTE D

Greek Writers on the Chase

THE Latin writers on the chase approached nearer in time to the Middle Ages than those of the great age of Grecian literature, but in spirit they were further apart. In the heroic age of Greece we now and then find some suggestion of ideas that afterwards found a place in chivalry and in *La Grande Chasse*. Homer has been accused—with Shakespeare—of indifference to the dog; in either case the charge is unfounded. In the wrath of Achilles, and in the battles in which Olympians took part, there was no place for the dog. But when he brought his heroes to everyday life, Homer had not got very far when the lover of the dog as the friend and companion of man stands revealed : and in his picture of the noblest form of sport known to the ancient world we see the hounds tracking a scent, and 'goodly Odysseus followed close on the hounds, swaying a long spear.'

When the wise Telemachus went to the assembly of the Achæans, ' holding in his hand a spear of bronze, not alone he went, for two swift hounds bare him company. Then Athene shed on him a wondrous grace, and all the people marvelled at him as he came ' (p. 16).*

Athene, ' in the semblance of a woman, fair and tall, stood over against the doorway of the hut of Eumæus, the faithful swineherd, and Telemachus saw her not before him and marked her not; for the gods in no wise appear visibly to all. But Odysseus was aware of her and the dogs likewise, which barked not, but with a low whine shrank cowering to the far side of the steading' (p. 264). This cowering of the dog, as if conscious of some unseen influence, has often been noted by his human companion, and spoken of as ' seeing a ghost.'

Argos, the hound of Odysseus, which of old himself had bred, when he was aware of Odysseus standing by, wagged his tail and dropped both his ears, but nearer to his master he had not now the strength to draw. The

---

* References in this note are to the translation of the *Odysseus* by Professor Henry Butcher and Mr. A. Lang.

story of the death of this faithful hound—fleetest in pursuit, and so keen in scent ' that there was no beast that could flee from him in the deep places of the wood when he was in pursuit '—must be read in the words of Homer or, if this cannot be, as they have been englished by my friend Henry Butcher and Mr. Lang, in a version worthy to take rank with the great translations of the Tudor age.

The same counsel may be given to one who would enter into the spirit of the hunting of the great boar which, before he was slain by Odysseus, inflicted a wound which left a scar whereby the hunter was made known to his loving nurse.

Odysseus could hardly restrain himself from leaping forth and dealing death to the wooers and their paramours. ' And his heart growled sullenly within him. And even as a bitch paces round her tender whelps growling, when she spies a man she knows not, and she is eager to assail him, so growled his heart within him in his wrath at their evil deeds.'

Scott among the great. writers stands first in love of the dog; but he nowhere gives proof of a closer study of his nature and manners than Homer does when he describes the cowering of the dog, as if conscious of some unseen influence; or (p. 264) when he compares the suppressed anger of Odysseus to the growling of a bitch on the approach of a stranger to a litter of her tender whelps (p. 330); and in his picture of the dying Argos when he was aware of Odysseus standing by (p. 284).

To Scott's bloodhound of black Saint Hubert's breed the hunted stag sinking, when scent should be best, was lost to hound's ken when dashing down a darksome glen (*Lady of the Lake*, canto i.), but Argos was a truer scenting hound, for from him the deep places of the wood afforded no refuge.

To the greatest of Greece's philosophers, as to the greatest of her poets, the chase was a subject of intense interest. Plato (*Laws*, vii. 823-824), after noting that there are many kinds of hunting—of creatures in the water and in the air; of land animals of all sorts, including such hunting of men as is practised by robbers—concludes that the legislator will have to praise and blame hunting with a view to the discipline and exercise of youth. Praise is assigned ' to that which will make the souls of young men better, and the censure to that which has the opposite effect.' In a pious wish for their welfare addressed to young men he expresses a hope that no ignoble kind of hunting will take possession of them. When Plato regards it as the duty of the legislature to exercise a wise discretion in its approval or disapproval of various kinds of sports, we can understand the place which they filled in the popular estimation of Greeks of his time, and of this we have further proof in the excellence of the books of sport which have come down to us. To the works of Xenophon mentioned in the text (pp. 240-244) may be added those written by Arrianus (born *c.* A.D. 90) which show the continuance among Greeks of an interest in the chase. He is known as the younger Xenophon, from the closeness of his imitation of his master in the subjects of his works, one of which, the *Cynegeticus*, was written as a supplement to Xenophon's work with which it was ordinarily printed, treating of Coursing, a subject which Xenophon worthily disdained in comparison with the pursuit of game with the aid of *odora canum vis.*

INDEX

Adrian, Cardinal, his poem on the chase attributed to Pope Adrian VI., 262

Albans, St., Book of, and English writers, 208-225; earlier books on venery in England, 209; importance of the book, 211; its contents, 211, 212; how far attributed to Dame Juliana Barnes, 212, 222; the question of authorship, 213; marks an epoch in social history, 214; teaches the language of sport to the new rich, 216-218; how this language was learnt by Ben Jonson, 218; how known to Shakespeare, 218; excellent reprints of the early editions available, 220

Albertus Magnus, 28-48; the father of scholastic philosophy and also of mediæval literature of sport, 28; the subject of tradition and legends, 29, 30; his work on falconry, 31; and that on horses, *ib.* (see Horse); early life of, 32-34; enters University of Padua, 33; how he acquired knowledge of falconry and horses, 34; his work a handbook of falconry, 36; corrects errors of earlier writers, 38; relations with Frederick II., 39; his book on horses the result of personal experience, 40; his ideal horse compared with Shakespeare's, 43; why his treatise not printed, 43; legend of his miraculous conversion, 92; foundation of

the legend, 44; compared with Budæus, 45; mistaken account of the date of his birth, 46

Alphonso XI. of Castile, book on hunting written by command of, 5

Baillie-Grohman, *Master of Game,* 3, 14, 49, 50, 55, 75, 76, 116, 117, 213, 273; *Sport in Art,* 8, 104

Barbarossa, Frederick, 226, 227

Bayle, *Dictionary,* 43

Bearn, union of, with Foix, 126-128

Beaumont, Jean Sire de, begetter of the chronicles, 106

Berners, Lord, his translation of the chronicles, 204-207; commissioned by Henry VIII., 204; merit of his translation, 207

Besant, sir Walter, his life of Froissart, 109

Black Prince, interview with Gaston, 176-182; at Limoges, 275

Blaze, M., 67, 68, 69, 75, 81

Blessing the hounds, a mediæval ceremony, 20; illustrated by Duchesse d'Uzès, 21

Bollstadt, birthplace of Albert the Great, 32, 34

Bouton, M. Victor, on the authorship of the *Roy Modus,* 51

Buche, Captal de, Note B, 271-273; a great mediæval nobleman, 273; his capture, 271; and death, 273

Budæus writes on sport, 3; great Greek scholar, 6

280